Risk-Free
Business
Re-Engineering

About the Author

Brian Dickinson is the founder and president of Logical Conclusions, Inc., a successful training and consulting corporation based in Lake Tahoe, California, with a branch office in Blackpool, England. Logical Conclusion's extensive client list includes many government agencies and major corporations throughout the world. Brian is also an active participant in the Citizen Ambassador Program and has represented the United States in China and Russia.

Brian has over 30 years of experience in teaching and consulting in Business Systems and all areas of Data Processing. He started his career in England with British Aircraft Corporation and then worked internationally as an independent consultant. In 1975 he moved to the United States and was one of the handful of people who originally helped spread the system engineering message across the United States. In this period Brian published papers and books, developed courses, and lead seminars on the emerging System Engineering techniques. Since then, he has consulted and taught globally on the subjects of Software and Information Engineering, Project Management, and Business Re-Engineering. He is also a popular international speaker on Quality System Development (or TQM) to organizations such as NCC, DPMA, ASM, and EDPAA.

In 1979 Brian wrote his first book on the subject of System Development Methodologies which was many years ahead of its time. This work was titled *Developing Structured Systems: A Methodology Using Structured Techniques*. It was translated into Japanese and it proved to be highly successful. Brian's next book was titled *Developing Quality Systems*. This work was published by McGraw Hill in 1989 as part of their Software Engineering Series. After writing *Developing Quality Systems*, Brian extended his focus into the area of Re-Engineering and published *Strategic Business Engineering: A Synergy of Software Engineering and Information Engineering* in 1992. To his latest book, *Risk Free Business Re-Engineering*, he brings the perspectives and insights of almost twenty years of experience in working with and implementing methodologies.

Additional Titles by Brian Dickinson

❖ *Developing Structured Systems: A Methodology Using Structured Techniques*

❖ *Developing Quality Systems*

❖ *Strategic Business Engineering: A Synergy of Software Engineering and Information Engineering*

Books in progress by the same author in the Business Re-Engineering Methodology Series:

❖ *Book II — The Business Re-Engineering Methodology*

❖ *Book III — Logical Business Re-Engineering Analysis*

The Logical Conclusions, Inc.
Business Re-Engineering Methodology Series

Risk-Free Business Re-Engineering

How to Re-Engineer Your Organization
Using Business Event Partitioning to
Achieve Ultimate Customer Satisfaction

by Brian Dickinson

Book One: *A Handbook to the*
Principles of Re-Engineering
for Business and Data Processing Professionals

LCI Press

Kings Beach, CA

A wholly owned subsidiary of Logical Conclusions, Inc.

Published by LCI Press
(a wholly owned subsidiary of Logical Conclusions, Inc.)
P.O. Box 699, Kings Beach, CA 96143.

Cover Design: Brian Dickinson

Cover Art: Brian Dickinson and Jeff Sparksworthy

Soft Cover ISBN Number: 0-9629276-1-9
Hard Cover ISBN Number: 0-9629276-2-7

First Edition

Produced and Printed in the United States of America

The publisher offers a discount when you order this book in bulk quantities or for educational establishments.

For information on Logical Conclusions' Seminars and Consulting Services in the fields of:

- Business Re-Engineering and Pre-Engineering,
- Business Process Analysis and Business Information Analysis,
- Computer Systems Design, and
- Project Management based on the Business Re-Engineering Methodology

call:

Logical Conclusions, Inc.

800 645-2226

Acknowledgments

In the late 1970s I wrote my first book on systems development. Back then, I felt the need to lock myself away in my office and work non-stop (I gave myself Sundays off) writing words of wisdom (or close to it). I didn't know that you were allowed to have people help you.

A couple of books later I got wise and, with this book, I was lucky to have some of my colleagues at Logical Conclusions to help ease the workload (as well as to constantly critique my thinking). Their help was above and beyond the call of duty and I would like to thank them here:

- Colt Rymer

- Doug Brown

- Ed Barstad

- Tony Stubbs

With this book I also had the luxury of receiving reviews from some folks who do real work for a living and who gave me their valuable input:

- Ed Socks and Mona Infield, Bureau of Indian Affairs, Albuquerque, New Mexico

- Jennie Hakes and Steve Hawrysh, *Star Tribune*, Minneapolis, Minnesota

- Jon Carter and Dave Barratt, A.C.T. Financial, England

- Mike Dwyer and E. K. James, Bureau of Land Management, Washington, D. C.

- Robert Brawn, Hewlett-Packard, Palo Alto, California

- Shari Aikens, National Inter-agency Fire Center, Boise, Idaho

I am amazed at the number of times I can change the same material and keep expecting my editor to re-edit it. So, for his patience and restraint in not laughing at my writing skills, I would like to thank:

- Jeff Sparksworthy
  PubTechs Consulting Services

I have been teaching these ideas for over ten years and I have had the great advantage of running them past thousands of students. Fortunately, they have been remarkably well received, and so, here I would like to thank all my students who helped me shape my ideas, with special thanks to the select few who believe in grasping new ideas and championing them in their workplace, invariably against all kinds of resistance to change.

Brian Dickinson
January, 1996
Lake Tahoe, California

Dedicated to all those who love to share their knowledge.

I'd like to start by explaining why I chose ***Risk-Free Business Re-Engineering*** *as the title of this book. Since I published my first book on the subject of Re-Engineering, "Strategic Business Engineering",*[1] there have been a number of articles in the press on Re-Engineering project failures. The negative impressions left by this coverage of project failures and their damaging impact on true Re-Engineering projects is a profound injustice. I find it difficult to believe that the failures being covered in the press were valid Re-Engineering efforts in the first place. I say this because I believe it's almost impossible to fail at Re-Engineering if your organization is more than three nanoseconds old (I'm only slightly exaggerating). This is why the first words in the title are: "Risk-Free."

I claim that it's almost impossible to fail at Re-Engineering because, based on over three decades of observing organizations, the vast majority of them have simply evolved to where they are today. This evolution was typically without any conscious "engineering" method applied to past growth. Therefore, the opportunity to Re-Engineer any established organization will produce many areas of significant improvement, and hence, a successful effort.

I believe that these, so called, Re-Engineering projects that failed weren't really true Re-Engineering projects. The initiators of these projects just used the banner of Re-Engineering to carry on the same "throw systems together," "projects as usual" practices. The goals of these bogus projects are often such things as: downsizing, cutting middle management, or implementing the latest computer or human-based technologies, and not to improve the service to their customers or to increase the quality of their products.

Risk in Re-Engineering

Of course, all projects have some risk. We simply need to reduce the risk to a negligible level at which we feel that the resources we will expend will result in an acceptable payback. Having said this, there are two types of risk in a Re-Engineering effort:

- Risk from a technical/systemic point of view, and

- Risk from a managerial point of view.

Now let me expand on these two types of risk.

Technical/Systemic Risk

The older an organization is, the more difficulties it faces in overcoming its own inertia. Any organization that finds itself in the position of needing to be Re-Engineered will already have a whole closet full of historical/hysterical systemic (design) limitations in place.

Some of the major limiting design aspects are the old system boundaries — both human and computer. These boundaries will be the organizations' biggest obstacles to customer satisfaction and re-vamping or eliminating these boundaries will also be the major sources of improvements when you apply Re-Engineering principles. In this book I refer to these boundaries as "partitions." [2]

I used "risk-free" in the title to mean there was no technical/systemic risk, i.e., there's no risk of failing to produce a better system. Technical/systemic risk is non-existent because, simply by replacing old technologies with those available today, you should see improvements in at least timing, capacity, or access to data, even if they're not dramatic. However, these are not customer-oriented improvements — after all, do your customers really care if you're using the fastest equipment with state-of-the-art technology? You can obtain far more benefits by improving the processes and data you use to respond to your customer's needs.

The gains achieved by switching technologies are often simply incidental improvements based upon this increased speed and capacity. Please note, however, the organization gains no competitive edge because their competitors can use the same technology, or even leapfrog by waiting and implementing the next generation of technology.

> *Any system built around a particular technology will last only as long as that technology before it requires rebuilding in response to the next new wave of technology and support systems.*

Unfortunately, what is all too often happening in these projects is that people are going from old designs to new designs without first having understood the business view (gained from necessary analysis) within the project scope, let alone understood the business view of the whole organization. In my past data processing career I've seen organizations implement and re-implement fads and new methods, models, and technology. They constantly change the designs of their systems, but the nature of their business rarely changes (or changes quite slowly).

Technology changes rapidly and the project that implemented the "last" technology is usually classed as a failure to justify the cost of that system's early replacement with the next technology. Sometimes the failure of these projects gets blamed on the preceding generation of technology used. At other times the blame goes on the old methodology used to build the existing system.

---

2   By "partition" I mean how an organization is divided up (for example, into manual divisions, departments , or jobs and/or by computer systems, programs, or macros).

One major reason for systems becoming obsolete early in their lifetime is that many of them are built around a particular implementation technology. That is, they are designed to run only within an existing departmental context or on a specific computer, use a specific database management system, or rely on specific system support software. Therefore, the advances in hardware and support systems that are constantly being announced lead to premature obsolescence and short lifetimes for these technologically dependent systems.

> *Significant and real business improvements will best be seen when an organization takes a complete look at its business and understands how it effectively responds to external things such as an outside customer's request.*

I hope that the preceding "key point" sounds obvious. The problem is it's not so easy to "see" the real business today. The older an organization is, the more it will have been covered by historical (*I prefer hysterical*) partitioning. The basis for these partitionings were, for example, human boundaries and their associated "politics", computer systems that were built in a haphazard manner in response to the latest fad (hardware platform, computer language, system development methodology), or which departmental manager carried the most budgetary clout. This type of partitioning is what I call "dysfunctional partitioning", in that it actually interferes with the business. What I hope you'll get out of this book is a clear understanding of what "functional partitioning" really is. The Re-Engineering discipline gives us tools to fundamentally improve the organization itself, and allows us to re-evaluate the very structure of the organization as it goes about its daily operations.

Managerial Risk

The managerial aspects of Re-Engineering are the only points at which risk becomes a factor, and even this risk can be minimized or eliminated using the concepts in this book. Managerial risk stems from someone placing arbitrary and uneducated limits on the project's Resources (time, people, money, support). Managers of Re-Engineering projects have a delicate balancing act on their hands. It's like trying to maintain an equal balance on a four-ended see saw (see the illustration below).

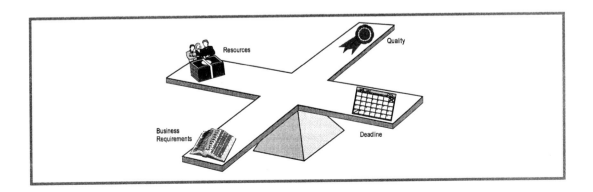

At one of the four ends of the see saw sits the Project Scope identified by the total set of Business Requirements and on another sits the allotted Resources. On yet another end of the see saw sits the effort Deadline. Sitting on the remaining seat is the resultant system's Quality.

Knowing the Re-Engineering project's scope (via the affected set of Business Events) is vital to its success. The ultimate scope is, of course, Re-Engineering the entire organization. However, it is perfectly valid to Re-Engineer a portion of an organization as long as you understand functional partitioning and don't simply Re-Engineer an existing, dysfunctional area of the organization's business. A small pilot project can be extremely beneficial by providing a success story to convince management that it can be repeated organization-wide.

If someone sets a restrictive project Deadline and the date set is not based on empirical data (from other, similar Re-Engineering projects), please realize that one of the other factors on the see saw has to "give" to maintain a realistic balance. With a preset Deadline you can achieve a balance if you can prune the number of Requirements (i.e., don't try to Re-Engineer the entire organization at once); or, if you can put more Resources (money, people, support tools, experts, etc.) on the project. Obviously, the same goes for any of the other factors; e.g., trying to increase the Requirements without increasing the necessary Resources upsets the balance as does trying to shorten the Deadline without upsetting Quality or one of the other factors. It's up to the project's resource providers to maintain this balance.

In my view, the most important rider on the see saw is Quality. If you lower Quality by shortening Deadlines (or skew Quality through a mismatch of Requirements and Resources on the other beams), you may as well throw in the Re-Engineering towel. This is where you may end up being chronicled as "another Re-Engineering project failure" when what has actually failed is not the concept of Re-Engineering itself, but rather the management of the project.

Why Call It Re-Engineering

When I first started teaching this subject, I didn't call it "Re-Engineering." Instead, I used the term "Business Engineering" because the word "Re-Engineering" implied that you already had an engineered system in place — something that I rarely found. However, since that time "Re-Engineering" has become the accepted term. Please note that in almost all cases, we're not Re-Engineering. Rather, in these cases we're actually replacing a historically/hysterically evolved system. In the vast majority of cases, a Re-Engineering project gives us the opportunity to finally do it right the second (or Nth) time.

The word "engineering" is extremely important to me. It is not just another word we tack on to somebody's work title (i.e., "Wednesday they were 'X'" and "Thursday they're an 'X Engineer'"). The word must have substance when we use it in a title or activity. From a process point of view it means that we're going to apply a discipline (not necessarily rigid) to ensure quality throughout a development effort to produce a final quality product.

Growth through Re-Engineering

To me, Re-Engineering's ultimate goal is organizational growth. I assert that by focusing on satisfying your customer's needs, your organization will automatically be more productive and will need to expand its human and technological resources to meet the expanding customer demand.

This does not mean that jobs won't change. We may re-train staff or repartition management tasks and bring in new technology, but this is what keeps organizations alive. Avoiding this constant (albeit, at times uncomfortable) improvement can have a catastrophic cost. For example, does anyone want to buy stock in slide rules? Keep in mind, however, if an organization that originally made slide rules evolved into making calculators — same **what**, different **how** — then it would still be in business.

Re-Engineering should also improve the quality of life — not only from a customer's point of view, but from both the employer's and employees' points of view. It should also ensure the longevity of the organization that provides the improved quality of life.

Hopefully, your organization is not simply planning a downsizing effort, or an effort to automate everything under the guise of Re-Engineering. If so, please don't call it "Re-Engineering." You may be just as likely to enlarge the staff as part of Re-Engineering if that's a better design for your organization. Downsizing is retreating from the competitive challenge of growth and it reduces the quality of life of everyone affected.

Think of Re-Engineering as a legacy project and know that it can take months and even years to fully implement (depending on the size, age, and traditions of the organization). Re-Engineering is not the quick fix that will make you the hero in the next quarterly report or this political term.

Re-Engineering is not a fad — unless you consider survival "faddish." Re-Engineering is important because often, the entire organization's continued existence is at stake. Remember, that history has taught us that there will always be another organization (or country) that's willing to take the long-term view and do it right.

I've "surfed" a number of industry fads over the years, myself, but this one isn't a fad. What really matters now is that we have a significant opportunity to change things for the better with this Re-Engineering wave.

Championing Re-Engineering

The success of Re-Engineering on a project-by-project basis and in the international arena depends, to a great extent, on a group of people I call the "Champions of Re-Engineering." These are typically the folks who have made my own business successful. These champions in each organization are the ones who want to "do it right" with the best techniques available (usually in the midst of chaos) and who often start the internal Re-Engineering revolution. This person can be at any level in the organization and their dedication to the goals of Re-Engineering is, at times, even pursued at their own expense. This book is also dedicated to these champions.

It is my belief that this book covers topics of vital concern to the Re-Engineering efforts in both the public and private sectors. In this book I wish to pass on the knowledge and insights I have gained from working on numerous Re-Engineering projects. Armed with this knowledge, you will not end up gaining notoriety as the scapegoat in some future trade press article about another failed Re-Engineering project. Instead, your project could be used as an example of how to do it right.

Contents

The Detailed Business Event Specification......... 167

B efore getting into the main content of the book, let me state two major concepts that I believe are essential for us to share if you are to fully understand and successfully use the ideas I'm trying to put across in this book. These key concepts are:

- the need to use an "engineering discipline" and
- the need for quality in manual and automated systems.

What Is "Engineering?"

Notice that the term "Business Process Re-Engineering" does contain the word "Engineering." This means making sure we start with a good mission statement with measurable objectives from the highest level of management. We, as professionals, then maintain and measure the quality throughout the entire development life cycle of any new system — all the way from inception to the final product (that is, down to a particular line of code or a procedure manual instruction).

Webster's Dictionary defines *engineering* as:

"The application of science and mathematics by which the properties of matter and the sources of energy in nature are made useful to man in structures, machines, products, systems, and processes."

The phrase *science and mathematics* gives us some clues about engineering discipline. The scientific approach entails using:

- Rigorous and proven methods.
- Models to make abstract concepts tangible.
- An emphasis on measurement and quantification based on the models.
- Objectivity (i.e., the ability to replicate a project and obtain the same resultant product, regardless of who conducts the project).

As we'll see, these features are also the cornerstones of any useful methodology (including the Re-Engineering methodology).

The definition also states that engineering deals with "properties of matter and the sources of energy in nature." The construction industry uses steel, concrete, and wood. Systems designers and implementors deal with human beings and their procedures and computers and their programs (and the data flowing between them).

In my view, the phrase "useful to man" in the above definition, is the most crucial. If our Re-Engineered products do not improve the quality of life, increase human and ecological safety, increase the cost-effectiveness of an organization, and so on, we are wasting both our time and the resources of others. All engineering disciplines have the potential to improve the standards of the society they serve. If we fail in that task, we cannot call ourselves professional engineers. To fulfill this obligation, the systems we develop (manual or automated) must be safe, reliable, provably correct, and "friendly."

Finally, with reference to the last part of the definition, the Re-Engineering task is to deliver structures, machines, products, systems, and processes that are useful (i.e., more useful than the old design). Obviously, the Re-Engineering task can potentially deliver all of these. So, as I just stated, Re-Engineering encompasses the definition of engineering, and therefore charters the people who conduct a Re-Engineering project and their management to commit to being professionals.

Applying a Strategic Engineering Discipline

For some time now systems development professionals have had an engineering discipline that allows them to build manual or automated systems in terms of their *business objectives and requirements* rather than their *implementation technology*. Systems that are built along business lines, with an engineering discipline are flexible and able to absorb change easily, simply because they are partitioned along the lines of the business they support. Using this discipline, we lay a foundation of "logical blue-prints" of business requirements that we can use to build any number of actual systems, be they manual or automated.

After teaching systems engineering techniques for many years, I felt the need and the responsibility to establish at least one unified view of all of these emerging systems engineering techniques. So, in the late 70's, I published my first book, *Developing Structured Systems — A Methodology Using Structured Techniques*. Over the following years (and four books later), I have refined my ideas and moved more towards understanding and satisfying the business person's needs. This book is the result of that refinement.

I intend this book to provide an approach that takes us beyond one single department or computer system to the very reason **why** the organization is in business, and **how** it intends to stay in business over the next ten years and beyond. We are, therefore, talking about Re-Engineering the business at a strategic level.

The Cost of Poor Quality

As stated previously, a high degree of Quality is a cornerstone in any Re-Engineering effort. If the system we're building is intended to last, then the quality has to be put in as we build it. Attempts to shortcut quality may lead to contempt (both internally and externally) for the system, the project team, and ultimately, for the organization that produced the poor-quality product. This reminds me of a sign I once saw bearing the following notice on the wall of a Colorado store:

> *"The Bitterness of Poor Quality Remains Long after the Sweetness of a Low Price Is Forgotten."*

Of course, we can throw a system together for a lower price. However, if we do, we should also factor in the cost of maintenance, dissatisfaction on the part of business people, and worse, the long-term loss of business from the lack of customer satisfaction.

As we shall clearly see by the end of this book, an "engineering quality" approach will lengthen a system's life span, thus improving the return on investment, as well as shorten the system development life-cycle (especially when testing time and time for "getting the bugs out" are included as part of development time). It will also deliver a system that reflects a commitment to quality.

The Cost of Quality

For many years in my early days of teaching I pondered the question: "What is quality?" In my own work it seemed to come down to "attention to detail", but that didn't ring true when I built something in quick-and-dirty mode, such as set of shelves made from concrete blocks and press-board planks, and knew that it satisfied my needs perfectly. Then I came across a book titled *Quality is Free* by Philip Crosby.

In Philip Crosby's book he states that "QUALITY IS CONFORMANCE TO REQUIRE-MENTS."[1] A set of requirements provides something against which we can measure our work, its quality, and our progress. When we develop a new system, there are requirements for analysis, design, and implementation of that system. We can apply this definition of quality to the development of a product, a service, or software.

The title of Crosby's book, *Quality Is Free*, means that quality costs nothing if it's built into the product at the time of manufacture. So, when we decide to build a system, we can choose either to build in quality as we go, or just to throw something together and worry about quality later with inspections and testing phases. We can take the latter approach if that's what our organization wants us to do, but we should frankly acknowledge that that's what we're doing and make sure management and business people document this approach as a Project Objective in a Project Charter. We should also make it clear that the cost of adding quality into a finished system/product is always much higher than building it in as we go. Unfortunately, we can't go to a store and buy a pound or two of "quality" to be added in after product completion.

Many studies have shown that correcting an omission in the final stages of the development life-cycle (typically where I see it performed) will cost significantly more than in an earlier stage. Therefore, building in quality from the very first stage of the development life-cycle, rather than trying to test and remove defects at the end, will actually save time and money, and deliver an overall superior product. So, I'd like to amplify Philip Crosby's statement and say: "QUALITY SAVES YOU MONEY IN DEVELOPMENT AND MAKES YOU MONEY IN PRODUCTION."

Building In Quality

Cost overruns and poor project statistics are also the result of not having a useful set of development and project management techniques.

Throughout the book I use real-life examples taken from my experiences in the building trades as extended analogies that may help you get a firm handle on some of the more abstract ideas being discussed. Since writing my first book on methodologies,[2] I have built two complete homes. On my first house, except for laying the foundation, I did the majority of the work myself — carpentry, plumbing, electrical, and so on. (I even developed muscles.) On the second house I contracted out some tasks and played project manager. Throughout this book, you'll find that I make much use of house building analogies because, having built many systems and then having built two houses, I clearly saw the parallels between the two processes.

---

1   *Quality is Free*, by Philip Crosby — see Bibliography.
2   *Developing Quality Systems*, by Brian Dickinson — See Bibliography

Let me ask you some questions relating to the concept of building quality in:

Have you ever seen a house being built?

Typically, a new house seems to go up very quickly, but what we don't see are all of the planning, up-front analysis, and design work that went on before the first load of concrete was poured for the foundation.

When the house was completed, did you ever see the entire construction crew pushing against a wall to see if it would fall over? Or, did you see them set up huge fans to see if it would withstand strong winds? Or, have you passed by when the fire department had hoses trained on the roof to see if it leaked?

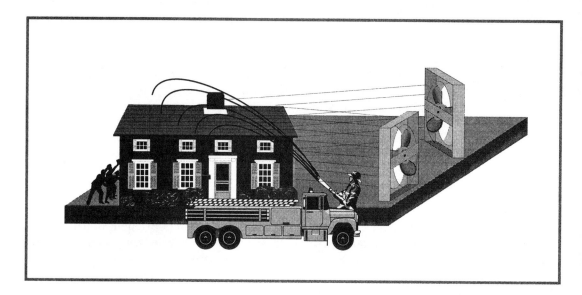

You haven't? Neither have I! We just don't expect to have to "test" a new house after it's built to compensate for poor building techniques. If any problems show up after the house is completed, it simply shows the poor construction methods and materials used during development and/or the lack of quality in the design.

I'm not saying: "Don't test systems.", but that after-the-fact testing is not a quality assurance activity and it should not be used as a substitute for thorough analysis and design.

My house building experience has taught me that "quality" is required and has to be demonstrated at all stages of the house project. For example, land recording/surveying, ground surveys, architectural drawings, blueprints, structural calculations, heat loss calculations, and so on, all have to be externally approved prior to any construction. Moreover, local government staff (the building inspector) also inspects every stage of the construction itself. Any aspect of the construction failing to meet the national and local building code standards must be brought up to code by law before we can continue. And, of course, as each stage is completed, the cost of making a change (such as modifying the plumbing or raising the ceilings) goes up dramatically.

Quality via Engineering

Established engineering disciplines are supported by business, system, and project models that allow potential errors and conflicts to be identified early in the development process. Here are some simple definitions of these terms:

Business Model: An essential or logical model of business rules and policy. This is a business tool for declaring an implementation-independent view of what has to happen to satisfy customer needs.

System Model: An implementation of the Business Model. This is a design tool for declaring how the organization runs in the real world.

Project Model: A methodology or life cycle for building systems. This is a management tool for declaring an organization's systems development standards.

These models provide a framework for defining issues, identifying the real conflicts, quantifying problems, and evaluating solutions in relation to the overall goals of a Re-Engineering effort. Also, they serve as the first point of reference in a future modification to a system.

Obviously, the house building analogy applies here in that each stage of the process is well documented. We need to make sure that the developers of a system have a good set of goals, and a Project Charter for any project that they undertake, as well as the skills and tools needed to do their job. The design of the actual human being environment should be created with the idea of satisfying the organization's business people and customers. In the past (as we'll see in the chapter on *Systems Archaeology*), human-based and computer-based systems have not been designed with the main intention of satisfying the customer, but more to satisfy the hierarchical implementation of the organization or the needs of the technology. This is what I call the "Clothes Have No Emperor Syndrome which I'll discuss later in the book.

The house building analogy I use may break down in places, but generally it works very well because house building and Re-Engineering share the following characteristics:

- Specific start and end points.

- Significant deliverables.

- A strong client/developer relationship.

- Periodic, intermediate quality assurance checkpoints.

- Risk (financial, project, and finished product).

- Dramatic escalating cost-of-change as the project proceeds.

Moreover, both house building and systems development:

- Involve many people and require complex coordination of many different skills and professions.

- Require specialized building tools, including "power tools."

- Use models for conceptualization, communication, and overcoming complexity.

- Use off-the-shelf, modular, and reusable components whenever possible.

I lived in the San Francisco Bay Area of California where I built my first house. During this task, I was pleased to see the building inspector come in periodically and tell me where I had not adhered to standards, and why. I looked upon the inspector's approval as a real benefit and, I had respect for his knowledge. The inspector showed up before the cost of change had escalated. The inspector ensured quality in the development cycle as opposed to being an exercise in after-the-fact testing. I was building the house for myself and I wanted to have a safe and long lasting home; my life may one day depend on it. *(California is beautiful, but it has its faults!)*

In October, 1989 a significant earthquake (7.1 on the Richter scale) hit Northern California during the evening rush hour. In October, 1994 a 6.0 earthquake hit a region 140 miles from the city of Hyderabad, India. Property damage in California was major, but limited to older buildings, and approximately 60 people were killed. The Indian quake (although smaller by a factor of over ten times), by contrast, killed 25,000 people even though the epicenter wasn't near a major city, a peak hour commute, or 52-story buildings. Why the difference? Of course, the emergency services in California responded magnificently, but the degree of damage in each place depended simply on the prevailing civil engineering disciplines.

In house building, the soil engineers, structural engineers, electricians, carpenters, plumbers, and all the other professions rely on each other to do their job correctly (e.g., you can have a wonderful home with beautiful carpentry and efficient plumbing, but if the wiring behind the walls is sub-standard, the house may burn down). In a Re-Engineering project, everyone must also rely on the others to do their jobs correctly. In the software world for example, the analyst must rely on the designer; the designer must rely on the application programmer; the application programmer must rely on the database technician; the programmer must rely on the compiler programmer; and the compiler programmer must rely on the operating system programmer, etc. This requires each manager and technician in the Re-Engineering task to employ professional practices.

I lived in my first house for ten years and had virtually no maintenance costs, even though I added on to the original house significantly over the years. Creating manual or automated system(s) that have virtually no maintenance costs is exactly what we should see as the result of a Re-Engineering project.

Knowing the goals, difficulties, and costs that we may face in a Re-Engineering project, we now need to talk about the method by which we can obtain the Re-Engineering goals. So, let me describe how I've laid out this book. Hopefully, this structure will ease your learning process.

How this Book Is Organized

This book is intended to provide the conceptual tools you will need to understand what your organization does, how to conduct Re-Engineering, and to model an organization's activities through analysis and design. Also, you will need to understand how to better implement the organization's Re-Engineered systems using an engineering methodology and discipline.

This book's chapters are organized into a series of building blocks to help you incrementally absorb the concepts of Business Process Re-Engineering.

- The initial chapter, *Attaining Business Re-Engineering's Goals*, discusses why we need to Re-Engineer the organization in the first place. This chapter lays out the goals of Re-Engineering and some of the potential difficulties.

- The next chapter, *Re-Engineering and Strategic Planning*, briefly introduces some of the strategic planning issues to consider in a Re-Engineering project. This discussion is important because a Re-Engineering effort that begins without a plan is almost certainly doomed to failure.

- The *Systems Archaeology* chapter focuses on how systems were designed and developed in the past, and how these designs are still haunting us today. This chapter exposes the ultimate reasons for Re-Engineering the organization.

- The chapter titled *Understanding the Nature of Systems* describes the basis of every system. In this chapter we look at ways to understand and describe the organization's current systems. This understanding is needed before we try to view a system and convey this view using an abstract model.

- *The Model IS the Business* chapter discusses why and how we model systems. This chapter provides examples of using graphical tools to analyze and model the organization's business. This knowledge is critical when it comes time to select the set of models that are most appropriate for understanding our particular organization. This chapter is also on learning to identify what we're seeing when we look at the organization using these conceptual tools and modeling methods.

- The next chapter, *Business Events — The Key to Ultimate Customer Satisfaction*, defines what a Business Event is and how it is what we model in our organization to be able to successfully Re-Engineer it.

- The chapter on *Partitioning by Business Events* describes what we need to know to functionally partition our model. We will use the concept of Business Events to partition our organization's model along business lines (as opposed to design or implementation lines). This is important because our initial partitioning of our model will dictate all subsequent classifications, and, will probably affect the future Re-Engineered systems' designs. This chapter shows you how to specify (document) every important aspect of the organization's actual business. These general-to-highly detailed specifications are what we use to communicate the organization's business essentials to others who have to make informed decisions about the Re-Engineering effort. The high-level specification provides an overview of the organization. We use the detailed-level specifications to break down complex Business Issues to make them understandable, and to spot potentially reusable data and functions. The next step is to analyze and document the ultimate detail of our business processing. Once again, this detail view, will be from a business point of view and not a design or implementation point of view (since this is a business task and not a technical task).

- In the chapter, *The Business Event Methodology — A Synthesis,* we build on the knowledge from the previous chapters. It is in this chapter that we talk about how we gain some incredible advantages by using a true engineering discipline in our Re-Engineering project. These advantages include such bonuses as Process Integrity and Data Conservation and can only be obtained by using this methodology. These benefits are only available if we have an engineered way to model and manage the organization.

- By this stage the hard part (the analysis) is over. The easy part is inventing a new design, and in the chapter, *Designing and Implementing Business Systems,* we will see how our new designs will be based on business (not technology) issues. This will lead to "seamless" business systems that give ultimate customer satisfaction, that are easily understood, that are easy to change, and that are ultimately more cost effective.

- After that is a discussion titled, *Strategic Planning via Business Events.* This chapter focuses in on the role of a Re-Engineering effort and how it affects the organization's long term survival. This next chapter revisits the Strategic Planning issues given your new found knowledge of the Business Event Methodology.

- Finally, there's a short chapter called *The Logical Conclusion* that shows how we can now satisfy the goals of Re-Engineering using the Business Re-Engineering Methodology.

- At the end of the book are appendices. The first appendix discusses the importance of quality and Total Quality Management (TQM) in all aspects of a Re-Engineered system. I've placed this subject at the end, but it can be read out of order if you're not already knowledgeable in TQM concepts. This discussion of Total Quality Management (TQM) is for those folks who want a summary and history of the merits of the TQM approach. A *Glossary,* a *Bibliography,* and an *Index* follow the TQM appendix.

A Word about Words

This book introduces and uses a set of words and phrases to describe various key Re-Engineering concepts. Some of these words or terms may be familiar to many readers while others will be more obscure. Please note that I have defined some words to have very specific and explicit meanings within the context of Re-Engineering. Wherever any of these words or phrases are used in this context, they are initially capitalized. I have taken care to provide my definitions for these terms where it seemed appropriate. In addition, any capitalized words or phrases are defined in the glossary.

As an example of my word use, I use the word "organization" in the book to cover both public and private sector enterprises and reserve the word "business" to mean the activities that organizations perform in the course of satisfying their customers needs. In this sense, a governmental postal service is in the "business" of delivering peoples' packages. Both the postal service and a private sector package service are "organizations" and each is in roughly the same "business."

Another important tenet of this book is the fact that the concepts and methods I advocate can be used to create or modify any type of system, manual or automated. I take pains throughout the book to make it clear that you can Re-Engineer human-based systems that rely on individuals following engineered procedures just as easily as you can use the latest technology-based tools to implement automated systems. For the purposes of Re-Engineering, human beings and computers systems are both means of *implementing* business needs. I want to show that what we're trying to improve are systems regardless of whether their CPUs are carbon-based gray matter or wafers of silicon.

Doing It Right

Now that you understand some of my ideals, you'll see why I stress:

- the use of a Re-Engineering methodology with professional methods and models, and
- having quality built in at every stage of the Re-Engineering effort.

I understand that you may have to back off from some of these ideals due to politics, budgetary constraints, limited resources, etc., but it's my task to put forth one comprehensive way of doing it right.

I hope you enjoy and profit from the contents of this book.

No problem can be solved by the consciousness that created it — we must work to see the world anew.

Albert Einstein

Attaining Business Re-Engineering's Goals

I hope this book changes your consciousness, or, by the time you've read this book, I hope it will provide the ammunition you need to replace the old consciousness of the skeptics in your organization.

In Business Process Re-Engineering, what we're really Re-Engineering are the systems that make up the organization, not the business itself. In other words, after Re-Engineering, we'll still be in the same business, so we Re-Engineer the organization by Re-Engineering its manual and automated systems. To do this, we will be involved in new systems development (typically known as a project). Projects produce systems which are then implemented, so let's agree on some terms before we state the goals of Re-Engineering.

Business Issues	These are those things pertaining to **what** the organization does regardless of how it's implemented.
System Issues	These are those things pertaining to **how** we design the organization to run its day-to-day operations. System Issues involve technology aspects (e.g., human beings, computers, robots, etc.).

We must be aware of these definitions when we involve ourselves in system development issues (i.e., Re-Engineering). These definitions help us delineate between analysis, design, and implementation (see Figure 1–1).

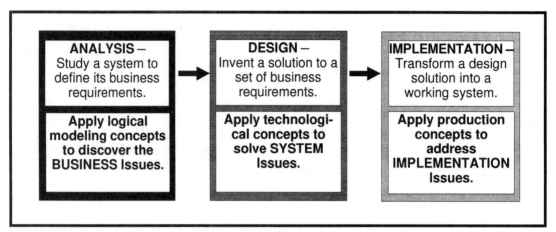

Fig. 1-1: High Level View of System Development Stages

The Goals of Re-Engineering

In this chapter we'll discuss the goals of Business Re-Engineering and how to attain them with the understanding that Re-Engineering applies to both human-based systems and computer-based systems. They are:

- To put the customer first — satisfy customers' needs and expectations by structuring our organization to "seamlessly" respond to these needs.

- To get back to business basics — focus in on **why** we're in business and on **what** we do (as stated in high-level form in the organization's Mission Statement) rather than on **how** we do it.

- To cut red tape — achieve dramatic and measurable improvements in the performance of the organization's old implemented systems by creating the most effective processes for delivering products and services.

- To Re-Engineer the organization by replacing old systems that may be hurting the organization today with quality engineered systems. The new engineered systems (be they manual or automated) will be faster and easier to install and maintain.

- To create systems that promote data conservation, and take advantage of the opportunities for re-using data and processing whenever possible.

- To attain the highest quality in the development and delivery of our products and services — use an engineering development discipline, empower employees, and use the best available technology in implemented systems.

- To satisfy the organization's strategic goals — allow for constant improvement in the organization by producing a flexible environment for future change. This means that we create an environment in which we can make business changes that will not affect technology issues, and where we can make technology changes without affecting Business Issues.

- Remove non-essential aspects — remove those aspects of your organization that do not directly satisfy the organization's strategic goals.

Re-Engineering Is Not a Technological Band-Aid

Many texts on Re-Engineering seem to imply that using new computer systems is the way to Re-Engineer our business (i.e., replacing manual systems). But, notice that we may accomplish the important goals above with no new computer systems. For example, we can go from an existing completely human-based system to a new human-based system, and can even replace an existing computer-based system with a human-based system.

Be cautious when thinking of technological solutions first when performing Re-Engineering. By the time you've read this book, you will realize that any technological, or even manual implementations, are not the subject of a Re-Engineering project. The design at which you arrive may indeed use such an implementation, but don't let any new technology obscure your view of what it is your organization actually does. The true nature of your business will almost certainly be unrelated to technological issues (unless your customers are machines).

The technology of the Information Super Highway in the United States can be a tragedy if all it does is connect every organizations' bad (non-engineered) systems. This is analogous to a four lane highway connecting a bunch of mud huts.

If your approach to Re-Engineering is to focus on new technologies as solutions to problems instead of analyzing and engineering the organization's Business Issues, then I recommend that the first thing you do is teach your entire staff how to perform the "three-fingered reboot" (Ctrl-Alt-Delete for you PC-DOS users) or how to find the "Big Red Switch."

It is our responsibility within our organization to Re-Engineer our internal systems. Others have taken on the responsibility to Re-Engineer the Information Super Highway that will link our systems with those of other organizations. However, it would be another tragedy to have our new wonderfully engineered systems connected by "dirt roads", so we can only hope that the highway's builders also apply an engineering discipline in their efforts.

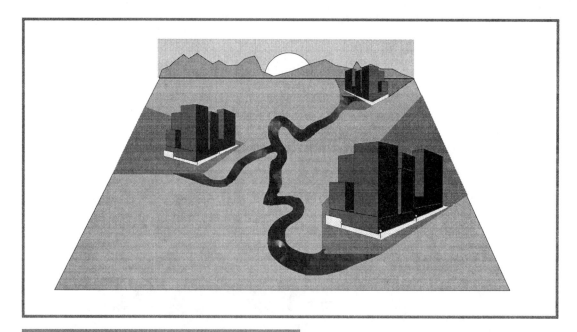

The Clothes Have No Emperor

We have a number of potential sources of failure relating to the goals of Re-Engineering. These are usually put in place by the existing organization's "powers that be." When an organization embarks on a Re-Engineering project, someone (usually a human being in a management position) has to declare the goals that define "success" in a Project Charter. Unfortunately, that "someone" in many cases has to put themselves in the hot seat and be willing to admit that they may be part of the "Clothes that have no Emperor." This leads us to a couple of major sources of project failure.

Much of what we see in place at an organization is there to support the "design structure." In other words, most systems were put in place to make the business run as designed for the real world at some point in the past. This structure is the biggest target for improvement in a Re-Engineering project. It is there, of course, to accommodate human systems and computer systems, as these are design aspects of an organization. These structures are the Clothes (the systems) that cover the Emperor (the business).

In many projects that have purported to be Re-Engineering efforts, I have seen their initiators declare the use of new computer technology as the major goal of the project (e.g., on-line automation of tasks, client-server computer systems, relational databases, use of the Internet, and such). This is technology "driving" the business, and it's incredibly common out there. In many cases these people have already mistakenly decided on a sexy new hardware solution before they've really analyzed the problem. They've lost sight of the fact that the hardware and/or software system issues are really only solutions to business requirements.

The same applies to any other design-oriented goal such as the human-oriented goals of downsizing, outsourcing, use of production teams, or flattening the management hierarchy. Don't get me wrong; these System Goals may be perfectly valid — IF the Analysis of the business reveals inefficiencies in the current implementation and these solutions will be the best in satisfying those inefficiencies.

I'm saying that if you're involved in a Re-Engineering project, it implies that you suspect there's something wrong today with the way things are and that you're going to apply an engineering discipline to discover what's wrong BEFORE proposing a new design. Don't start proposing new designs as long term solutions until after the analysis is complete. Even then, please realize that designs aren't the goals of the project, but merely a part of the solution. If we do not conduct an accurate analysis as the primary part of a Re-Engineering effort, we will probably fail to remove our blind acceptance of preconceived design notions of "normal business practices" of the past. These "normal" practices include human structures such as divisions, departments, agencies, and bureaus (and their "turf wars," etc.). They also include their computer equivalents such as Order Entry systems, Accounting systems, Edit/Update/Print programs, Input/Process/Output programs, 4Kb subroutine, etc. (and the programmer/D.P. mentality that perpetuates these structures).

This failure will lead us to Re-Engineer a system or a significant part of a system that should have been tossed out long ago. In fact, this failure to see through the old designs leads us to create faster bad systems and hence from any measure, brands the project as a failure.

I do realize that one of the problems is that strategic planners must often make decisions regarding long term equipment acquisition, site management, facilities expansion, and so forth based on the needs of the proposed design. Even so, please don't let this lead to the myopic view that it's the new equipment that matters most. This view also often sets up false Re-Engineering projects for failure.

Re-Engineering vs. Outsourcing or Downsizing

If Re-Engineering is being done at all, it is because the existing implementation of an organization's systems is perceived to be (or actually is) inefficient, ineffective, or more costly than a system we can Re-Engineer to take its place.

The potential tragedy of not Re-Engineering, for you who are reading this book, is that you may have your job (and maybe your whole department's jobs) outsourced. Outsourcing is the practice of using an external agency or vendor to perform tasks that were previously performed by an organization's own staff. This short sighted management approach may result in a quarterly report that looks good because we've eliminated "N" jobs off the payroll. However, we may in fact have done a disservice to our customers by internally fragmenting our response to their needs. If your department's tasks are outsourced, the organization loses some control over satisfying the customer's needs, and we may not even realize any real savings. I've seen this happen in the era of downsizing. Remember, every vendor has to mark up the price of their services to obtain their profit.

By the way, this book is intended for your potential outsourcing vendors too. They must put themselves in the position where they can impress on your organization's management that it is more cost-effective for the organization to use them instead of you. What I'm describing here is the nature of competition, which I find very healthy, also, it is inevitable in a market-driven environment. Any organization that sits back on its laurels will eventually suffer for their complacency (especially in hard times). These trends do not sneak up on us as we've witnessed in the global competitiveness of German and Japanese companies.

When I speak of outsourcing, I'm not talking about forming strategic alliances with our organization's existing vendors. This is a good Re-Engineering strategy. Rather, I'm talking about outsourcing to a vendor the tasks that your department currently performs.

You have to prove to your management that you are the best possible implementation for your customers' needs and that you are more efficient and cost-effective than any vendor can be, so that downsizing or outsourcing are ridiculous options.

I'm the president of Logical Conclusions, Inc., and, in all honesty, if there's an aspect of my business that I could outsource to better satisfy the needs of my customers, I would be a fool not to outsource it (especially if it cost less). However, I'd be a bigger fool if I didn't give my staff at least one chance to Re-Engineer their operation. After all, the knowledge and skills of my staff are one of LCI's greatest assets.[1] In the face of downsizing, some of your best people are the first to find new jobs rather than waiting for the inevitable axe. The people who are savvy enough to be in control of their own destiny don't wait to be downsized.

Some of the Challenges of Re-Engineering

The following section summarizes the obstacles, risks, and benefits of Re-Engineering a system (or an entire organization) for upper management, middle management, and for workers.

The legacy of everyone in an organization today is to keep the organization's founder's vision alive. With the exception of those organizations that were intended to be temporary, the ultimate tragedy of not Re-Engineering would be to see the loss of all the effort and struggle your predecessors went through to make the organization what it is. Even though Re-Engineering will be challenging, costly, and time consuming, the ultimate benefit is that your organization keeps its doors open and hopefully provides a pleasant environment for its workers and benefits to its community. Note that because realizing the full potential of Re-Engineering could take many years, the successors of the initiators may be the ones who reap the credit.

I want to emphasize here (as I do in my seminars) that Re-Engineering systems is a lot easier than Re-Engineering values and management practices. The challenging part involves everyone overcoming obstacles such as:

- Resistance to changes of management style and reporting structures (especially at the middle management level).

- Politics, i.e., empire building, turf protecting, us vs. them, etc. (especially at the upper and middle management levels).

- Fear of job loss (throughout the organization).

- The need for instant results as reflected in the quarterly profits obsession, and the need to immediately appease the stockholders/taxpayers.

- The lack of a clear vision of purpose as expressed (or not expressed) in a Mission Statement.

Even though the ultimate benefit is keeping the organization's doors open, there are other benefits including:

- We can create an organization that truly fulfills its mission.

---

1   The management of one company that I know of, when faced with a reduced demand for their products and services, gave their employees one year to re-invent their jobs.

- People benefit by producing results in a Re-Engineered environment because people should ultimately be rewarded for meeting customer needs as opposed to rewards based on internal management whims (such as pleasing superiors, having tenure, or on meeting unrealistic deadlines).

- Ultimately, your organization should be able to deliver services and produce products faster, making the employees and the organization appreciated.

- As an employee you should obtain more job satisfaction by being empowered and staying up-to-date by using new technology.

- Being proactive instead of reactive to produce a less stressful environment (no more putting out internal fires).

- No re-work and re-inventing the wheel because of the engineered environment.

So, put your staff back into a comfort zone by stating that we want to grow; not close the doors. Employees who are not informed of what's happening, and their resultant resistance to change are probably the biggest factor in the failure of Business Re-Engineering projects. Therefore, be honest and openly discuss your organization's "politics." The greatest resistance will probably come from those folks who are at the organization to build their own private empires, not to accomplish its mission. In spite of their resistance, the effort must succeed because, ultimately, Re-Engineering will keep the organization in business and foster future growth.

Having the right and the resources to overcome the above challenges and being able to realize the benefits is predicated upon having top management directly involved in championing the Re-Engineering effort.[2] Everyone must be totally enrolled in the process. A real Re-Engineering effort does not simply start with a memo by the water cooler from on high, declaring that an organization will be Re-Engineered next year. There needs to be a watershed defined when the Re-Engineering effort begins, and to affirm that management is fully behind the Re-Engineering effort.

The start of a Re-Engineering effort requires that everyone is informed of the goals, the direction, and the progress in as positive a light as possible.

Under the Business Event Methodology, an organization's top-level management must assume a new role and adopt new leadership techniques. Their new role is what I refer to as the *Business Policy Creator*. This role, which is really an extension or redefinition of their previous duties, is to decide which customer needs their organization will respond to.

---

2   In fact, I believe that the word "management" should be abolished in the business world. We should instead have the concepts of leaders and facilitators. These are not new concepts. Theodore Roosevelt said: "People ask the difference between a leader and a boss...The leader works in the open, and the boss in covert. The leader leads and the boss drives." I'd like to emphasize that the titles that we put on people and use are important. We don't want to manage people; we want to lead people. "Management" to me implies a control or top-down view. Whereas "Leadership" implies "at the same level" and "I will guide, help, and facilitate you in getting the job done."

Once they have defined this set of customer needs and their organization's overall responses, the Business Policy Creator must then determine the data and processing that their organization will use in these responses to their customers' needs.

This level of decision making may involve the Business Policy Creator in dealing with (either directly or by delegating) some of their organization's low-level "nuts and bolts" data and processing details. This is not to say that they will become micro-managers who play watch dog over their staff. Rather, they will need to shift their approach from that of a "boss" to that of a "leader" who works closely with their staff to carefully formulate their organization's responses to each customer's needs.

In this methodology, they must cease looking at their organization as a set of discrete departments and numbers, or workers. The new leadership paradigm will be for them to look at those systems and people in their organization who must work as a team to satisfy their customer's needs, as a single, seamless customer satisfaction unit.

Assessing the Difficulty of Re-Engineering

Please realize that the attainment of these goals (i.e., the journey towards Re-Engineering an organization) will be easy, or hard, depending on how the organization currently runs its business.

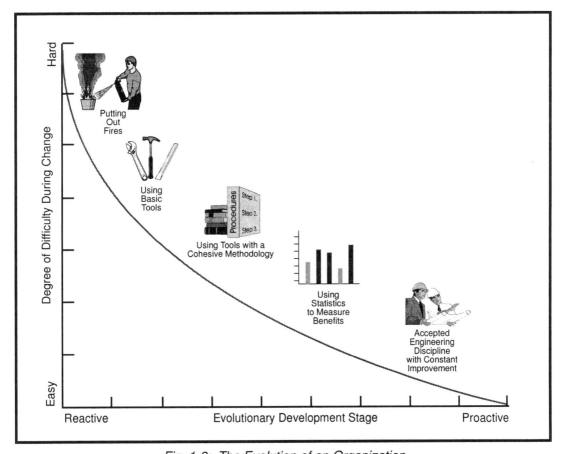

Fig. 1-2: The Evolution of an Organization

Figure 1–2 depicts the level of difficulty in implementing Re-Engineering. In general the larger and more steeped in its own history an organization is, the more challenges a Re-Engineering effort will face. [3]

- If an organization's standard operating procedure is to expect and respond to internal emergencies (i.e., planning is non-existent), then the systems in this organization (human- and computer-based) will have been built in the same haphazard manner. This reactive rather than proactive method of operation poses the most difficulties for Re-Engineering because of the large differential between it and an engineered environment.

- If an organization is using standardized development methods and models to run its day-to-day operations (manual and automated), then it still faces challenges, but not as hard as those in the first scenario. This is because this organization at least acknowledges the potential benefits of using standardized tools even though it may not use the same methods and models in the Re-Engineered environment.

- If the organization defines an all-encompassing method within which to use standardized tools (i.e., it adopts a practical methodology), the task will be even less daunting because this organization is used to having structure in its operating procedures.

- The next easiest environment to Re-Engineer is one in which standardized tools, and a methodology are firmly in place, and the organization gathers statistics and measures results to see what works, and what doesn't; i.e., it uses metrics (statistics) to plan and measure its successes.

- The easiest type of organization to Re-Engineer is the one in which an engineering discipline is already accepted as the standard method of operation, and the environment accepts constant improvements (even though the current methods may change after Re-Engineering takes place). With my definition of "Re-Engineering", this last example is the only one to which the term really applies, because we are Re-Engineering an existing engineered organization.

If you are low on the above organizational evolutionary scale, don't let this deter you because you will also realize the most benefits from Re-Engineering. However, be aware that your investment will be the greatest as other training will be needed to support Re-Engineering (for example, Total Quality Management, people/team skills, and training to facilitate change).

Re-Engineering is the methodology that we apply to an existing organization to make it more customer focused. However, you may be asking if we can use the same concepts on a startup company. After all, it would be an especially bad scenario to start a brand new (and heavily capitalized) venture that fails to compete with an older organization that has been Re-Engineered and that vies for the same customers as you. You can ensure your venture's success by conducting what I call "Pre-Engineering" in which you use the same engineered analysis, design, and implementation techniques used in a Re-Engineering effort. There are some obvious differences between these two forms of engineering. However, the methods and methodologies are fundamentally the same.

---

3   A similar view to this is given in Watts Humphrey's book, *Managing the Software Process* — See Bibliography

A non-existing (new) organization will be easier to Pre-Engineer than it will be to Re-Engineering an existing organization because there are no systems in place that obscure the essential business. Also, there will be no political or other institutional roadblocks to overcome in terms of historical/hysterical partitioning or archaeological wrong turns.

If the person tasked with a Pre-Engineering project has been taught "standard business practices" while they were in school (e.g., "every organization needs an Accounts Department, a Personnel Department, etc."), then they are pre-disposed to take the same archaeological wrong turns listed in chapter three and, in fact, won't be conducting true Pre-Engineering at all.

Another aspect of Pre-Engineering that differs from Re-Engineering is that when starting to design a business from scratch, you have no existing systems from which to "dis-cover" the logical Business Model.

Perhaps the major difference between a Pre-Engineering and a Re-Engineering project will be the scope of the activities. In a Pre-Engineering project, you have the luxury of performing what I call the "big bang" in that you get to perfect the entire organization at once so that nothing is "outside" the scope of study. In this mode you have no existing Design Issues to accommodate in your modeling. Also, you do not have to be concerned with taking pains to ensure that the project does not impact the day to day operations on non-engineered systems that are outside the scope of study. Only in rare cases, will a Re-Engineering project have these same freedoms of action and scope.

Pre-Engineering reminds me of the message I gave to my audiences on my trips to Russia and China with the People to People Citizen's Ambassador Program. This message was that you don't have to go through the last twenty to thirty years of history to get today's best engineered implementation of a business. You can leapfrog and start today without historical partitioning or pre-conceived notions of what constitutes a computer system (or to some degree, a human-based system).

Maximizing Your Organization's Effectiveness

Achieving dramatic and measurable improvements in our organization's effectiveness by streamlining processes can be difficult or easy on a case-by-case basis. In this respect it is just like the overall improvements realized by applying an engineering discipline to systems development.

These objectives can only be accomplished if you:

- Take care of *Project Issues* with such things as having a clear and measurable Mission Statement.

- Take care of *Product Issues* with such things as building quality into the product by building quality into each step of the systems development process (as opposed to relying on after-the-fact inspections or debugging tasks).

- Take care of *People Issues* with such things as open communications, empowered employees, and effective leadership (see Figure 1–3).

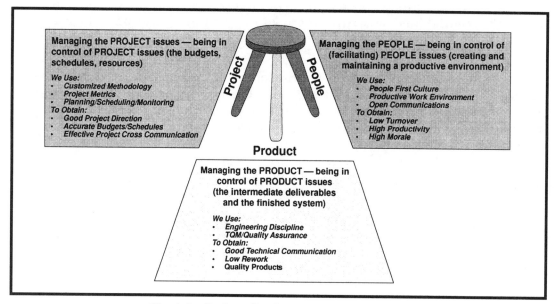

Fig. 1-3: Project, Product, and People Issues

When we embark on a Re-Engineering project, we have an opportunity to change the existing implementation to a better implementation. Therefore, each participant in the project must be accountable for their part of the project — both technical and managerial (see Figure 1–4).

PLAYER	DELIVERABLE	GOAL ORIENTATION	METHODS/MODELS
Strategic Planners/ Upper Management	Mission Statement	Strategic/Organizational	Long Range Forecasting/ High-level Business Models
Project Manager	Project Charter/ Customized Methodology/ Project Plan	Project	Metrics/Communication/ Organizational Methodology
Project Team	Manual & Automated System(s) (via Analysis, Design, & Implementation)	Technical	Development Models/ Implement Technology
Business Policy User/ Operations	Completed Work	Production	Manual & Automated Systems/ Schedules

The Mission Statement dictates

The Project Charter dictates

The Analysis Requirements dictates

The Design Solution dictates

The Procedures Manuals/ Computer Code dictates

The Implemented System

Insuring Quality at each and every stage of these dependent deliverables avoids pollution in the final product.

Fig. 1-4: The Waterfall of Accountability

> *Management has the responsibility for declaring standards, realistic deadlines and quality levels, and for monitoring compliance.*

I would like to acknowledge here that various product, project, and business goals affect the work of an engineer, and often these goals conflict. Everyday we see the results of this conflict, and occasionally we see major examples, like the near-meltdown at Three Mile Island and the explosion of the space shuttle Challenger.

In Book II of this series, *"The Business Re-Engineering Methodology"*, I address managing conflicting goals like meeting client requirements within a specified time-frame and budget, while achieving the highest level of quality.

Justifying the Cost of Re-Engineering

The three main financial justifications for Re-Engineering are:

- Staying in business.

- Increased business revenue, greater market share and therefore increased satisfaction of shareholders or taxpayers, etc., due to improved customer service and competitiveness

- Reduced operating costs through efficient systems and improved quality.

I have to note here that I'm not a believer in downsizing. I am, however, a believer in right-sizing (which could just as well mean the need for more staff or less staff in certain areas). I find the people who set downsizing as a goal only see their organization as numbers of people. If you're measuring people as the cost of your business, you will cut people in lean times. If you measure in terms of quality and quantity of responses to the needs of your outside customers, you can then cut unnecessary and non-critical responses. Rather than cutting a percentage of people, you may actually find a better solution is to relocate resources to more profitable and critical areas of the business. In this respect, I believe that management should budget **what** the organization does as opposed to **how** it's implemented (i.e., don't budget departments, agencies, systems, etc.). Later in this book, I'll recommend a more business-oriented view of budgeting. We can best save costs by removing unnecessary waste caused by historical systems and their maintenance.

Summary

Re-Engineering is an excellent opportunity to introduce an engineering methodology for the development and production of manual and automated systems, and to launch a continuous quality improvement program. However, the underlying focus is on achieving as perfect a match as possible between the needs of the customer and the organization's responses.

A successful Re-Engineering effort may preempt any kind of reactive, short-term-profits driven downsizing, or outsourcing, because we will have the option of proposing a better design based on a rational study of the organization. I'm sure that everyone would rather grow their organization than shrink it.

The hallmarks of a Re-Engineering program are:

- Bold, measurable business goals (e.g., "Obtain *the* best rating within our industry within three years," "Win the Demming or Malcomb Baldridge Award within five years," "Immediately introduce a continuous improvement program," "Set up a Reusable Library of zero-defect data and processes immediately and reward its use by every project").

- A potentially total, top-to-bottom overhaul. A continuous and possibly fast-paced effort is most beneficial to minimize the period of disruption during which only some parts of an organization's response to the customer's needs may be Re-Engineered. Please note that the parts of the organization being Re-Engineered must interface with the organization's old systems during the entire effort.

- A charter from the highest organizational level, along with a well-thought out strategic direction/plan available to everyone in the organization.

- An entirely new way of looking at the organization as consisting of a set of partitioned, cohesive processes that satisfy the specific needs of a customer. By the end of this book you may want to consider conducting a fundamental repartitioning of your organization's internal boundaries.

We should note, however, that Re-Engineering is not a solution to a crisis. Crisis thinking usually calls for immediate answers to specific problems. Re-Engineering is a solution to a problem that has crept up on most organizations over several years, probably decades, and the full benefits of Re-Engineering may take years to realize.

Recently, some people have been talking about the need to shift the basis for organizational structures away from the paradigms derived from the writings of Adam Smith[4] and Frederick Winslow Taylor[5]. The key question in this line of thinking has been to identify what new paradigm to use as a replacement. I am going to propose that the shift be to an organizational partitioning based not on human departmental or computer system boundaries, but to a paradigm that is more fundamental to the true business view. I believe that the Business Event Methodology, as described in this book, reveals a true business view, and as such, it can be the basis for Re-Engineering organizations that will grow and last as long as the businesses they were created to support.

Now that you know the goals of Re-Engineering and the level of difficulty facing your organization, and you still want to proceed, the first step is to consider some Strategic Planning issues as outlined in the next chapter.

4　　*The Wealth of Nations*, by Adam Smith — see Bibliography

5　　*Scientific Management*, by Frederick Winslow Taylor — see Bibliography

The world will not evolve past its current state of crisis by using the same thinking that created the situation.

Albert Einstein

Re-Engineering and Strategic Planning

In today's competitive environment, organizations are trying to bring their products and services to market faster than their competitors, or to respond more quickly to customers' demands. Speed often spells the difference between success and failure, or growth and stagnation of an organization. In banking, for example, the first bank to modify its systems to support a new financial service, or to take advantage of new legislation, can corner the market. Or, a delivery service might save a significant amount of time by seeing through the old design and implementing the same Essential Business needs with a new design to deliver items more quickly and/or for a lower price.

Strategic Planning is a planning approach aimed at organizational issues which addresses where the organization is today, and where it expects to be in the next decade and beyond.

Very often, how an organization has partitioned its existing business (i.e., how it is currently divided up) can mean the difference between a fast modification to engineered systems, versus months of patching a mishmash of already patched systems. In turn, this can mean the difference between a warehouse full of slow moving goods and a swift response to customer demand. To set and maintain its competitive edge, an organization must do two things:

- Create a new line of business as quickly as possible in response to the market place (possibly even anticipating market demand).

- Minimize the delay in its current satisfaction of customer needs by streamlining the organization's responses into "seamless" systems.

Of course, this relies on the organization having a specification of its Essential Business needs available in order to take advantage of new business opportunities, new designs, and new technology.

For swift response to a new or changing environment, an organization should ask some strategic questions:

- How quickly can we introduce a new line of business, or an extension/modification to an existing line of business?

- How much of our existing systems can we re-use?

And, to maximize profitability on existing products and services, the organization should ask:

- What are our key lines of business?

- Which ones are the most profitable?

- How can we streamline these areas of business to reduce response cost and time?

These strategic business questions are answered more easily in a "customer-aligned" organization than in one with a traditional, hierarchical/fragmented design. Under the traditional regime, several systems in different locations may play a part in responding to a customer's need. Applying the Business Engineering Methodology as outlined in this book will give management a tool for streamlining the whole organization for ultimate customer satisfaction.

To support Strategic Planning, we need a method for determining the Essential Business to which the organization must respond now and in the future, and for evaluating how well its internal configuration enables it to make those responses. The heart of such a method, I believe, is in the methodology stated in this book. With it, we can:

- Produce a specification of the business that shows **what** has to take place rather than **how** it happens to take place, in terms the business community understands.

- Re-Engineer an organization to provide ultimate responses to its customers' needs.

- Produce a Business Model in which changes to departmental boundaries, job descriptions, or implementation technology would not affect Business Issues.

- Enable both business and technical staffs to provide realistic resource statistics for how the organization responds to its business, and provide statistics for the cost of new lines of business and potential changes to existing business.

- Clearly show where changes in business policy will require modifications in the Business Model (and hence its implementation), making it easier to identify and manage changes.

- Easily add or remove entire business products or services with minimal confusion.

- Easily assess the costs and impacts of any technology changes.

- Support the re-use of functions and data.

- Support system integration. Bringing systems together at some future date, or identifying the effect of a new business on all systems is easier than with traditionally designed systems.

- Support system dis-integration, that is, repartitioning of a poorly partitioned organization where several separate Business Issues track through the same system.

We will see in this book that many systems in place today were based on a faulty understanding of the business they were intended to support. These systems were built for reasons of design and internal politics. Unfortunately, new systems are built simply to replace old systems that were themselves based on the partitionings of earlier manual and automated systems, so that the effects of old partitioning still haunt us today. Many of today's systems reflect how an organization partitioned its activities and information several years, if not decades, ago.

The fact that an organization's systems may support its response to *today's* business, however, is not enough to protect it from the devastating effects of not being able to support its response to *tomorrow's* business. Having invested huge sums in manual and computer systems, an organization may encounter the disaster of inflexible systems that stifle the fast reaction time needed to respond to changes in the market place from both a business and a technological view. Trying to change a crucial system to offer a new product or service can become a quagmire of *ad hoc* quick fixes that buries an organization in ongoing production and maintenance problems and even greater inflexibility. That's why I advocate using the Business Event Methodology discussed in this book as part of Strategic Planning.

A Basis for Strategic Planning

We live in an age of specialization, and in business each specialist sees the organization from the viewpoint of his or her particular specialty. If an organization decides, for example, to offer a new product or service, the accountant may look at the change in terms of new line items in the general ledger; the production manager in terms of new production schedules; the procurement manager in terms of new parts to be ordered; the sales manager in terms of new promotional programs to be launched; and the Data Processing (D.P.) manager in terms of new transactions and programs.

These specialized views, when implemented separately, fragment the overall response to new Business Issues or to changes in the existing business. The senior management of an organization needs a more strategic view for overseeing the introduction of a new product or service and for restructuring the existing organization.

This new view should enable managers to see the organization as a unified system that responds to outside customer needs, which is, after all, the main reason why the organization exists. Only then can the organization perform two vital functions: first, the identification and manipulation of the variables that are important for the mission of the organization (that is, Strategic Planning); and second, the efficient processing of the data used in its day-to-day operations.

> *It's imperative for Strategic Planners to have available to them a model of the business, unencumbered by any design and implementation characteristics.*

There are various techniques for identifying the organization's operations, but many of them focus on an organization's internal functions, rather than on its interaction with the outside world. They concentrate on mapping processes and data onto *existing* departments, and on the proper configuration of *existing* procedures, including human and material resources. Even techniques like data normalization and functional decomposition were too often performed on the implementation data and processing of old environments. In this, they fell short of being true *strategic business* tools.

Providing a Competitive Edge

Telecommunications and computers are already dissolving the old boundaries around organizations. Today, the technology is available to allow a company to install terminals at its customers' sites for direct order entry, or to order materials directly by hooking into its suppliers' computer systems. But, removing the physical barriers between systems requires an organization to understand the *Essential Boundaries* between systems versus the *Non-essential Boundaries*. Essential Boundaries are those over which we have no control — they must exist for the business to run. Non-essential Boundaries are those based on some implementation or historical reasons.

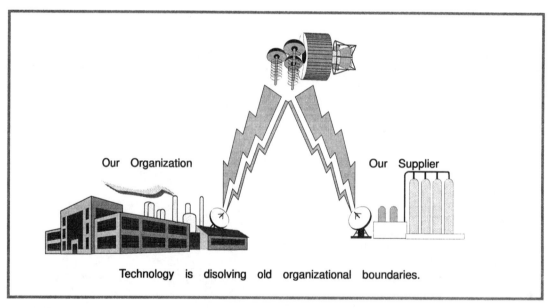

Technology is disolving old organizational boundaries.

Needing to rewrite whole systems to benefit from new technology, such as erasable optical disks or voice recognition, is ridiculous and unnecessary. Similarly, not being able to absorb a complete new business product or service is equally ridiculous. An engineered system should accommodate both new business and new technology readily, and it should give an organization a significant head start over any competitor with a non-engineered environment.

In a medium-to-large organization, it's typical for people to be overwhelmed by the volume and complexity of its current implementation, and to not know the essentials of its true business functions. Organizations spend much effort on untangling disorganized existing systems when the effort could be applied to building new, engineered ones. Until an organization introduces well partitioned, engineered systems, and keeps comparative statistics of the old and new designs, the degree of wastage will not be known, and senior managers will continue to be deprived of the tools they need for effective Strategic Planning.

A Strategic Business Planning Approach

The focal point of any Strategic Planning approach is the set of organizational objectives that defines where the organization is today, and where it expects to be in the future. Without this set of goals, the organization cannot define the processing and information it needs to support this movement.

The Key Organizational Questions

Figure 2–1 shows the strategic questions that an organization must answer. They are discussed briefly in this chapter and returned to in the *Strategic Planning via Business Events* chapter. The details of "how to" accomplish them are discussed in *Book II: The Business Re-Engineering Methodology*.

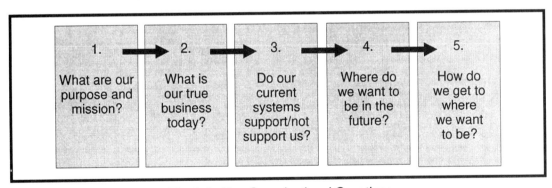

Fig. 2-1: Key Organizational Questions

1. What Are Our Purpose and Mission?

This is a description of the business our organization is in and what we want to be or do in current terms. This may be an overall purpose, or it can be broken down into a set of Organizational Objectives. To be meaningful and useful, these objectives should be quantifiable and measurable. They contain the "vision" of the strategic planners. All projects use them to develop individual objectives. The objectives, as stated in the Mission Statement, should be displayed throughout the organization. A Mission Statement is a brief, clearly stated expression of an organization's reason for being in existence. It is this that each and every employee is working to support.

2. What Is Our True Business Today?

We have already mentioned that the managers in each department of an organization will typically have their own view on what the actual business is.

The heads of an organization cannot take any particular department's view, so I recommend answering this question with:

- A list of all stimuli at the boundaries of the whole organization to which it has decided to respond, and definitions of existing business boundaries between the organization and the outside world.

- Identification of critical line(s) of business. Define the set of cohesive Business Issues that are our reason for being in business, or our main revenue generators. (In a resource crunch, these issues would take priority.)

- A high-level map of our existing implementation (e.g., departments, divisions, computer systems, and computer platforms).

- An Organizational Business Objective or set of objectives for each line of business using the list of our organization's stimuli. These Organizational Business Objectives are quantifiable, measurable statements of a specific line of business' required performance. The objectives must be stated such that it will be quite clear when they are, or are not, being met.

3. Do Our Current Systems Support/Not Support Us?

We must evaluate how well the organization achieves its purpose and mission. We do so by analyzing how the systems currently implemented respond and contribute to the organization's purpose and mission.

One way of assessing how we are doing is to see how much any specific customer request is fragmented across existing systems (manual and automated). Also, given each business objective, we should be able to assess how we are meeting these objectives by projecting the optimum response/performance statistics and compare them with the current statistics. (*I tend to find that organizations have reasonable statistics or metrics of their operating costs for their manual systems, but not for their computer systems. So, this step may be difficult, but nonetheless essential, for the computer environment.*) Thus, the organization's purpose and mission objectives decompose into specific business objectives, which in turn decompose into specific Business Policy for each customer request.

4. Where Do We Want to Be in the Future?

In addition to evaluating the organization's current position, we must also identify what changes, additions, or deletions are required for future business opportunities. These can also be stated in high-level terms, but again, they must be measurable.

Whenever I think of future measurable strategic objectives, I remember the one declared by John F. Kennedy on May 25, 1961:

> *"I believe that this nation should commit itself to achieving the goal, before this decade is out, of landing a man on the moon and returning him safely to the earth."*

This was a succinct and measurable organizational objective.

The strategic planner is not just responding to the competition's actions. An organization's leaders need to set new directions, but this is not easy when they themselves are typically blinded by the existing design of their organization.

I have found that when an objective, logical view of the organization is developed, this view provides a platform for many new products and services to be introduced. Seeing the essentials of the organization, as opposed to how it is currently implemented, opens up a world of opportunities for expansion and improvement.

5. How Do We Get to Where We Want to Be?

Unfortunately, we can't do a "big bang" repartitioning of an organization without completely shutting it down, so we have to Re-Engineer the organization's activities *in situ* via a Re-Engineering Plan.

Preparing a Re-Engineering Plan presents us with an opportunity to examine the relevance of existing partitioning with objectivity, to select what works, and to replace what doesn't, all with the overriding goal of optimizing the organization's response to its customers for its critical areas of business.

Objectives Vs. Requirements

Objectives can be looked upon as achievable goals for the project. I would like to distinguish. between Requirements and Objectives here. If it doesn't sound too esoteric:

- Objectives are a description of measurable reality as of a future instant in time.

- Requirements are data flows, data stores, data relationships, and processes, that must be in place for a system to work. These requirements, operating through time, satisfy the objectives.

Let me clarify this by using another one of my analogies. When we build a system, it's kind of like building a radio. We have requirements for what the radio must do. We design the radio around those requirements and implement/build the radio. Now, just like systems, the radio isn't exactly what the customer is looking for; they're looking for music or news, etc. to come from the radio. When we put a system in place, the code is the radio. By running data through it, we produce the necessary output(s) that the client really wants.

We recognize business objectives as being applicable to what the resulting system should accomplish for the business, in business terms. They are measured from day one of production onwards. They are typically measured against current system statistics.

For example: Reduce by at least 50% the turn-around time between customer order and delivered product and accomplish this with no more than a 5% increase in existing operating costs. We can measure from day one of production the new operating costs compared with the old.

We recognize project objectives by the fact that they apply to the project issues such as planning, scheduling, budgeting, etc. and can be fully measured by the last day of the project (i.e., the day before production).

For example: The project must not exceed a cost of $1,000,000.00, and must follow an engineering development discipline.

We recognize system objectives as being design related, usually technical, and are further recognized by the fact that they are accomplished and fully measured during the project, usually in the design and implementation stages.

For example: The system must use the in-house data-base management system and be implemented with client server architecture.

The organization conducts projects in order to produce systems and systems help the business.

Summary

In many organizations, systems have grown historically over the decades. These originated mostly from manual methods and old technology. We will see how this is a particularly poor basis for any future partitioning of the organization. Add to this the lack of Strategic Planning and increased competition, and we see organizations that need Re-Engineering in order to remain viable.

To gain the optimum benefits, it is imperative that Re-Engineering be an organization-wide issue rather than a system-by-system issue. The core team responsible for Re-Engineering should not be aligned with any particular organizational unit.

Job redefinition and departmental change will challenge the status quo and is likely to result in conflict and resistance if not handled correctly. In order to obtain the necessary support, the implementors of a Re-Engineering program must have the full backing of senior management, and they must be reasonable and sensitive to the human issues of change.

An organization *must* be prepared to change at every level. The hardest part to change will be the business culture. Business Process Re-Engineering is merely the facilitator of human change, and human change requires that all staff identify with the big picture of improving customer service, meeting the challenges of global trends, and increasing the quality of life.

Thus, new techniques and technology take second place to human relations as we Re-Engineer the organization. Eliciting the whole-hearted support of staff is a leadership function, and requires a campaign of information sharing. Re-Engineering that is felt by the staff to be externally imposed may be immediately rejected. *People are really good at identifying the ten reasons why they should not do something while ignoring the twenty reasons why they should.*

Now, let me give you my succinct definition of "Re-Engineering" and then modify the definition in *Chapter 11* after explaining the methodology's concepts.

Re-Engineering is the re-alignment of an organization and its resources with the ultimate goal of satisfying its customers' needs.

What perception sees and hears appears to be real because it permits into awareness only what conforms to the wishes of the perceiver. This leads to a world of illusions, a world which needs constant defense precisely because it is not real.

When you have been caught in the world of perception[,] you are caught in a dream. You cannot escape without help, because everything your senses show merely witnesses to the reality of the dream...

We look inside first, decide the kind of world we want to see and then project that world outside, making it the truth as we see it.

A Course in Miracles
The Foundation for Inner Peace[1]

Systems Archaeology

I believe that the vast majority of systems in place today are badly designed. This statement applies equally to manual and computer systems. These badly designed systems create many problems for the overall business and a serious Re-Engineering problem.

If we look carefully at these old systems (and especially how they are partitioned), we see that they cause business problems like:

- *Slow Response to Customer Needs* — because the separate systems wait on each other.

- *Inflexibility in the Face of External and Internal Change* — because processing and data are fragmented across systems.

---

1   The quotation on this page is from the Preface to *A Course on Miracles* ®, © Copyright 1975, and is reprinted by permission of the copyright owner, Foundation for Inner Peace, Inc., P.O. Box 1104, Glen Ellen, CA 95442.

- *Unnecessarily High Costs of Doing Business* — because the organization is supporting the systems instead of the systems supporting the organization.

- *Duplicated Processing* — because one system receiving data from another may not "trust" the source system's accuracy and repeat some of its processing (i.e., validation) out of self-defense.

- *Duplicated Data* — because individuals and computer systems tend to have their own redundant sets of data accessible for their processing (coupled with expensive or no consistency checks to support this duplication), individual data elements up to whole files are duplicated.

Even though many existing systems have the above problems, we can't just throw them away. First, because they represent billions of dollars of investment and can't be replaced overnight, and second, because poor documentation often leaves these dinosaurs as the only existing repository of business logic. This especially applies to old computer systems, but these previous decades of non-engineered systems present an enormous obstacle to organizational flexibility and competitiveness. There is even a benefit to studying these old systems, as George Santayana said:

Those who cannot remember the past are condemned to repeat it.[2]

Historical Partitioning of Systems

Let's begin with a look at how we've built systems in the past, and move from there to how we might build them in the future. Our problems arise when we try to analyze the existing system to ensure no loss of business function while we implement a new system. The first questions we can ask are "What were the criteria used to form our existing systems?" and "How are these criteria still haunting us today?" Let's answer these questions in the following sections.

Knowing Who's the Prisoner

In my younger years, I traveled the world and, on one of my sojourns, I ended up in India. Many of the ways of thinking I encountered there have stayed in my memory. A person by the name of Ram Dass (a former Harvard University professor) also traveled to India. His experiences — like mine — changed his life. In his book, *Be Here Now*, he quotes George Gurdjieff who once said:

"You don't seem to understand. You are in prison. If you are to get out of prison, the first thing you must realize is that you are in prison. If you think you're free, you can't escape."[3]

I believe that many of the ways we have implemented a business in the past imposed prison-like restrictions on us. Knowing we're restricted like this is the first step to changing things. I hope this book demonstrates that we are trapped by old, outdated designs, and that the book offers some means of escape.

---

2   *The Life of Reason*, George Santayana — See Bibliography

3   *Be Here Now*, Ram Dass — see Bibliography

What Obscures the Essential Business?

Many existing systems, be they manual or automated, are still partitioned for historical reasons. *(Remember, I prefer to call them "hysterical" reasons.)* Often this historical partitioning obscures the true nature of the business. Everyone can relate to the term "government bureau" as well as to "corporate department" — they both obscure the mission of the organization:

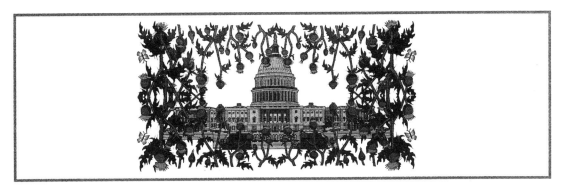

The first (and most major) step in Re-Engineering is to "dis–cover" the underlying business purpose. Then we can engineer a new design that will support this essential business view and not just use new technology to re-implement the old system faster. The original needs of the organization we are Re-Engineering may be buried in the undergrowth of the organization 's processes and data (as shown in Figures 3 –1 and 3–2).

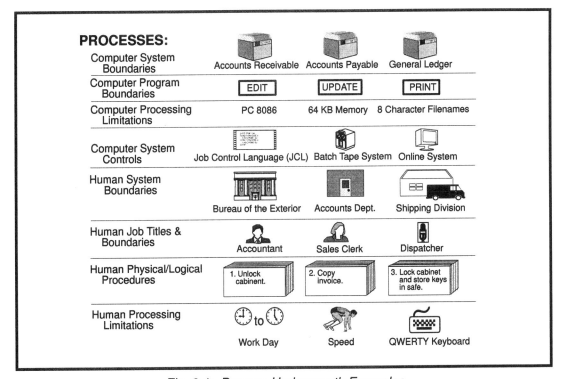

Fig. 3-1: Process Undergrowth Examples

Of course, we reveal the organization further when we remove the undergrowth associated with the data the organization's systems keep.

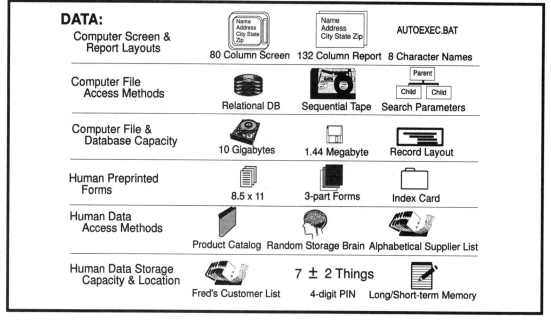

Fig. 3-2: Data Undergrowth Examples

All of this "undergrowth" crowds us from seeing an *Essential* or *Functional* view of the business). Figure 3–3 shows the phases in the system development life cycle that also deliberately obscure the essential business. When not seen as old Design Issues, these partitions tend to lead designers of new systems into the trap of "cloning" outdated, bad designs.

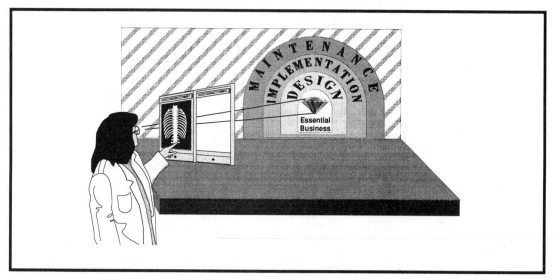

Fig. 3-3: Discovering the Essential Business

Before I talk about these poor partitions, however, let's briefly examine a little of the history of functional partitioning. Then later in *Chapter 7 — Partitioning by Business Events*, we'll arrive at a definition of *Business Functionality*.

My background in data processing took me through computer programming then into computer systems design and then system analysis. In systems analysis I realized that it didn't matter whether the system I was analyzing was currently implemented with human beings or computer programs. Both of these "implementation" views had to be removed to get a non-corrupted view of the business.

> *Deriving a view of the business that removes any*
> *implementation details is the most important*
> *step in Re-Engineering.*

What Is Functional Partitioning?

In the late 1960s two people in the Data Processing Industry, Ed Yourdon and Larry Constantine, got together and defined in their book, *Structured Design*, seven levels of "cohesion" of a module or process. They defined the best level of cohesion as "functional." A piece of software at this level of cohesion does only one thing and has minimal coupling (interfaces) to other pieces of software. Figure 3–4 illustrates the difference between a nonfunctional "do everything" software module and a functional, "single-minded" module. The main point here is that by looking at the data that couples modules together, we can evaluate the functionality of those modules.

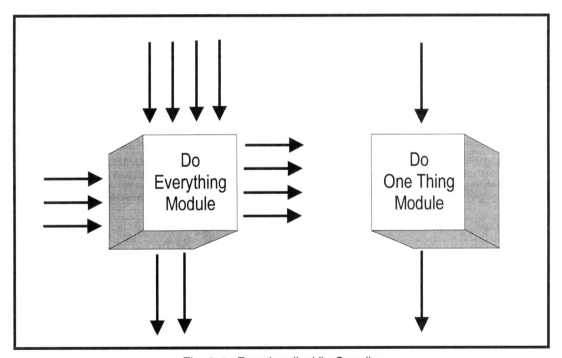

Fig. 3-4: Functionality Via Coupling

In the late 1970s another D.P. professional, Tom DeMarco, wrote the book, *Structured Analysis and System Specification*, and in it defined the most functional business process as the one with fewest interfaces (Data Flows). The book advocated constantly re-partitioning the Data Flow Diagram (DFD) to obtain minimal Data Flows for one complete task. Figure 3–5 illustrates the difference between a non-functional and a functional process. Again, the main point is that too many inputs and outputs indicate poor functionality.

Dysfunctional   Functional

Fig. 3–5: Functionality Via Interfaces

Just based on the above definitions, we can see that one functional view, or *partition*, would be based on grouping together only the processing and its essential data that our organization needs in order to satisfy a single request from outside the organization. That is, given one interface from outside our organization, we bring together into a single partition all necessary business logic and only the data needed to support this logic.

In contrast to this view, suppose we took an incoming Customer Order and followed it through a **typical**, traditionally partitioned system (a non-engineered system), we would probably find:

- A ridiculous "trail" left over from poorly-fragmented designs.

- A series of poorly implemented, quick fixes.

- A history of poorly planned system development efforts.

- Massive duplication of processing and mass redundancy of data capture and storage.

We could draw pictures of this incoming order, charting it as it bounces through the various programs and systems (see Figures 3–6 and 3–7). Figure 3–6 shows a simplified representation (model) of a typical organization's order processing. In this type of environment each order has to find its way through a variety of totally distinct departments and systems, before the customer receives their requested product or service.

If we took the same order going through the same set of departments and systems, and we modeled the processing using a Data Flow Diagram (see the *Model IS the Business* chapter), it would look like the tire tracks left by a demolition derby (see Figure 3–7)!

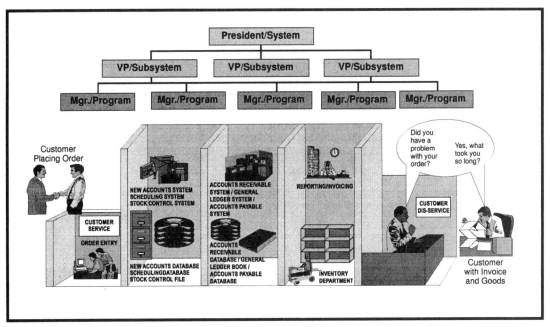

Fig. 3-6: Old Partitioning to Fill Customer Orders

Note that Figures 3–6 and Figures 3–7 do not show a functional partitioning of systems, even though this common partitioning is called "functional" in many organizations. Although we might expect this chaotic partitioning in a human-based system, this poor design is often perpetuated into automated systems as well.

Our first task in Re-Engineering is to remove these historical system barriers — both technical and managerial — that stand in the way of providing ultimate customer satisfaction.

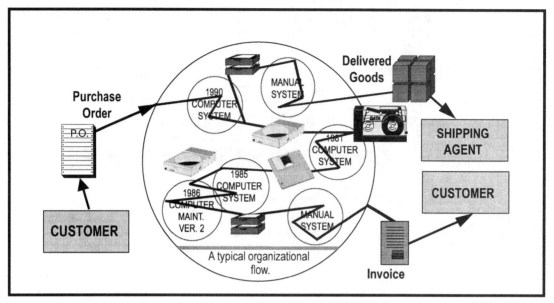

Fig. 3-7: Tracking a Customer Order

The Need for Good System Design

It's not uncommon to see front page headlines and/or a TV news commentary on an organization's silly procedures that sometimes have devastating results in the outside world. For example, a utility's customers would be irate if they were double-billed or had their service cut off due to a computer system bug. Or, an employee following poorly-designed procedures "to the letter" could cause discontented customers. In these examples somehow the implementation of the procedures corrupted the intent of the Business Policy Creators.

Of course when one reads of these failures in the newspapers, it brings home the fact that we need good design in computer and human systems. Despite the fact that we now have the tools to **engineer** manual and automated systems, we still find today that we're rewriting computer systems from the last decade, and even some that were built less than five years ago. In addition, we see organizations revamp their procedures and management structures constantly. The useful life expectancy of some systems is often not worth the development investment.

> *We should be building systems that last "as long as the business they support."*

So, how did we get in this situation and how is it affecting the business we support? Designers of systems (myself included) have made a number of mistakes. These mistakes (the "undergrowth" I listed in Figures 3–1 and 3–2) can be summed up as a series of what I call: "Archaeological Wrong Turns." They include:

- **Wrong Turn #1 — "People" Partitioning in Manual Systems**

- **Wrong Turn #2 — Computer Partitioning in Automated Systems**

- **Wrong Turn #3 — Program Partitioning in Automated Systems**

- **Wrong Turn #4 — Data File Partitioning in Automated Systems**

- **Wrong Turn #5 — File Partitioning in Manual Systems**

- **Wrong Turn #6 — After-the-fact Quality Control**

Wrong Turn #1 — "People" Partitioning in Manual Systems

Imagine that we are system archaeologists digging about in the remains of a typical existing organization. What might we find? How did it get to be designed like that?

An "archaeological dig" of an organization partitioned with human beings in mind might uncover the reason for partitions. These include reasons such as being divided into an Accounts Department, a Stock Control Office, a Manufacturing Division, and so on. Figure 3–8 shows the structure and lines of communication that we might find in our archaeological dig of a typical manual environment.

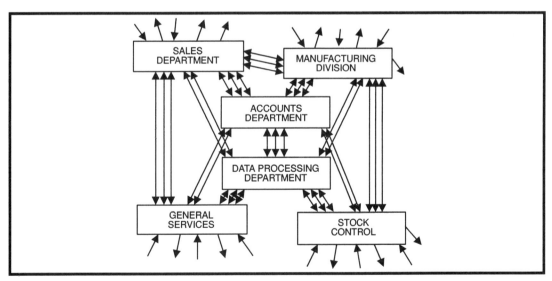

Fig. 3-8: Typical Manual System Partitions

The partitions of Figure 3–8 are very common in organizations for a number of reasons:

- People with the same kinds of skills get grouped together. For example, people who are good at selling get hired into the "Sales Department", people who are good at bookkeeping are assigned to "Accounting", and people who can write computer programs have glamorous job titles and get to work late in their cubicles in the "Programming Department." (In the past, putting together all the people with certain aptitudes and skills made a lot of sense from the point of view of economy of scale in a manual environment.)

- People or facilities may be concentrated in one area, building, or branch location based on the location of raw materials, ease of transportation, or customer base distribution.

- Physical space availability may have split a group of people up into different buildings or cities, or forced different groups into being situated together regardless of having different functions.

- Security considerations often isolate one group of workers from others. For example, Payroll is often a separate group, physically as well as administratively, because it processes sensitive, confidential information and money.

- Historical reasons such as "It's always been that way." (*I call this a "hysterical" reason because it's the irrational response usually given when someone asks why things are grouped unreasonably.*)

- Political reasons, such as when a manager of a division who has the political power to create departments under him or her captures work that really belongs to another division. This gives the manager more power in the organization.

These implementation issues are often the sole basis for many *so-called* "business" partitions. Although these are all valid *manual* partitions, and the structure of Figure 3–8 is an extremely common partitioning, it's not a *functional* partitioning. The most common partitioning basis in the above examples is *similarity of task*. We will come to see that this is not a functional partitioning. I hope to convince you that similarity of task, and the other rationales I listed above, are very poor reasons for grouping functions together and **do not reflect a well-engineered business view**.

---

*Similarity of task is not the basis of a truly
functional partitioning.*

Wrong Turn #2 — Computer Partitioning of Automated Systems

If we extend our archaeological dig, we find a remarkable similarity between the partitioning of computer systems and that of manual areas. Figure 3–9 shows the structure and lines of communication we might find in an automated environment. Notice how this is a similar partitioning to Figure 3–8. The exception is the General Services Department. Apparently it didn't get computer system support, possibly because it had no budget or insufficient political clout.

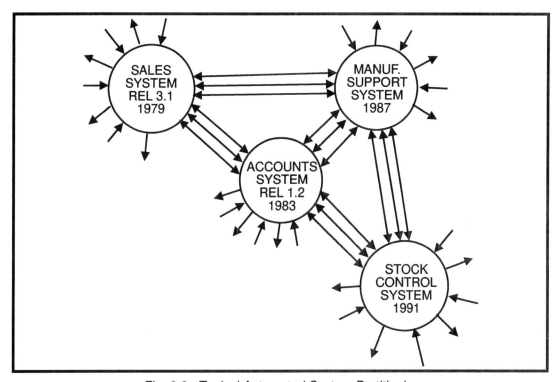

Fig. 3-9: Typical Automated System Partitioning

Of course, the reasons for putting manual systems together were blindly used as reasons for computer systems or programs. This leads to systems that were counterproductive and the "reasons" were quite silly when looked at using computer system partitioning reasoning. For example, we don't put all mathematical logic together in one program because of the math skills of that program — all programs can do mathematics (i.e., they have the same skill). So, it's ridiculous to use this old manual partitioning for computer system or program partitioning.

The partitions of Figure 3–9 are very common in computer systems for a number of reasons:

- *Automated systems have traditionally been built along manual system lines — accounting systems, sales support systems, stock control systems, and so on.*

  It seems only natural to assign project teams to build systems along the lines of internal boundaries, such as Accounting, Sales, Stock Control, and Manufacturing. After all, that's how the money for systems development is usually partitioned and acquired — by the internal departmental boundaries and their management. *(This could have been salvaged by a "neutral" D.P. Department budget, but if the department had a budget, it was very often used to buy computer hardware and support software, or to rewrite bad batch systems into faster, bad on-line systems.)*

- *The availability of machine time and capacity often led us into batching system functions together.*

  Even though a function might logically belong on its own, the lack of machine capacity may have forced the designer to squeeze together functional units that did not really fit. Functions which could be separated on-line, such as individual information retrieval, found themselves batched with other functions into a reporting system to keep the number of separate computer jobs down and save machine time. In this category there are many old design reasons, and all of them are very strange when you think about it. For example, how about the practice of putting a system together just to enter all orders (i.e., an Order Entry System)? *That's as bad as forming a department by putting together all of the people who come from the same town or who wear red socks!* Grouping different orders together is as bad as grouping different reports together.

- *Political boundaries are as influential here as they are in manual systems.*

  In my consulting work, I've often encountered systems that would have been far more business-efficient if their boundaries could have been stretched a little to complete some functional processing that was outside the project scope. The complexity of budget administration is often so great that it forces system boundaries to align with the budgets of the project requester's departmental boundaries. Also, a manager of one department may not want to give away any power or have their budget used to study a competing department. So computer system boundaries matched political power boundaries.

- *External constraints often affect system boundaries.*

  Government deadlines, for example, may mean that we must focus all our efforts on the immediate scope of the mandated change, or new requirement boundary. It may also mean that we can't afford the time or resources to look beyond it. Given the time to study further, we may fold-in the new requirement into existing functional areas instead of separating it out with duplicate extracted data files and processing.

- *The packaged software industry and PC hardware often imposes its own partitioning.*

Software packages obviously have to target specific, already existing departmental partitions, in order to make sales. So again, they follow traditional departmental boundaries for their packages to sell to department management, and hence reinforce those boundaries. Also, PC hardware and PC-based software packages are often "kludged" onto an existing system (as opposed to being engineered in). This often results in fragmented and duplicated data processing efforts.

Our data processing systems are rarely based on true functional partitioning, but rather on old manual design boundaries or new technological boundaries.

Wrong Turn #3 — Program Partitioning in Automated Systems

Let's now go one layer deeper to look at program boundaries inside a typical computer system. In Figure 3–10, we see that boundary partitions were based on similarity of tasks, such as the "edit-update-print" or "input-process-output" structures.

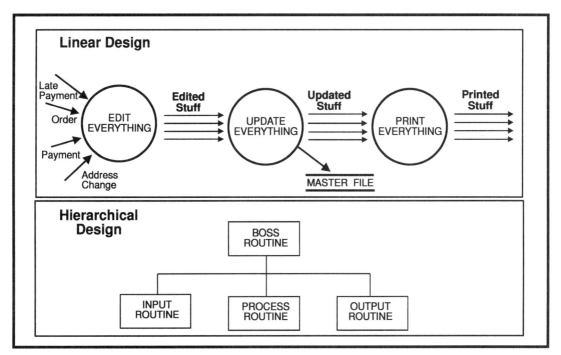

Fig. 3-10: Traditional Automated System Partitioning

Obviously, these programs were large because everything traveled through them. There are still programmers and file designers who believe that "big is best," and that partitioning is a waste of time and leads to inefficient systems. With this type of design, multiple inputs are passed through common system partitions, such as one huge, hard-to-maintain, monolithic edit program or an "everything but the kitchen sink" program.

Many computer programs are also poorly partitioned because:

- *Technology constrained design.*

   Historically, the D.P. Industry began by focusing primarily on the *processing* aspect of automated solutions to business problems, and the data aspect was seen as secondary — something to be addressed by the programmers. The low speed of early computers and peripherals meant that system jobs had to be batched into monolithic "lumps" and a programmer would strive for "efficiency" by processing as much as possible with one program or job. The data was lumped together into large transactions and master files to be fed to the monster, nightmare 10,000-line plus programs. (Be aware that some of these unreadable programs still cause organizations problems today.)

   Another excellent example of the constraint of technology is the anachronism of the QWERTY keyboard layout. This keyboard was originally arranged to slow down typists on old, manual typewriters, otherwise the strikers would jam together. This layout is still around and still limiting keying rates, even though there are no strikers to jam on today's electronic keyboards. We're therefore stuck with a keyboard layout purposely designed for slow input and hence, is the worst possible design for today's needs.

- *Programmer skills often constrained early systems.*

   It's obvious that if you're skilled in only one technique, such as how to build batch systems, you'll keep building using that technique. I still see many on-line systems that have internal logic from batch processing days. Another example would be to have somebody who was good at a particular computer programming language (e.g., COBOL or Assembler) lump logic together to accommodate the structure of a language.

- *Highly-procedural programming languages also constrained processing structure.*

   Languages constrained the way in which business systems were viewed by program developers. This is why Object Oriented Design and Programming views can be difficult to pick up by programmers who started with a Process Oriented language view. Also, some old computer languages dictated the design of your program (e.g., RPG and COBOL with its internal sort feature).

- *Programs were often built around a master file or a particular file structure (e.g., sequential or hierarchical).*

It is not uncommon to find a "monster" program into which every function that wanted access to master file data was incorporated. (This is analogous to a manual system that revolves around, say, "Fred's Ledger", and the only way to access the data in this ledger is to work your way into Fred's busy routine.)

- *Resource availability often influenced the structure of a system.*

Some program designs may be based on the availability of file data, machine speed, storage capacity, and machine availability. These are ridiculous reasons, when you think about them, for structuring new business systems. You know this hardware platform will be obsolete in a few years and then the programs will have to be re-written for the next platform.

Using the house building analogy, I ask in my seminars, "Can you tell how many carpenters worked on building a house by counting the number of rooms?" Of course not. A house's structure is not based on such an arbitrary physical partitioning as how many people were available to build it. But, if you look at Figure 3–11 and ask, "How many programmers worked on this system?", the answer is likely to be four or some divisor of four because there are four programs. If the project team had consisted of five programmers, we would probably see five programs. Creating separate programs for each programmer working on the project is definitely not a functional partitioning — it's based solely on implementation resources.

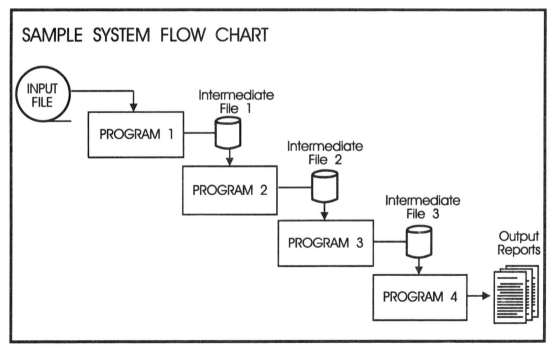

Fig. 3-11: Programmer Availability and Programs

Wrong Turn #4 — Data File Partitioning in Automated Systems

So far, we've been concentrating on the processing side of our archaeological dig. However, we see exactly the same problems when we start digging through old data partitioning. We see old automated file boundaries based on:

- *Everything anyone could ever want to know in one record.*

  This is the old "kitchen-sink" master file containing a record structure of several hundred or even several thousand characters (bytes). On one of my consulting assignments, I encountered a 22,000 byte-record customer file, built initially with the best intentions of satisfying one system's needs, but which just grew and grew over the years as each new application wanted to store more data. This file is typical in that it contained masses of "dead" data no one had ever removed because they assumed someone somewhere might be using it.

- *Limited storage devices which limited the file structure.*

  This reminds me of when I was a young programmer, working at a company where the D.P. Department owned only two tape drives and no disk storage. We were *forced* into batch processing — reading from one tape drive and writing to the other. But then, when direct (random) access storage devices became available, what did we do? We just put the batch file structure onto disk with no structural changes! The resulting structure looked something like Figure 3–12. It's unfortunately quite common to see a blind evolution from old file designs to new file designs, without taking advantage of the opportunities for improvement.

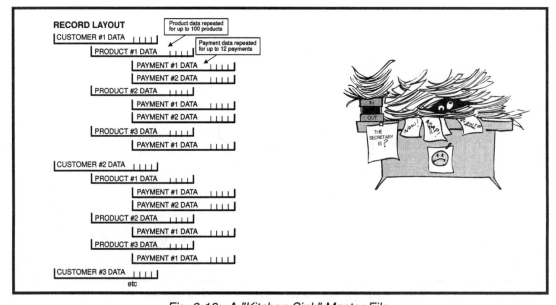

Fig. 3-12: A "Kitchen Sink" Master File

These files contained bundled information and arose when the previous designer grouped separate sets of data together for the sake of efficiency. This was very common of the files used in "edit-update-print" computer systems, because this data partitioning was based on process bundling for technology and efficiency. In Figure 3–10 the data between the processes Edit-Update-Print would typically be bundled into the Edited data file and the Updated data file. The analyst must break up these bundled stores (typified in Figure 3–13) , and assign their Data Elements to cohesive data groupings or Entities during business data repartitioning.

Customer 1
    Product 1
        Payables
    Product 2
        Payables
    Product 5
        Payables

Customer 2
    Product 1
        Payables
    Product 3
        Payables
    Product 4
        Payables
    Product 5
        Payables

Supplier 1
    Product 1
        Part Number
    Product 2
        Part Number
    Product 3
        Part Number

Supplier 2
    Product 5
        Part Number
    Product 7
        Part Number

Supplier 3
    Product 9
        Part Number

Fig. 3-13: Examples of Bundled Stores

- *Misguided access efficiency decisions.*

  This produced file structures based on the least number of READ instructions in a program, so that the data we needed was all "right there" in one record. *(When combined with the "kitchen sink" master file wrong turn listed above, the resulting huge record structure dimmed the computer room lights whenever a program READ statement was executed. This is like receiving a phone book and having to find someone's name when all you are given is their phone number.)*

- *PC/Local Workstation Partitioning.*

  With PCs becoming so inexpensive, it's easy for the average organization's employees to requisition computers to store and process data at their desks. Of course each PC user then needs to have data that is really *global* in nature stored *locally* on their machine (and in their software packages' formats). This leads to mass data redundancy, stored dead data, and data synchronization problems (e.g., they have a customer's new address on their *local* PC, but the company's *global* data doesn't get updated with this new address and besides, it's in the wrong format). Client/Server technology is helping with this, but again only when analysis is performed first, not when the flaws of old designs are brought forward in new designs.

Wrong Turn #5 — File Partitioning in Manual Systems

We can find the same monster file in a manual environment (e.g., tub files), but it is more common to see the opposite — fragmented data files, resulting in mass redundancy (e.g., my name appears in five files at my bank) and non-synchronized data (e.g., my address is potentially different across all five files). In Figure 3–14, we see Accounts Receivable, Manufacturing, Customers, Collection Offices, etc. all have their own "local" files. The old system's designers had to create these files so that one department could accumulate documents while waiting until the scheduled time for another department to pick them up. Notice between each and every old design boundary there will be some kind of store. This store is usually unnecessary in the Re-Engineered business world. If the analyst does not recognize this old design characteristic, the old store is very likely to become part of the requirements for a new file/database. This will perpetuate unnecessary stored data and the housekeeping processes associated with it, such as Creating, Deleting, and Updating data.

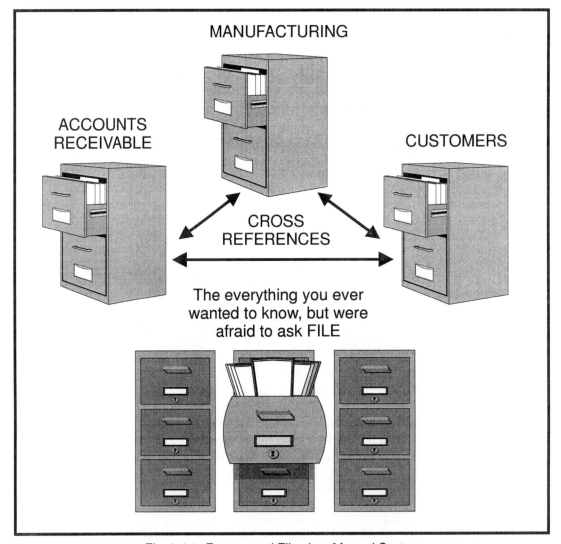

Fig. 3-14: Fragmented Files in a Manual System

There are many other reasons for the fragmentation and lumping together of manual data. Some you may hear are:

- "It's always been that way, and besides, it's my private file."

- "We lock our files up overnight in separate locations for safety reasons."

- "I look entries up by name and they look them up by account number."

- "We keep multi-part paper copies for backup and security, but of course, no-one uses all the data on each form."

With these local files in Figure 3–14, it's common to find the same customer information in all of the files. Customer details may appear in three places in the name of easy manual access, because to deal with a customer inquiry in Sales, the Sales staff must have access to Customer Orders without running over to Accounts or Manufacturing. Similarly, the Accounts Department staff must have access to Customer data without going to the Sales Office. If a customer sends in a change of address, the chances are that only one file will be updated — the file in the department that happened to receive the notification.

Wrong Turn #6 — After-the-fact Quality Control

When we put managers in charge of workers, we introduce another wrong turn where the workers get the feeling that inspections and after-the-fact processes are needed to produce a quality product — in other words, that they need to be managed. Since the product they are creating is going to be inspected, this introduces a double-edged sword where workers don't put their ultimate effort into doing the job right the first time. They know that somebody else will possibly catch their errors. This of course leads to less quality up front. The very reliance on after-the-fact inspections simply indicates that something was wrong upstream that produced that product. Since after-the-fact inspectors are expected to find errors down the line, the product/system developers are put into the frame of mind that these are a fact of the human process.

Of course the inspectors have the inverse view. They assume the folks who were putting together the product knew what they were doing, so that they, as inspectors, don't have to scrutinize every detail.

This wrong turn is the result of thinking that it's automatically necessary to have inspections and audits as "after-the-fact" quality assurance measures for both products and services.

It's not uncommon to find in the manual environment that we inspect products after we've built them to see if their quality is up to scratch. We will find the data (i.e., the product) being looked at by a particular partitioned area (typically known as Quality Control or the Inspection Department).

In the automated world, it's typically seen during systems development where we see testing phases which outnumber the other development phases. Testing phases often include unit testing, system testing, performance testing, acceptance testing, etc. On the other hand, we typically have only one analysis phase and one design phase.

What were the reasons for putting inspections after the fact, or insisting on management approvals and sign-offs? Obviously, the reason was because under the old paradigm, we thought that human beings needed to be watched and were not empowered. Management was always "higher" than the technical tasks. A lack of trust was also an issue. We didn't, for example, trust another department, so we inspected their result when it came into our department. A lack of skilled workers or training also led to the feeling that inspections after the fact were needed. Possibly the biggest *hysterical* "reason" of all is that it's always been that way. All the textbooks told us that inspections were part of how we implemented a manufacturing organization or managed a development process.

When people who came from the shop floor (or from the technical ranks of programmers) were made managers, they were already indoctrinated into the old methods of testing after the fact. Also, from the customer point of view, we expected defective returns and even set up a special department to handle returns, to track numbers of errors per thousand, etc. Again, like Quality Control, this department was self supporting. It was expected to have statistics on defects and to be a growing department. In some cases the idea was to put more people into processing returns than into putting more effort into the development of the product itself.

What this leads to is poor customer satisfaction. We may never even hear from those who don't return the product, or like our service, but they will never do business with us again. Poor satisfaction could also result from wrong data (such as errors on bank statements or mixed up airline reservations) leading to loss of business.

Another factor leading to after the fact inspections was the wastage. We came to accept that a certain amount of the product is going to be thrown away. Therefore, the cost of producing that product and the amount of materials going into that product is already factored into purchasing and ends up being scrap.

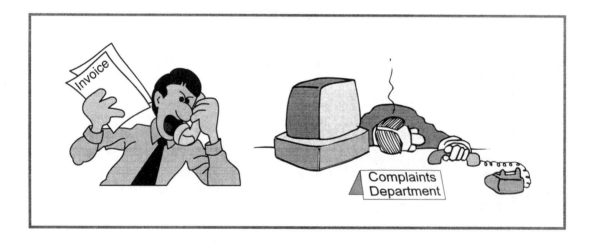

Of course, duplicate processing is also one of the causes of this problem. Whoever developed the product should be making the product right the first time. However, the inspectors after the fact are going to be looking at the exact same processing as it took to create the product in the first place.

This redundancy can be self-perpetuating, such as the case of finding people monitoring the phone calls to the people in the Complaints Department to see if these people are doing their jobs correctly. In this case we have quality control of the Complaints Department. *(It's amazing to me at the time of this writing the number of times I call the Technical Support Department for a PC hardware or software product manufacturer where the line is constantly tied up for days. What does that tell me about the product?)*

We also have duplicate data where we will overproduce a product anticipating returns, or to have them on the shelf as replacement parts. In the automated world we have duplicate processing in things such as re-editing data and cross checking the last system's output (which is our input). Obviously, this is also a problem from the duplicate data point of view (i.e., backups, tapes, many generations of backups, histories, etc.), because we don't trust the software or hardware.

All these inspections and audits are not Business Issues, they are System and Implementation Issues.

Summary

Of course, none of these wrong turns are unique to the systems building world. House building started with mud huts and no architectural plans. It was only when houses fell down and "outside" government mandates were introduced, that the building industry started to apply an engineering discipline. Only then did the industry adopt the mandating of detailed requirement specifications prior to building and the documenting of codified regulations for the profession.

Now, what can we do about all this? Obviously we need to repartition (Re-Engineer) these old design boundaries. We also need to improve our application software to match the tremendous advances made in hardware and support software technology during the last decade.

Business Re-Engineering professionals would be doing a disservice to the business people using the resulting systems if the system design procedures make systems any more complex than the business functions they are supporting. The sooner we start building manual and computer systems around Business Issues instead of technological, or old design issues, the sooner we will be able to end the short payback periods of today's systems. Also, business people will be able to relate to automated and manual system designs, thus enabling modification and system building to be no more complex than the business at hand.

The first step towards language was to link acoustically or otherwise commutable signs to sense impressions... A higher development is reached when further signs are introduced and understood which establish relations between those other signs designating sense-impressions... When man becomes conscious of the rules governing relations between signs[,] the so called grammar of language is established... When language becomes [thus] partially independent from the background of impressions, a greater inner coherence is gained. Only at this further development where frequent use is made of so called abstract concepts, [does] language become an instrument of reasoning in the true sense of the word.

Albert Einstein
Out of My Later Years
The Common Language of Science

Understanding the Nature of Systems

Most organizations have become too complex to comprehend by one person without some representation with an abstract model. One major complexity is the design that covers the essential business functions.

When we are given a Re-Engineering project, it's important that we first study (analyze) the nature of the business (the **what**) before we introduce a new design (a new **how**) for that business. We need a clear understanding of **what** the business is doing before going from an old **how** to a new **how**.

Systems analysis is critical for Business Process Re-Engineering. In fact, once we understand what our organization does, we may not use any new technology and still Re-Engineer the organization.

Re-Engineering without analysis is not Re-Engineering.

It always seems ludicrous to me when I encounter an organization that doesn't know the details of what it does. By *details*, I don't mean manual procedures, rule books, program flow charts, and such, but a **Business Model** of what the organization does. Such a view tells which data are used where, what processing is performed where, and so on. Only with a fully-engineered business view of the organization can we effectively identify what processing is going on, what data is being used, or what changes in data and/or processing are necessary to respond to a business change.

The point is to be able to pinpoint where modifications are necessary in our response to a business change, and to make those changes with minimal disruption to other parts of the business. When the managers of an organization can't find quick answers to business questions, or fully understand how the business itself is implemented, it's time they developed some engineered Business Models.

One dictionary defines *system* as:

> *"A connected or related set of activities that works toward a result."*

The definition works for me during analysis because, from a fundamental systems view and from a purely business perspective, data are the *connections* between the set of *activities* or processes. And, I see the *result* as the satisfaction of the customers' needs and the strategic mission of the organization. The task of analysis is to determine what is required of the system in terms of its business data, processing, and control (all of which are devoid of any design issues). This results in an implementation-independent Business Model.

Everything You See Is a Design

What I mean by "Everything you see is a design" is, when you look at a system, be it human- or computer-based (never mind inanimate objects), they are "implementations" of requirements (either humans' or Mother Nature's).

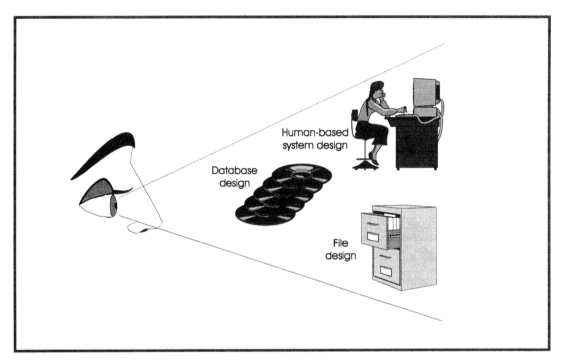

In other words, I guarantee that 100 years from now, everyone in your organization won't be there. I'll also guarantee that any software system won't be there, but the exact same business can still be running. So, what is it that's running when you remove the human beings and computer systems? The "business" is what's running.

The problem is, you never see the business, you always see the implementation of the business. I'm sorry if this sounds a little metaphysical, but, you can't see the business itself. In other words, you can't see an analysis. You can see a design, but you can't see an analysis.

My basic premise is that a non-redundant set of facts describing the business should underpin any organization. We can represent that set of facts in many ways.

Business Issues as Conceptualized by Humans

The question is: "How do humans conceptualize the organization's Business Issues?" We have a problem as human beings trying to view analysis/Business Issues because we're all designers. For those of us who fall into "solution mode" — trying to solve problems as soon as we find them — it's very difficult to understand what analysis is and what its deliverable is.

It's actually quite difficult to see an analysis. In fact I find the sentence: "Show me an analysis of a chair." awkward to say. Somebody might ask: "Do you want me to show you a specification that results from analysis?" To which I reply: "No. Show me an analysis of a chair." It sounds strange. And yet if I said: "Show me a design of a chair or of a system.", it's an easy thing to do. But what was the analysis of the chair?

Now, if you take the identification of the requirements for a chair as a mental exercise (as I've had my seminar students do many times), it's actually quite difficult to define the requirements. What I've arrived at in my discussions with these groups is that a chair is a product that will support a human body in a seated state comfortably. It can be movable. It should support the back, etc. Given those requirements, we can have a chair that we kneel on, we can have a bean bag chair, and, most importantly, we can invent something we haven't seen before. So, there are many designs that satisfy the requirements of a chair once we give the requirements.

Because we can't see an analysis, we have to produce some kind of specification that models what we want. It's also rather difficult to use the *Oxford* or *Webster's Dictionary* to help during analysis because the dictionary itself is design oriented (i.e., the dictionary uses design words and defines design issues). That doesn't mean that there aren't any logical analysis terms in the dictionary; it just means that the vast majority of terms are related to design because those are the kinds of things we see out there in the world (and hence are defined in a dictionary). So, we are forced into thinking about analysis using design terms. In my seminars, the best I've been able to do in simple definition terms is to talk about **what** we want verses **how** we implement the **what**.

The chair is **how** you've implemented the requirements. The requirements are as I stated before. It seems implicit in the design of a chair that we have the requirements. So, if you do a model of a chair, you're usually drawing a design model and not necessarily a model of the requirements of the chair. It gets even more difficult to develop the model of something that's intangible, it's hard enough with a tangible chair. For example, how do you model a system or a service?

The Stimulus-Response Nature of Systems

All systems we encounter have some fundamental characteristics in common — they're all *stimulus-response* mechanisms and they all have *process* and *memory*. The stimulus-response aspect occurs on the outside edges of the business and defines the organization as viewed from the outside. The process-memory aspect occurs within the organization and represents the organization's internals.

The stimulus-response nature of systems applies to all types of systems — physical, biological, and informational — and gives us a "black-box" view of a system. In other words, we can view the organization from just **what** it does in response to its inputs and outputs without getting involved with **how** it is implemented. Figure 4–1 shows this stimulus-response nature of a system with the system shown as a "black box."

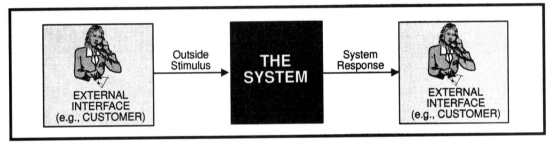

Fig. 4-1: The Stimulus-Response Nature of Systems

For example, the physical automatic doors we see at airports and supermarkets are systems. The *stimulus* is the body heat or motion of a person coming towards the door, or the weight of the person stepping on the sensor mat. The *response* is the opened door.

An example of a biological system is that of a person accidentally hitting his or her hand. Pain is the stimulus to the brain and rapid withdrawal of the hand is the usual response (often accompanied with a verbal response).

This stimulus-response view, of course, applies to an organization also. An example would be a mail order company that receives a stimulus (a purchase order) from the outside world and responds by shipping products and an invoice. *(I used to use a rock as an example of what is not a system, but the more I've begun to understand ecosystem management, I've realized that rocks are also stimulus-response mechanisms. If you don't believe that, take a look at the Grand Canyon.)*

The Process-Memory Nature of Systems

The response to an external event may alter the system, so that a system may not respond in exactly the same way to two identical stimuli. For example, if I have four hundred dollars in my bank account and stimulate a banking system with a three hundred dollar withdrawal request, the response will be a successful transaction. But if I try to withdraw three hundred dollars a second time, the response will be different. As part of the first transaction, the *process* updated the system's *memory* and retrieved the updated memory as part of the response to the second occurrence of the event (see Figure 4–2). From an analysis point of view, the same system was invoked, but with different values for the memory. The business rules didn't change, just the values, and hence a different part of the business logic was executed.

Fig. 4-2: Varied Responses from Identical Stimuli

A *process* is the set of forces, actions, laws, rules, and operations that act on a stimulus, generates the response, and usually alters the state, memory, or material within the system. *Memory* maintains a record of the internal state and the relevant data that the system needs to retrieve and update in response to a stimulus.

A system's processes are implemented by procedures, tasks, and computer programs. Its memories are implemented by records, human memory, files, tables, and databases (see Figure 4–3).

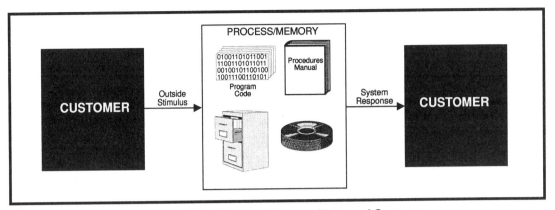

Fig. 4-3: The Process-Memory Nature of Systems

"Process typically needs memory" and "memory is processed" so they are not necessarily distinct from one another. However, recognizing this distinction is valuable for understanding the system and the business.

Be careful not to isolate process and memory from each other (especially into two groups of people dealing with them in the organization). At some organizations I have seen the situation where one group may believe that it can understand a business by looking only at what the business needs to retain in its memory, that is, a *data-only* view. Another group may believe that it's only necessary to look at things from a process-only view. Each view believes that the other is important only in so far as it supports the primary view. The truth is, the two should not be looked at in isolation, especially when the goal is to support the business.

Notice that I started this discussion by talking about stimulus-response but, as soon as we begin to look inside a system, we must acknowledge process and memory. Unfortunately, the classical analysis techniques have tended to focus almost exclusively on *process-memory* aspects of a system (*for most of my early career I also fell into this view*). Looking at Table 4–1 shows the past emphasis on an organization's internal processes and data in analysis and design without any focus on what happens on the outside.

	TYPE OF VIEW	ASPECT VIEWED
BUSINESS VIEW	Business Process View	Business Policy
	Business Memory View	Business Stored Data
DESIGN VIEW	Design Process View	Process Architecture
	Design Memory View	Data Architecture

Table 4-1: Internal Business and Design Process and Memory Issues

Summary

So, systems are merely stimulus-response mechanisms regardless of how they are implemented (human systems, computer systems, biological ecosystems, etc.), and we need to acknowledge the process and memory associated with the system's stimuli and responses (see Figure 4–4).

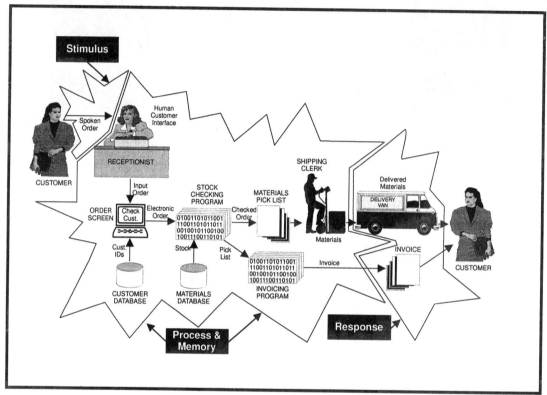

Fig. 4-4: Physical Aspects of Process/Memory

To get a meaningful, seamless view of an organization, the stimulus-response, process, and memory aspects need to be looked at in total and specified as the result of the analysis. Therefore, our problem is how do we represent these aspects of the business. If you realize from our previous discussion that everything you see is a design, we need some way of removing this design and seeing only the analysis requirements (see Figure 4–5).

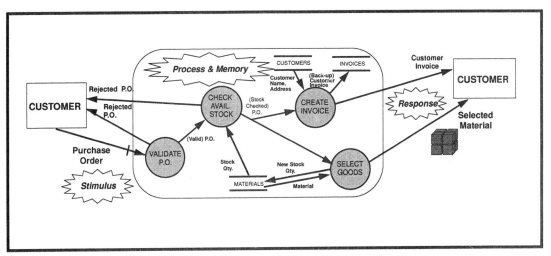

Fig. 4-5: A Stereotypical System

The model IS the business.

The next chapter covers one way to represent this stimulus-response, process-memory view of an organization using models.

If your only tool is a hammer, the [whole] world looks like a nail.

Abraham Maslow

The Model IS the Business

As discussed in the previous chapter, we need some way to get to the essential view of a business without seeing the implementation of that view. We need to use a model because the business is not its implementation. In fact, that's what we use models for; to conceptualize something that might not be easy to visualize. Now, to deliberately contradict this chapter's title, any model we produce isn't really the business. However, models are the closest we're ever going to get to seeing the business until we can do Spock-style mind melds by touching the side of an office building (*for all you Star Trek fanatics*).

When I go out to a consulting assignment and someone tries to explain their business to me, the first thing I do is to try to "picture" it using a graphical model. There have been many models introduced over the past few years that can represent the basic set of business facts. However, I have found it useful to select from a variety of different models, depending on who is going to review and verify them and what I am trying to model. *I didn't want to make this chapter too long, so topics such as how models relate to Total Quality Management are covered in the Quality in Re-Engineering Appendix.*

The basic families of models described in this chapter are: Process Oriented Models, Data Oriented Models, Hierarchical/Network/Relational Data Oriented Models, Process and Data Oriented Models, and Control Oriented Models.

If the people I talk to are trying to describe their organization (or part of it) from the point of view of what data are stored and the relationships between that data, a data model is a good choice. If they're trying to describe something that's based on complex control issues, I'll use a State Transition Diagram or Control Flow Diagram. If they're trying to describe something that involves data flowing through a system and the transformation of that data, I'll use a Data Flow Diagram. If they're trying to describe their organization by relating to the things in it and all of the processing that can act on these things, I'll use an Object/Class Model.

When we represent the aspects of an organization in a model, we must take human issues like readability into account. Using one model to identify all the details (facts) in a house, for example, can produce a complex, unreadable model because a single diagram including structures, wiring, plumbing, heat loss calculations, structural calculations, drainage, topography, etc. would not be very readable. This is also true of Re-Engineering models.

Obviously when dealing with Business Re-Engineering, we need some sort of model to be able to communicate between the business people and customers (the users of the product or system), the analysts and designers (the people who will build the product or system), and those who perform system maintenance (those who will modify the product or system as the needs of the business change).

In many situations graphical models are superior to text as a communications tool. Most engineering disciplines emphasize the importance of drawing graphical models before building actual products. This is because it's too expensive to build the real system before we are sure that we correctly understand the business requirements. Especially in the case of some particular physical product, it's vital to test the product on the model before manufacturing it in volume. This is analogous to drawing the blueprint and getting it approved by the customer before building the house.

It's worth noting here that, although graphical models provide a clear, understandable specification, they don't stand alone. Text is still usually required, but it no longer appears in huge, monolithic blocks. It is used, instead, as backup documentation for parts of the graphical model and is organized along the same lines as the model.

We must acknowledge that we human beings can't effectively assimilate and comprehend large, monolithic specifications. Presenting these for customer review invites uninformed consent, allows errors to pass undetected, and leads to reduced quality because the business people can't confirm that the product or system as specified will conform to business requirements.

Unfortunately, the most commonly taught modeling tool has been text. This tool was given to us by our country's educational system. Text is perfectly fine as a tool to describe something that flows in a linear manner. For example, text is adequate to describe the flow of linear control (what do I do next?). In the English Language we are automatically given the idea of going to the next line to carry on reading. Text is also perfectly fine if we are telling a story. However, text is not very good when we try to use it to "picture" something to do with a system. As a modeling tool, text has a number of undesirable characteristics. The following table contrasts the weaknesses of text as a modeling tool versus the strengths of graphical models.

TEXTUAL MODEL SHORTCOMINGS	GRAPHICAL MODEL STRENGTHS
Linear — It must be presented linearly and is usually read from start to finish. Systems, on the other hand, can be both synchronous and asynchronous networks of processing and data does not flow linearly through them. It's only when we get down to a fine enough level of detail that some systems may appear to be linear.	**Depict non-linear systems** — Graphical models make it possible to represent non-linear structures and such processing features as concurrent tasks.
Monolithic — It is not naturally partitioned although we do have the concept of major and minor breaks: chapters, sections, paragraphs, and sentences.	**Support partitioning** — They allow easy representation of the natural partitions of systems and their interfaces, leading to tangible, measurable deliverables and task allocation along the natural lines of business systems.
Difficult to change — correcting errors and omissions is extremely laborious, time-consuming, and error-prone because text is linear. Also, it's difficult to spot a global or referential change (e.g., page 63 disagrees with page 328).	**Flexible** — Graphical models are far easier to change than narrative text. Also, associations and referential integrity can be depicted easily.
Verbose — A word is one thousandth of a picture.	**Succinct** — A picture's worth a thousand words.
Not measurable — Lines of text in a requirements specification are difficult to use to quantify completion.	**Verifiable** — Graphical models support the validation and review activities during system development via easily-changeable representations of the system.
Ambiguous — The English Language is deliberately rich and therefore has the potential to be vague and misinterpreted.	**Unambiguous** — Graphical models break the language/semantic communication barrier by using specific symbols — the universal language.
Subjective — Almost all text is subject to individual interpretation.	**Non-subjective** — No interpretation is necessary given the rules of the model's symbology.
Not easily leveled — Textual material consists entirely of two-dimensional details.	**Can easily show levels of detail** — Graphics can support a diverse audience and depict high-level, abstract views and low-level, detail views.

Table 5–1: Text vs. Graphics for Models

Effective System Modeling

We obviously use models to:

- Aid our own thinking and understanding.

- Be able to analyze something because we can picture it using the model.

- Communicate our ideas into the minds of others. For example, we use models (blueprints) to communicate the design from the architect to the person who will actually build the house. Also, the architect uses models to communicate the design into the mind of the customer to make sure that the architect understands the desires of those who will live in the house.

- Defer detail in order to get a high-level view before we get drawn into the lower-level details.

It's important to keep in mind that any models we produce need to be specified to the necessary level of detail for the reader (whoever they may be) to be able to verify their requirements for analysis, design, or implementation.

The audience for the model may be ourselves who at some point in the future may need to refer to the model to remind ourselves why we did something in a particular way.

Using a graphical model helps to make an intangible problem tangible. Even though the final product is still intangible, we can conceptualize the problem more easily with these modeling tools. This is no different than an architect drawing a line on a blueprint to indicate a wall. When we see a meter on the side of our house or apartment, showing how much electricity we've used, it's not showing us the electricity; its dials or gauges are simply models of the electricity — a representation of the electricity that we've used.

Figure 5–1 shows the symbology used in a DeMarco-style and a Gane/Sarson-style Process Model.[1] [2]

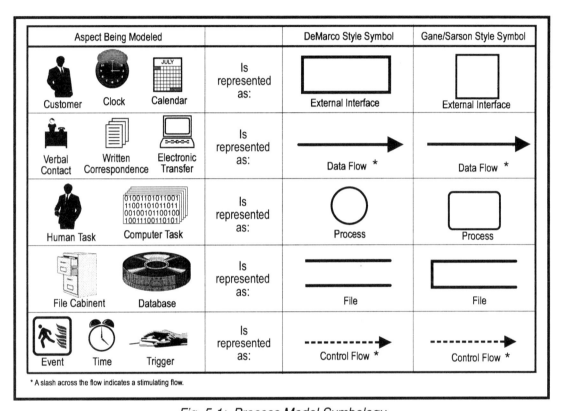

Fig. 5-1: Process Model Symbology

---

1   *Structured Analysis and System Specification,* Tom DeMarco — See Bibliography

2   *Structured Systems Analysis: Tools and Techniques,* Gane, C. and Sarson, T. — see Bibliography

Figure 5–2 shows the symbols used in a Chen-style Entity Relationship Diagram and in a Bachman/Martin-style Information Model.

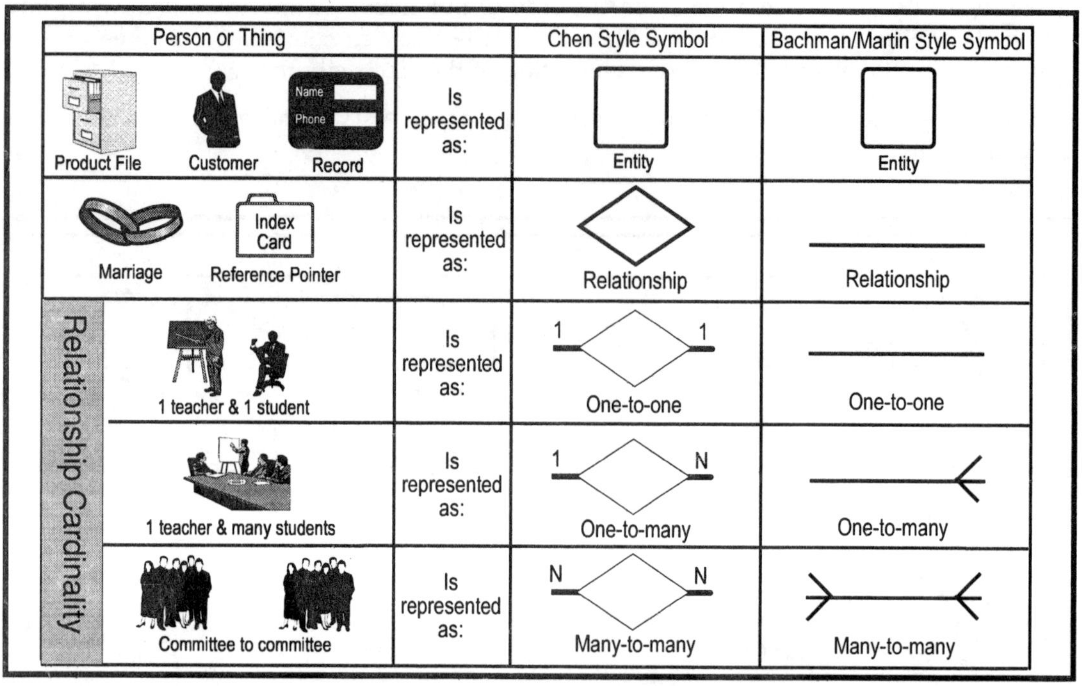

Person or Thing			Chen Style Symbol	Bachman/Martin Style Symbol
Product File Customer Record		Is represented as:	Entity	Entity
Marriage Reference Pointer		Is represented as:	Relationship	Relationship
Relationship Cardinality	1 teacher & 1 student	Is represented as:	1 ◇ 1 One-to-one	One-to-one
	1 teacher & many students	Is represented as:	1 ◇ N One-to-many	One-to-many
	Committee to committee	Is represented as:	N ◇ N Many-to-many	Many-to-many

Fig. 5-2: Information Model Symbology

> *It is vital to Re-Engineering that we have the ability to model businesses and systems. Our success depends on the suitability of the model for the job at hand.*

You're probably already familiar with using models to depict real-world issues. For example, your family tree as represented in a hierarchy diagram is a model. We are all used to this use of models. I'd like to bet the reader that they can read a map of their town, or of the U.S.A. As we look at the map, we understand that the lines represent roads. The thicker lines (or, in some cases, the red lines) may indicate freeways. The size of the text may also indicate size of towns. Once we understand the model's symbology, we can read that particular model.

Models for Analysis

There have been a number of models introduced over the years for modeling systems. In fact, the profession that I'm most used to (Data Processing) has gone through an evolution of its modeling techniques. A number of proven models emerged from this Data Processing methodology evolution that we can use in the Business Re-Engineering process. In fact, analysis itself is a Business Issue rather than a System Issue, so we can use the same analysis methods and models that were developed as part of D.P.'s evolution quite effectively.

However, in many cases the models used within a project methodology are dictated by the methods that you use for the project. For example, if you use Process Analysis, DFDs tend to be the main model of choice. If using Object Oriented technology, then Object Oriented diagrams are obviously the model of choice. Figure 5–3 shows sample Analysis methods and their view of models.

Process Analysis views the Business from the point of view of Data-on-the-Move by modeling:
- ❖ Data <u>flowing</u> through the organization
- ❖ Data <u>stored</u> in the organization
- ❖ Processes <u>transforming</u> Data
- ❖ Sources and Receivers of Data (the System Boundary)

Information Analysis views the Business from the point of view of Data-at-Rest by modeling:
- ❖ Entities (Data held in cohesive units)
- ❖ Relationships between Entities
- ❖ Data Elements (facts about Entities)

Object Oriented Analysis views the Business from the point of view of interacting Objects by modeling:
- ❖ Objects (Encapsulations of Data and Process)
- ❖ Methods (reusable processes acting on shared variables — Data or States— within an Object)
- ❖ Messages (Communication between Objects)

State Transition Analysis views Business Issues from the point of view of control by modeling:
- ❖ The State of the system being modeled
- ❖ Transitions that show what causes a State to change and the action to take based on that change

Fig. 5-3: Modeling Business Systems

When performing Pre-Engineering, you would use either a Process Engineering, Information Engineering, or Object Oriented Engineering's methods and models because these are all techniques to capture the essential business information. Once you have discovered your initial Business Event Partitions, by all means evaluate which technique is most suitable (if one is not already dictated by an existing requirement).

Modeling Business Systems

The vast majority of business systems deal with both data and processing (and some control issues) that are part of the analysis requirements. So, we can put on our analysis hat and take a look at data (the information that flows and that we keep regarding a system) and model that information. Also, we can look at the logic (the processing of data) and model that processing.

A number of methods (each with their recommended models) have been proven to be of help to the analyst in D.P.: *Process Engineering, Information Engineering,* and *Object Oriented* methods. Each of these analysis techniques can use a State Transition Diagram to supplement the specification when business control issues are a factor.

These methods and their associated models were proffered by their authors to help understand analysis details, design details, and implementation details. Figure 5–3 shows the points of view of each modeling technique and its associated model.

What we'll see in the *Partitioning by Business Events* chapter is how these models can be partitioned from a natural business view.

The Inadequacy of Conventional Models

Let me talk about some of the models that have become popular over the past few decades. I do not intend to teach the details of each of these models, but let me make you aware of a few and describe their orientation. Figure 5–4 enlarges upon a previous diagram to show how these three phases are accomplished. This figure summarizes the three major activities in the development of any system.

The common denominator of all the methods employed in Figure 5–4 is that they all use models as a means of communication. Please realize that everything we perceive can be classed as a model or view. From one point of view, our minds merely model reality for us in terms of vision, hearing, smell, and so on. The models we draw using symbols simply aid the process of understanding and communicating with the symbols representing abstracted aspects of reality.

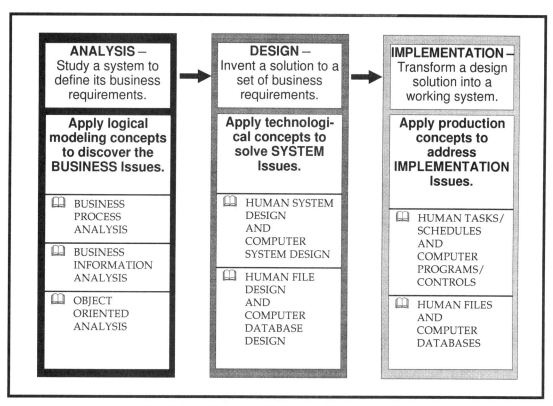

Fig. 5-4: A Common Platform of Understanding

The Characteristics of an Effective Model

What, therefore, are the characteristics of an effective model?

To effectively represent the complexity of business, a model should be:

Comprehensive	We need to use our model to represent both the process-memory (inside view) and stimulus-response (external view) aspects of our business completely.
Partitionable	We want to avoid complex models where we have to understand everything in order to understand anything.
Supportive	The model should assist us in dealing with complex and voluminous information that exceeds the capacity of human memory.
Intelligible	Graphical symbols, especially, help understanding because — do I need to say it? — a picture can be worth a thousand words. The few words we do use should be concise, precise, and specific.
Non-redundant	If we have more than one model of the business, such as a process view and a data view, they should not duplicate each other. They should complement and correlate with each other.
General and/or Specific	The model should be able to show levels of detail from the highest to the lowest; for example, from an organization-wide enterprise model down to individual fields or Data Elements (attributes).
Abstract	We should be able to represent and describe an idea, or the qualities of a thing apart from the thing itself. For example, the memory model should allow us to describe the types of data we hold about our customers, quite separate from the *actual data values* describing each customer occurrence.
Economical	We should be able to simulate a business, or those aspects in which we are interested, without going to the expense of creating the business itself. Obviously, a wind-tunnel model or a computer simulation of an airliner is much cheaper, safer, and more convenient to work with than flying the real thing into a hurricane.

Table 5–2: The Characteristics of an Effective Model

What follows is a review of a number of models that can be helpful to a person analyzing (which involves understanding the old design) and specifying an organization and its systems. I've categorized these models into four areas: Process Oriented, Data Oriented, process and Data Oriented, and Control Oriented. Let me enlarge on these types of models in more detail.

Process Oriented Models

Flow charts like the one in Figure 5–5, are what I'd call a Process Oriented model.

Flow Charts

It's actually quite rare to find someone who does not know what a Flow Chart is and who does not recognize its symbology. A Flow Chart's intention is to depict processing in a linear (flow-of-control) manner. [3] In this respect Flow Charts and text are very similar in that they both declare a control structure of verbs.

Unfortunately, Flow Charts are one model not very well suited to depicting businesses because they are a one-sided view. They show processing only with its flow of control. I call them a Process Oriented model because they don't show data. This doesn't mean we can't put data in the boxes and say, for example, "IF X = Y, THEN..." (where "X" and "Y" are the data). However, that data are not given a symbol in the model. For example, the lines are not the data, they are "GO TOs."

Flow Charts are also detailed diagrams (i.e., they are typically used when figuring out detail issues to do with processing/logic). They are not really useful for modeling high-to-low leveling issues or complex control structures. What we need is a model (or set of models) that can show both the data and processing sides of businesses.

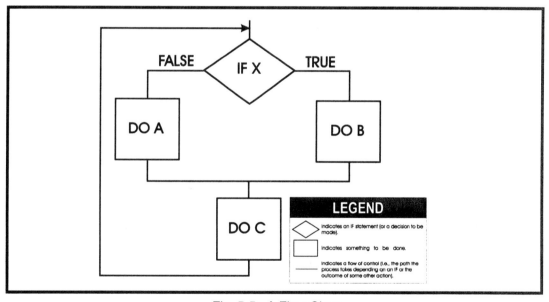

Fig. 5-5: A Flow Chart

---

3   By the way, that's my excuse for not being able to cook. If you read a linear text recipe from top to bottom, it may say: "Prepare the vegetables by steaming them until you can stick a fork in them." I do just that and get them ready and then it says: "Meanwhile, prepare the meat." Then I ask: "What do you mean by 'meanwhile' prepare the meat? The vegetables are ready?" Of course, if they reversed the steps, the meat would be ready before the vegetables. Text is obviously linear. Even if you give the sets of steps side by side, people would still read them from left to right instead of knowing to perform the tasks concurrently.

Functional Decomposition Diagrams

Another Process Oriented model is a Functional Decomposition Diagram (see Figure 5–6). These are also a process-only view and are a good way to decompose a process or system and to break down that process or system from a high level to a low level view.

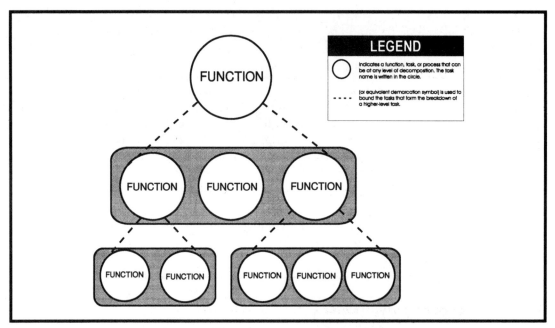

Fig. 5-6: A Functional Decomposition Diagram

Functional decomposition concentrates on processing and its breakdown. For example, we might use a Functional Decomposition Diagram to show what's involved in a process called Calculate Net Pay. We might break down this process into Calculate Gross Pay, Calculate Overtime, Calculate Taxes, etc. If I didn't understand what was involved in Calculate Taxes, I could further decompose that process to Calculate Federal Taxes, Calculate State Taxes, Calculate Local Taxes, and so on. Again, if Calculate Federal Taxes was a complex process, I could break that down further into Calculate Taxes for Single People, Calculate Taxes for Married People, etc. As you can see from these examples, Functional Decomposition Diagrams are process oriented and do not show data.

Process Hierarchy Diagrams

Many of us are fairly familiar with Process Hierarchy Diagrams (see Figure 5–7). Everyone of us is represented in part of one type or another. Everybody has grandparents and parents who are higher in the hierarchy in terms of their ancestry. That is one use of a Process Hierarchy Diagram. Process Hierarchy Diagrams are good for modeling top-down control to show who is in charge of whom. This is a very common model for organizations where the big bosses are at the top, middle management is below them, and the staff is below middle management in the hierarchy.

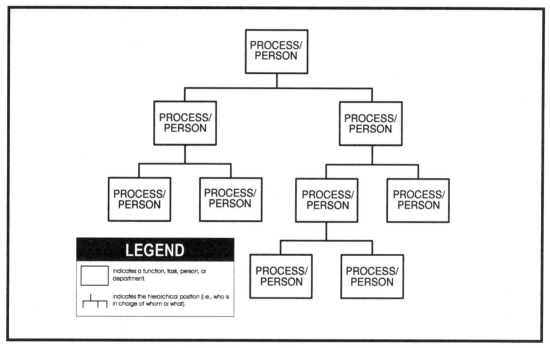

Fig. 5-7: A Process Hierarchy Diagram

We also see Process Hierarchy Diagrams used in the Data Processing Industry when modeling the structure of computer systems to show "boss" modules and "subordinate" modules that are invoked by these "boss" modules.

Data Oriented Models

There are also models that are completely Data Oriented as opposed to the three Process Oriented models I just described. Data Oriented models (see Figure 5–8), which are typically referred to as data models, show entities and relationships (typically two-way relationships).

These diagrams also show the cardinality between these entities. For example, one employee may work on many projects, so we have a "one-to-many" relationship in this case.

Typically, Data Oriented models are good for seeing cohesive blocks of data and their binary relationships. They serve as a good design tool for implementing computer databases and human file systems.

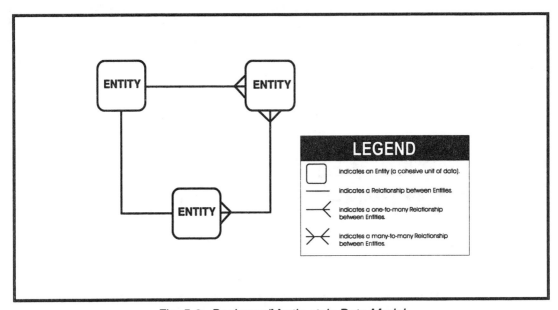

Fig. 5-8: Bachman/Martin-style Data Model

Entity Relationship Diagrams

An Entity Relationship Diagram is another model that shows entities (blocks of cohesive data). However, rather than being limited to showing binary (two-way) relationships, these diagrams show "n-ary" (multiple) relationships (i.e., many entities can be associated with one relationship). They also show the cardinality of these relationships (see Figure 5–9). For example, we may use these diagrams to represent a 3-way relationship between a Contract for a certain set of Products with one particular Client. In this case the business relationship can be shown with these three entities together to avoid a disjointed binary view.

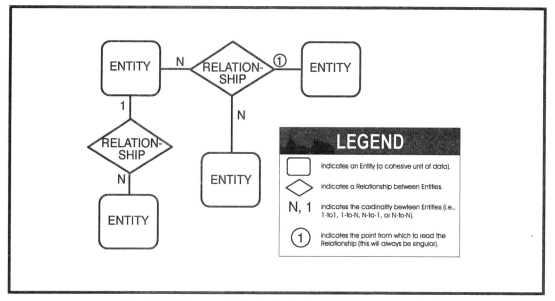

Fig. 5-9: Chen-style Entity Relationship Diagram (ERD)

Hierarchical/Network/Relational Data Oriented Models

In addition, we have a number of Data Oriented models to show the design structure of a database or file cabinet system (see Figure 5–10). We can use a hierarchical model to refer to a parent-child structure of data. For example, we can represent a Customer (parent) set of data as being "over" all that customer's Account (child) data. This would indicate that we can access all Account data given a particular Customer.

Another example of a Data Oriented model would be a network structure where we can access one entity (set of data) from any other. Still another type is a relational data model, typically represented as rows and columns where we can create dynamic tables that bring together sets of data related to other sets of data.

These last three data models are good for modeling a specific type of data structure in an organization.

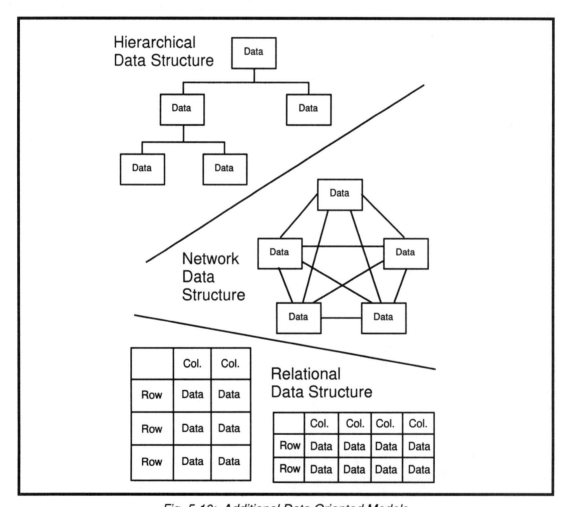

Fig. 5-10: Additional Data Oriented Models

Process and Data Oriented Models

Data Flow Diagrams

I've just covered Process Oriented models and Data Oriented models. There are models that combine the two. A Data Flow Diagram (see Figure 5–11) is an example of a model that is both Process and Data Oriented. This particular model allows us to look at the data and the processing acting on that data as it travels through a system.

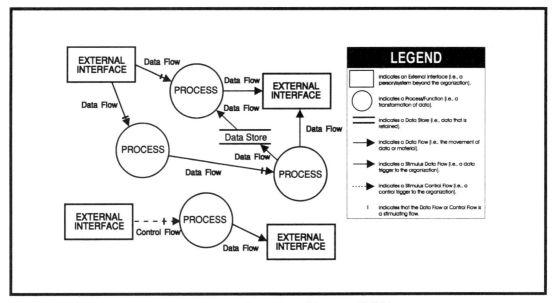

Fig. 5-11: A Data Flow Diagram (DFD)

These diagrams can also be represented at various levels of decomposition. You can have a high-level Data Flow Diagram that just depicts a single process and its data for what is involved in a payroll system, for example. You could further decompose this single-process view into a low-level diagram that shows a more detailed view with the particular data and processes involved in calculating taxes, pensions, etc.

Object Oriented Models

An Object Oriented Model (see Figure 5–12) also shows data and processing. To me, the Object Oriented Model is the inverse view of a Data Flow Diagram. They are similar in that they both model data and processing and the stimulation of that data and processing. They vary in that the DFD looks at a specific flow of data (and at just the processes acting on that flow of data) while the Object Oriented Model shows data at rest encapsulated with all of its processes and the messages that stimulate specific processes within an Object.

An Object Oriented Model focuses in on interacting Objects (Encapsulations of Data and Process). Objects can contain Methods (reusable processes acting on shared variables — Data or States). In addition, Object Oriented modeling tracks Messages (the Communication between Objects).

Object Oriented Models are good for modeling systems where the focus is on an Object (e.g., a thing) first and the Object determines the processing.

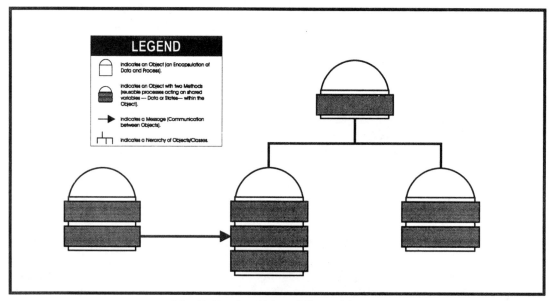

Fig. 5-12: An Object Oriented Model

Control Oriented Models

Control Oriented Models typically depict states and the transitions between those states.

State Transition Diagrams

There are other models we may need when we start to represent all aspects of a system. A State Transition Diagram (STD) is a Control Oriented Model (see Figure 5–13). State Transition Diagrams are good for modeling the flow of control between different states. We could look upon a State Transition Diagram as a high-level Flow Chart. This model may show the state that a particular device is in and what causes the device to transfer from one state to another.

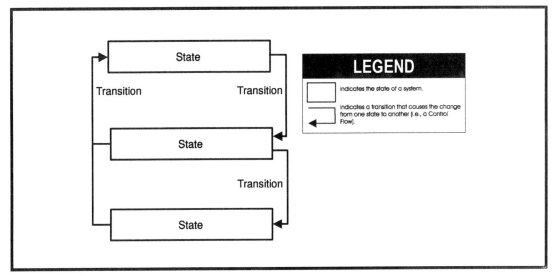

Fig. 5-13: A State Transition Diagram (STD)

For example, when you go to an automatic teller, the device may be in a wait state. When you insert your card into the machine, it transfers from the wait state into a validation state. If you enter a wrong Personal Identification Number (PIN) three times, it may transfer into a state in which it takes your card and goes back into a wait state. If you enter the correct PIN, it may enter a menu state in which it asks you what you want to do.

Control Flow Diagrams

A Control Flow Diagram (CFD) is a Control Oriented Model that can also show data movement or is tied to an associated Data Flow Diagram. This model is helpful for modeling the complex control issues of a system (see Figure 5–14). For example, in a system that controls an intelligent set of traffic lights, the decision to change the light and the order of the change can be governed by sensing the flow of traffic, the volume, the time of day, and the number of waiting vehicles at any particular location in the system.

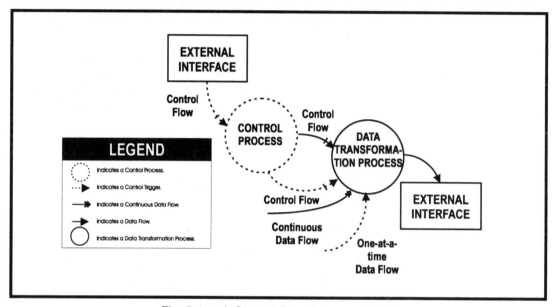

Fig. 5-14: A Control Flow Diagram (CFD)

Choosing the Right Model

When we find ourselves analyzing a department and/or a computer system to determine how, for example, a purchase order gets through them, we are instantly involved in a "flow-of-data" problem. In this case, an ideal model to use would be a Data Flow Diagram. This model shows data on the move.

If I wanted to see how the files were organized in that department, or computer system and how one file related to another, then I would prefer to use an Entity Relationship Diagram. This data model would show that we have supplier information, that certain products come from particular suppliers, that the suppliers deliver to certain depots, and so forth. This model shows data at rest.

If I wanted to study something in the department or computer system (an Object) and see all the processes that can be performed on that object, I would use an Object Oriented model. For example, if the department was involved in editing text books, I may want to see all of the activities that can be performed on text (e.g., delete it, change its font, underline it, etc.).

If I wanted to see the step-by-step detailed logic that transforms gross pay into taxes, I could use a Flow Chart or even linear text. There are obviously other models. However, those I've listed should be an adequate set for modeling in Business Re-Engineering.

A major consideration when conducting analysis is to use the appropriate modeling tool or tools for the particular job. This is especially important if we are conducting analysis with a customer who is non-technical and from whom we require confirmation of the requirements.

If we are trying to gather and verify some information from business people or a customer (and they are not familiar with a particular technical model), try to use the model that best represents the business and train them if needed to understand that model. So, we may need to become a part time trainer if we want to model a business and communicate that view to verify its accuracy to someone unfamiliar with the model we are using.

An Example of Using a Model

Let me show an example of using a couple of the models discussed in this chapter. The ones I'm going to use are the models that I've used frequently over the years *(and to that extent, I have become somewhat warped by them).*

Let's look at a theoretical warehouse environment in which someone sits at a desk waiting for shipments of books to come in from suppliers. When the books come in, they have notes attached from the suppliers. The person at the desk deals with orders for these books (some of which are pending and some of which are completed). Their job is to validate the incoming shipments with a pending order, create accepted orders, and to file the accepted books on particular shelves. Figure 5–15 shows a sketch of this physical environment.

Fig. 5-15: A View of a Warehouse Environment

If we have the luxury of taking everybody who might ask what this environment looks like back to the actual warehouse and its occupants, we don't need to bother drawing a current design model of it. Or, it would be perfectly valid if we created a comprehensive video and did not bother with modeling the actual physical/implementation view of this environment.

But, if we then wanted to move to a non-implementation (logical) view in which we removed the existing design aspects of this human-based system, we could capture the book delivery and model it through its transformations using a logical Data Flow Diagram.

As you can see from Figure 5–16, we might represent this small system in a single-process DFD. The diagram would show Books coming in. It may also show us rejecting Books if they weren't ordered (by comparing what comes in with Pending Orders or by checking our Supplier list). If something is wrong, we send back the Books. If everything is fine, we change our Pending Order to an Accepted Order, put the order into a different file, and store the Books on the shelves.

After we validated this model, we could add any new data or processing needed for the new business view (if any) and use it to identify a new design to support this part of the business.

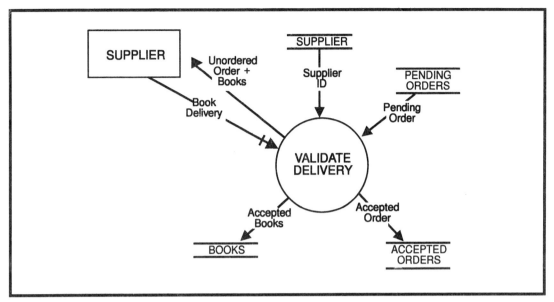

Fig. 5-16: A Logical DFD of the Warehouse Environment

I could also look at this small system from a "data-at-rest" point of view using an Entity Relationship Diagram. Using this model I would see (as shown in Figure 5–17) that this one shipment of Books involved one relationship where a Supplier sends me many Books. Part of this delivery relationship is to retrieve an Accepted Order and to produce a Pending Order.

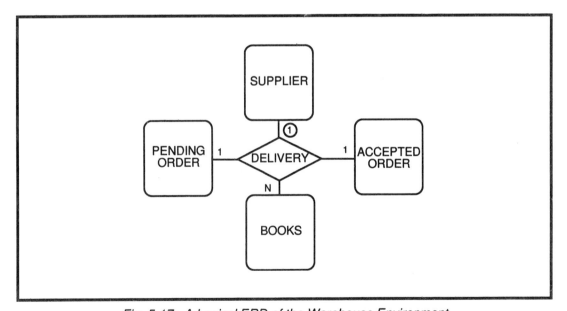

Fig. 5-17: A Logical ERD of the Warehouse Environment

The way we read this diagram is; a Supplier (the circled one is an anchor point from which we read the relationship) is involved in a Delivery relationship with many Books and an Accepted Order and one Pending Order. After we validate this model, we can again add any new data, or relationship features, and we can use it to identify a new design.

To me, the process and data models should not be separated. In other words, when I have entities on the Entity Relationship Diagram, they should correspond one-to-one with a store on a Data Flow Diagram.

Of course, we can change these models and introduce another model (such as an Object Oriented Model), or use another collection of models with which we felt we could validate the requirements with the customer/Business Policy Creator. The only constraints are that the models must not be ambiguous and they should satisfy the criteria established earlier in this chapter for an effective model.

The type of model is not what's important.
What is important is understanding the
business via the model.

I also want to emphasize that if someone comes along with a new model three years after you've read this book, it doesn't make the book (or your use of the old model) obsolete. Simply absorb the new model in your methodology/toolkit if the model is superior to any of the others that have been used. *I thought that Flow Charts were the greatest thing since sliced bread when I first started in Data Processing. Then I realized that they were very restrictive when I was trying to look at concurrent processing and model systems that weren't linear.*

Physical Design and Logical Analysis Models

So far we've looked at a number of different ways to model systems. Business Re-Engineering allows us to bring together these different models into one unified methodology. But, our model must do more than just combine the stimulus-response and process-memory aspects of businesses. It must allow us to represent the issues we talked about in the previous chapter (i.e., Analysis Issues vs. Design Issues).

System development involves a progression of specifications from gathering objectives in a Project Charter, to requirements in an Analysis Specification, to solutions in a Design Specification, and on into Implementation Specifications.

*When playing the role of analyst in a
Re-Engineering project, the most important
concept to grasp is the distinction between
Business Issues and System Issues.*

My brain associates Business Issues with one set of words and Systems Issues with a different set of words, based on my experience and education. Table 5–3 shows these associations. I hope these are helpful associations for you as well.

BUSINESS ISSUES	SYSTEM ISSUES
Analysis	Design
Requirements Oriented	Solution Oriented
Implementation Independent	Implementation Dependent
Logical	Physical

Table 5–3: Business/System Synonyms

Let's briefly examine the distinction between Business Models and System Models. Let me show examples of physical and logical models if you haven't seen them before using Process Oriented and Data Oriented Models.

Physical Design Models

Physical models show **how** a business is, or will be, designed. They are partitioned by design issues such as departmental boundaries or computer system boundaries, and they depict physical details such as media, job titles, computer programs, and form layouts.

The Process Analysis world has a physical DFD to model the existing system design. In the mid 1980s, in papers and talks, I proposed the use of a *physical* Entity-Relationship Diagram (ERD), equivalent to a physical Data Flow Diagram to model the current data design. We use this to derive the *logical* ERD, just as we use a *physical* DFD to derive a *logical* DFD.

So, physical design DFDs and ERDs depict the actual details of **how** the system processes and remembers. It declares actual people, locations, files, forms, documents, and materials. To illustrate this, we could depict a package delivery service environment with a physical DFD (see Figure 5–18) showing the actual people and processes. We can also use the physical ERD showing the actual captured data and their relationships (see Figure 5–19). These models assist an analyst/designer in verifying the existing and future environment with the business person or customer of the system.

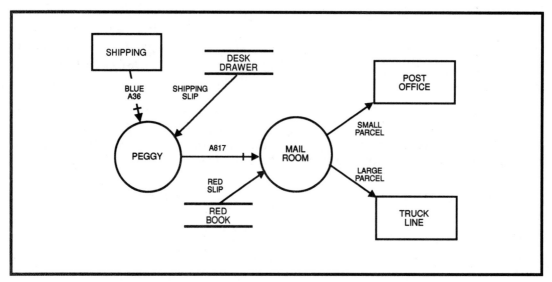

Fig. 5-18: A Typical Physical Process Model (DFD)

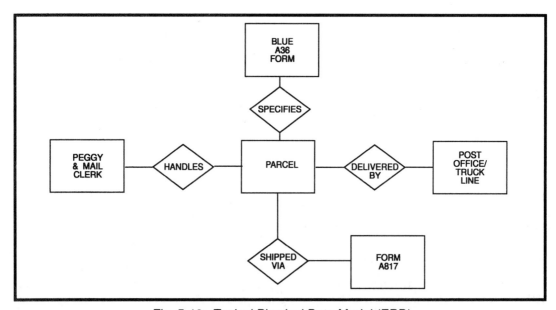

Fig. 5-19: Typical Physical Data Model (ERD)

Logical Analysis Models

Logical models depict the *essential* details of **what** the business does and remembers, either currently or in the future. Logicalizing is the process of removing any physical (design and implementation) issues from the business view. There are obvious and subtle physical issues that get in the way of a purely logical view of Business Issues.

- **Obvious Physical Issues** can include things such as paper and forms, computers and computer screens, etc.

- **Subtle Physical Issues** can include things that may not even be part of the current design or implementation. Things that are not part of existing systems are often the most difficult to see. Nonetheless, it's important to ask questions such as: "Why don't we have real-time payroll?" or, "why don't we pay suppliers when the ordered materials arrive instead of waiting until the bill is actually due?"

We can use two types of logical models for modeling a business:

- Using our previous physical process model (see Figure 5–16) , we can derive a *Logical Process Model* consisting of a set of *Data Flow Diagrams* that declares the business without any implementation (design) issues. The process model is supported by a *Data Dictionary* which defines every data flow on the DFD and *Process Specifications* which define the business policy (or rules) for data transformation. Figure 5–20 shows a sample logical process model (DFD).

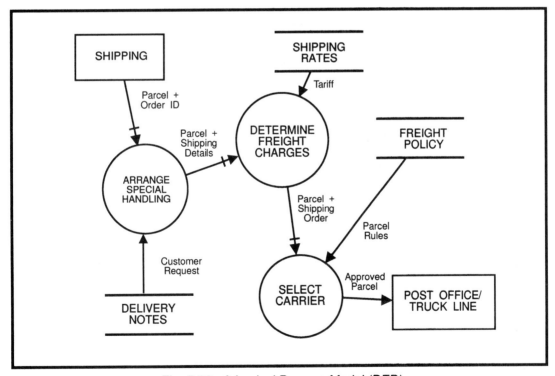

Fig. 5-20: A Logical Process Model (DFD)

• Again using our previous *Physical Data Model* (Figure 5–19), we can derive a *Logical Data Model* consisting of an *Entity Relationship Diagram* that declares the business without any implementation (design) issues. This model is supported by an *Entity Specification* for each entity on the ERD, an optional *Relationship Specification* for each relationship between two or more entities, and *Data Element Specifications* for each item of information about an entity. Figure 5–21 shows a sample *Logical Business Data Model* (ERD).

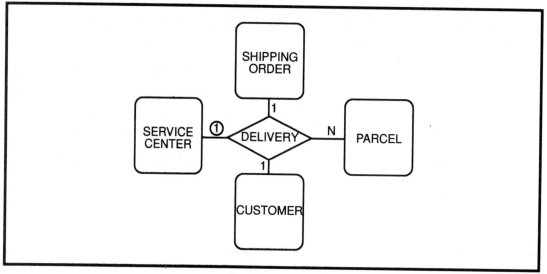

Fig. 5-21: A Logical Data Model (ERD)

We can use both types of Business Models (process and data) for analyzing and modeling the business. As we'll see, the power that Business Re-Engineering brings to these two modeling methods stems from how we partition the business being modeled.

The next chapter will show how to partition these models based on the stimulus-response view presented in the previous chapter. We will also get into the key principles and discipline of Business Re-Engineering. And, in the *Partitioning by Business Events* chapter, we'll see how we can use this discipline to Re-Engineer a portion of, or even an entire organization.

Summary

The Business Re-Engineering professional needs to use models just like all other professionals. This chapter has proposed some proven models that, with a little training, should be easy for a business person to understand. The important thing is to select the appropriate model for the problem at hand and to partition that model along business lines as described in the following chapter.

6

The customer is the one who supports us. Study his needs; get ahead of him.

W. Edwards Demming
Last published interview via "Industry Week" Magazine

Business Events — The Key to Ultimate Customer Satisfaction

I n this chapter, we examine the concept of the *Business Event* and, we see that functional partitioning based on Business Events provides an objective model of the true nature of the business. This definitions chapter is where I hope to give you the ability to comfortably recognize Business Events in your environment apart from the myriad of events that obscure the nature of the business.

The Foundation of Business Event Methodology

From one point of view we could say that any organization has simply decided to respond to a set of customer needs that occur in the external world. As examples:

- An airline company decides to respond to customers' travel needs in which they, or goods, must be moved.

- A bank decides to respond to customers' needs for storing and manipulating money.

- Logical Conclusions, Inc. has decided to respond to customers' needs for consulting or training in subjects such as Business Re-Engineering.

From within an organization, we never know why the need was generated. That's why we classify it as *outside* of our organization. What makes a customer want to withdraw funds from our bank, for example, is literally none of our business. For example, a funds withdrawal could be made in order to go on vacation, pay a bill, or just have expense money for the day.

A system (a manual operation, a computer system, or even our entire implemented organization) has no control over external customers' needs. But, at the same time, it is obliged to respond to the arrival of stimuli caused by a customer's needs.

Without any stimulus from the outside, our organization and its systems remain inactive and are essentially meaningless, and our organization will eventually close down. No organizations are self-perpetuating. Even non-profit government systems respond to external needs as their reason for existing. We call these needs *Events*.

> *All organizations rely on stimuli from outside*
> *events as their reason for existing.*

A Little History of the Concept of Events

In the 1970s the Systems Engineering techniques that were being proffered were somewhat disjointed, mainly because the ideas originated with different authors (and their sales staffs). That same decade I was lucky enough to join a young company called Yourdon, Inc. involved in generating and spreading these new ideas in the area of Systems Engineering. The company's emphasis was on data processing except when it came to systems analysis. During those earlier years of teaching new tools we didn't quite have the techniques down. For example, we knew how to draw a Data Flow Diagram and we understood the usage rules of each symbol, but we didn't give much advice on how to produce a well-partitioned Business Model. (The size of the drafting surface — a page — and the human limitation of keeping track of seven plus or minus two things per page were somewhat the extent of our partitioning rules.)

In my seminars I could convince my data processing students that any new partitioning of a systems model was good, mainly because almost all existing partitioning of programs and systems was arbitrary anyway. *(D.P. was a new industry and almost any programmer was allowed to partition their programs and systems as they saw fit.)* This arbitrary partitioning was not so true for the business community. Of the seminars I taught for Yourdon, Inc., the ones teaching analysis subjects were the only ones where I would expect a business person to be present. They at least had a longer history and established reasons for how and why they partitioned their departments, people, and tasks. We had to have good reasons for repartitioning these established organizational boundaries.

I and a few of my colleagues who taught analysis seminars for Yourdon, Inc. used a technique called *Stimulus-Response Modeling* as a means of partitioning a Logical Data Flow Diagram. This was a means of getting away from any of the physical/design partitioning of the old environment. We used the analogy of a "string-of-pearls" to illustrate a stimulus data flow triggering a chain of continuous processes connected by intermediate data (indicated by lines and circles on a Data Flow Diagram).

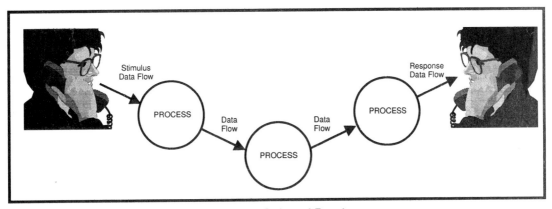

Fig. 6-1: String of Pearls

In Figure 6–1 we see an external stimulus initiating the execution of the set of processes (the string of pearls) required to respond to the event that produced the stimulus. Once initiated, the set of processes runs its course without further stimulus until a response is returned to the outside world. Because all these processes, and *only* these processes, are triggered, we can see that they make up a highly functional partition in that they perform a "single-minded" overall function from the point of view of the external customer. This basic concept has evolved into the contents of this book built around the central theme of the Business Event.

A High-level View of Business Event Methodology

Before going any further, let me establish a Common Platform of Understanding regarding the Business Event Life Cycle (Methodology).

I have heard many discussions/meetings go awry when people use the terms "methods" and "methodology" erroneously. Figure 6–2 shows that methodologies contain methods, and methods recommend models.

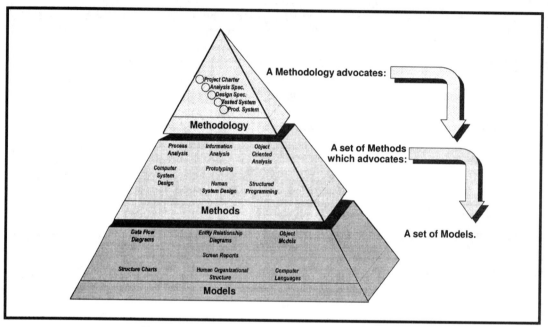

Fig. 6-2: Methodologies, Methods, and Models

Players in the Methodology

There are number of "players" (see Table 6–1) and tasks associated with those players in the Business Event Methodology. These players could be different people in a development project, or they could be one person wearing different hats.

- The Customer has the need.

- The Business Policy Creator identifies which needs the organization will respond to and the data and processing the organization will use to respond to these needs. (In other words, the organization's decision makers determine the business policy.)

- The Systems Analyst models/documents this business policy. The Systems Designer designs the implementation of this business policy.

- The Systems Builders (Technical Writers and Programmers) implement this business policy.

- And finally, the Production Systems (People, Technology, etc.) accomplish the customers' needs through time.

CUSTOMER	BUSINESS POLICY CREATOR	SYSTEMS ANALYST	SYSTEM DESIGNER	SYSTEM BUILDER	PRODUCTION SYSTEMS (PEOPLE & TECHNOLOGY)
Has the Business Event Need	Creates the Business Policy to Satisfy the Customer's Need	Analyzes and Models the Business Policy	Designs the Implementation of the Business Policy	Implements the Business Policy	Accomplishes the Customer's Need through Time

Table 6–1: The Players in the Business Event Methodology

The Types of Events

In the Business Event Methodology there are five types of events: Strategic Events, Business Events, Dependent Events, Regulatory Events, and System Events. Determining the type of event we are analyzing is important to understand because some types affect the Business Model in different ways. Some events don't belong on the model at all, while another type actually changes the model. You could create separate models for Dependent Events and Regulatory Events, but I recommend you don't when you're new to this methodology, because the processing and memory parts of a Business Event will be due to regulatory and/or dependent reasons. For example, the process "Calculate Taxes on an Order" is part of a Business Event, but given our choice, we might not want to do it. It may be a good idea to indicate the different types of events that do belong on the Business Model (Business, Dependent, or Regulatory) by using different colors on the Business Model.

Table 6–2 lists a series of questions whose answers will help us determine the type of an event under analysis. In addition to the questions in the table, the following simple rules may help you to differentiate between the types of events. Strategic Events cause the Business Policy Creator to add or delete nouns (data) and verbs (processing) on the Business Model. Business Events (including Dependent Events and Regulatory Events) activate the existing nouns and verbs on the Business Model. We will talk about each of these event types later.

Key Questions / Event Type	Does it come completely from beyond Our Organization?	Does it Modify the Business Model itself?	Does it Stimulate the Business Model into Life?	Are We in Control of it in any Way?	Does it Contribute to Fulfilling Our Organization's Mission?
Strategic Events	—	Yes	No	—	—
Business Events	Yes	No	Yes	No	Yes
Dependent Events	Yes	No	Yes	Yes	No[1]
Regulatory Events	Yes	No[2]	Yes	No	No
System Events	No	No	No[3]	Yes	No[4]
[1] Only indirectly as it helps fulfill a Business Event.					
[2] If a Regulatory Event does modify the Business Model, we class it as a Strategic Event.					
[3] It can stimulate the Business Model into life only via some aspect of the design.					
[4] Only when the System Event is used to trigger a fragment of a Business Event.					

Table 6–2: Questions for Determining the Type of Event

Events also have a hierarchy in terms of their of importance to the Business Event Methodology (see Figure 6–3).

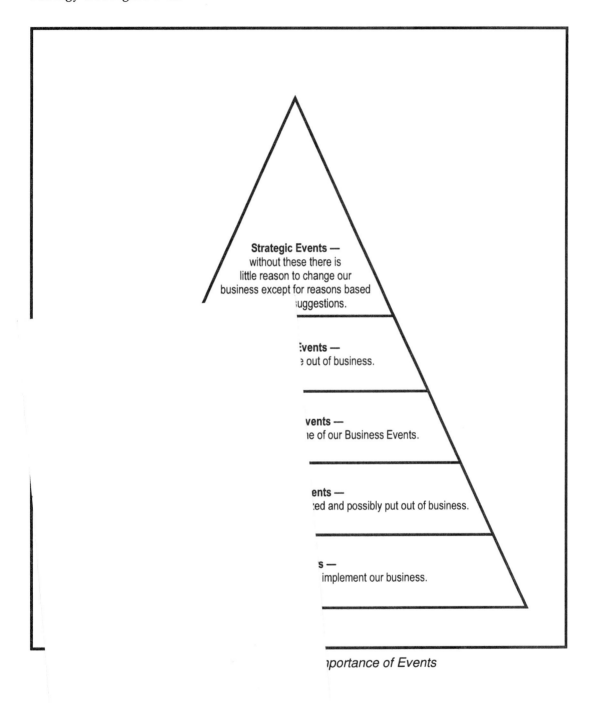

Strategic Events —
without these there is
little reason to change our
business except for reasons based
 suggestions.

:vents —
out of business.

vents —
le of our Business Events.

ents —
ed and possibly put out of business.

s —
implement our business.

iportance of Events

Identifying the Customer and Their Events

The type of customer often dictates the type of event to which our organization has to respond. We can identify three major types of customers — Business Customers, Regulatory Customers, and System Customers. Each of these types has a corresponding type of event: Business Event, Regulatory Event, and System Event. You can also call the latter "Internal Events", but I call them System Events because they will always be associated with an implemented system issue. Strategic Events and Dependent Events do not have associated customers in the same sense as do the other events.

- Business Events are the most important event to the Business Re-Engineer.

- Strategic Events can't be ignored, but they are not the main focus of the Business Event Methodology. Strategic Events typically originate with our organization's management via the Business Policy Creator. Note that the management may have initiated the Strategic Event based on our competition doing something to which we need to respond. This impetus to the management could also originate at an agency whose laws affect our organization.

- Dependent Events typically originate with the vendors used by our organization.

- Regulatory Events are imposed on the area of business to meet legal operating requirements, such as a government tax regulations, or the rules of an external regulatory agency.

- System Events are invented and imposed on the area of business to meet management and design needs.

I don't classify Regulatory Events or System Events as true Business Events. So, we want to filter out System Events and separate Regulatory Events from Business Events. I also separate Dependent Events from Business Events in that we have some measure of control over them (see Figure 6–4).

Notice that this diagram is indicating that we're trying to focus in on true Business Events as our organization's mission, but, we have Strategic Events and System Events in the way of our business view. We should filter out these from our business view as shown in Figure 6–4. We will keep Dependent and Regulatory Events in our Business Model, but we should identify them on our model by categorizing them as Regulatory Events or Dependent Events. Even though they appear on the Business Model, they are less important than Business Events because they are not our main focus for "keeping the doors open."

In the majority of the remaining chapter we will define these types of events with the understanding that the Business Events are the most important ones to the organization's success. I'm not going to define these types of events in the order they appear in the diagram, but please understand that Strategic and System Events are the types we want to filter out first. Then we categorize Regulatory Events and Dependent Events in order to get to Business Events.

The tasks of data gathering and modeling to document Business Events are the prime focus in this chapter. Please note, however, that everything we say regarding Business Events can be applied to Dependent Events, Regulatory Events, and even Strategic Events.

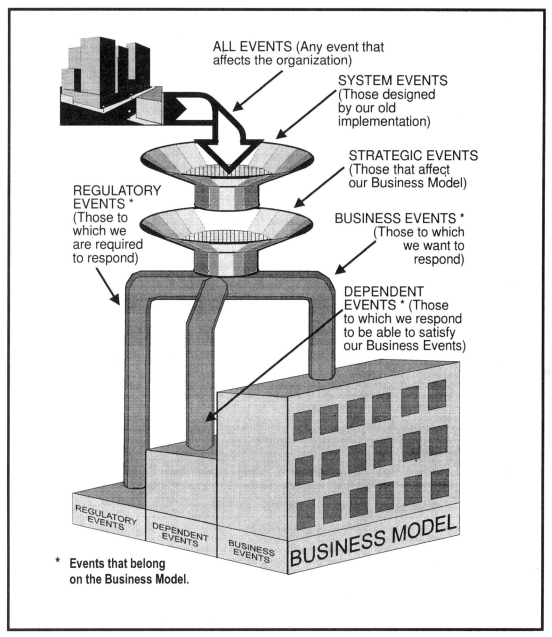

ALL EVENTS (Any event that affects the organization)

SYSTEM EVENTS (Those designed by our old implementation)

STRATEGIC EVENTS (Those that affect our Business Model)

REGULATORY EVENTS * (Those to which we are required to respond)

BUSINESS EVENTS * (Those to which we want to respond)

DEPENDENT EVENTS * (Those to which we respond to be able to satisfy our Business Events)

REGULATORY EVENTS

DEPENDENT EVENTS

BUSINESS EVENTS

BUSINESS MODEL

* **Events that belong on the Business Model.**

Fig. 6-4: Filtering and Categorizing Events

Before any of the definitions, I want to make sure we don't confuse an event with its implementation. A phone call, a piece of mail, a fax, or a customer walking up to a counter are all Implementation Issues. Phones, the mail, a fax, or a personal visit are just the means for communicating the customer's need (i.e., Design Issues). We need to concentrate on who the external customer is, why they are there, and what events they generate to stimulate our organization.

The Business Policy Creator and Strategic Events

When we, as analysts, create a Business Model of our organization, the purpose is to help conceptualize the logical view of **what** our organization does in its day-to-day business, in order to respond to our customer's request. We, as analysts, create and modify models using Strategic Events. The request (Business Event) is outside our organization, but the Business Model will mostly show our internal response to Business Events.

As I've previously stated, there are other kinds of events that stimulate us. One in particular is what I call a Strategic Event. Similar to Business Events, this type of event will affect our Business Model, but in a different way than does a Business Event. A Business Event stimulates a portion of our model into life whereas a Strategic Event will change the Business Model itself. Therefore, we must be careful not to confuse Business Events with Strategic Events.

As I stated previously, Strategic Events can be initiated by either the Business Policy Creator, who makes decisions that affect how we respond to our customer's needs, or by our organization's competition, who may stimulate us into changing our business policy. The result of either of these stimuli would be for us to change the Business Model.

Even though Strategic Events cause the Business Policy Creator to change the Business Model, they do not belong on the Business Model. It is the responsibility of the Business Policy Creator to respond to Strategic Events and to model them on a separate model. This model is what we call a Meta Model. (Remember, you're not in Business to respond to System Events, so they do not go on the Business Model.) This Meta Model contains the organization's response to Strategic Events that the analyst will use to Create, Update, or Delete parts of the Business Model itself.

Definition of the Strategic Events

A Strategic Event is an external event that makes the Business Policy Creator change the way we do business and hence change our Business Model in some way.

Recognizing Strategic Events

I find that Strategic Events are a difficult concept to convey, so I'll use analogies to make the point. When I built my house, I created a model of it before construction. That model showed my requirements (the customer's) for my particular needs, but there were other requirements that had to be on the same model that were necessary to satisfy the local government's building codes. I, as a customer, could change my requirements, but obviously not the local government's requirements. In other words, I had my needs satisfied within the needs of the local government's. The person who created the Uniform Building Codes Manual for house builders is an entity we're going to call the *Business Policy Creator*. They can change the building codes from time to time, which in turn changes the manual, but they are not the people who want the houses.

When we conduct analysis during Re-Engineering, we are mostly concerned with customer's requirements. However, we must be aware of the role of the *Business Policy Creator* who is actually stimulated by Strategic Events (see Figure6 –5). This is the person authorized to state the data and processing required within the organization to satisfy the customer's needs. This person's role must be viewed separately from that of the customer. They could be an organization's manager, but I don't want you to look upon them as playing a management role in this context. I want you to look upon them as the "prime mover," the person who creates the business policy.

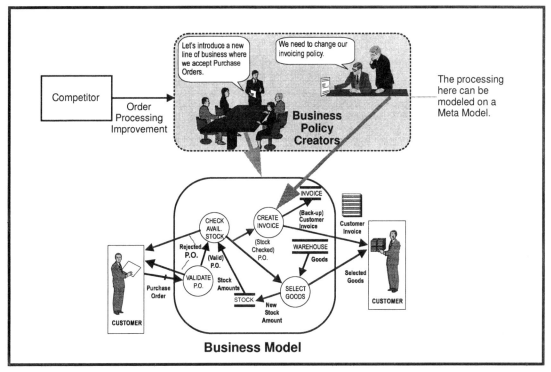

Fig. 6-5: A Sample Strategic Event

Again, the *Business Policy Creator* affects our Business Model, but in a different way than do our customers. Our customers stimulate the model into life, while the *Business Policy Creator* creates and changes the model itself — they never stimulate it into action (see Figure 6–6). So, Strategic Events can be mistaken for Business Events. I have consulted on projects where I have seen the *Business Policy Creator* classed as an External Interface (under a name such as Management) and therefore shown as stimulating the model. A request from them will obviously change the Business Model. For example, the Business Policy Creator may say: "We need to change our business policy for Special Orders in response to the competition's changes. So, we're now offering lower prices on Special Orders." This makes the Re-Engineering analyst change the data and processing for Special Orders on our Business Model, but this is not a Business Event. We call these Strategic Events (*I also think of these as Meta Events because they affect the Meta Model*). These are events that dictate how your organization and its model respond to Business Events.

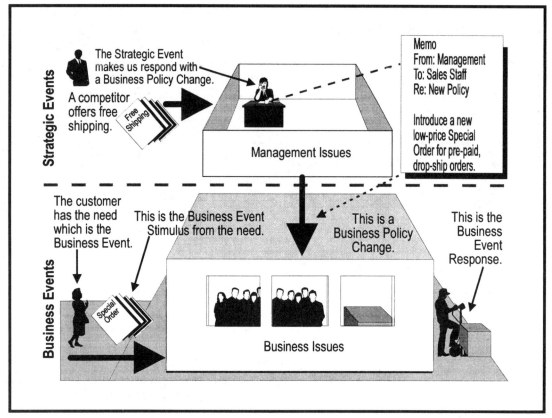

Fig. 6-6: Strategic Events vs. Business Events

To clarify further, an example that seems to bring this to light is the case of the government where a Senator requests a valid Information Event or Create, Retrieve, Update, or Delete (C.R.U.D.) Event of an agency. "How many spotted owls reside in the Pacific Northwest?" The Senator can also introduce a new law to protect spotted owls. The first request stimulated the Business Model and its implementation into life. The latter changed the actual model. The former is valid and necessary to appear on the Business Model; the latter is not. Keep in mind that when our competition brings out a new line of business, or changes their pricing structure, this may make us change our Business Policy rather than due to the direction actions of the Business Policy Creator.

If you're reading this book from a Strategic Planner point of view, then for Strategic Events, you can form a parallel view of everything I'll say in this chapter regarding Business Events and the Business Model. That is, you can produce a model showing how you will respond to such Strategic Events as the company's workers going on strike, a key supplier going out of business, or competition's changes to which you wish to respond. So, to model Strategic Events, you may gather its stimulus, its processing, its stored memory, and your responses (see Figure 6–7). Remember, changes to government's or any other agency's regulations that make you change your business policy are also Strategic Events.

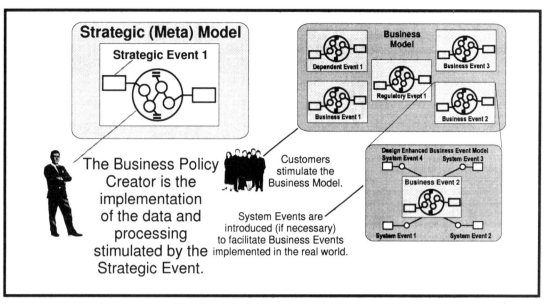

Fig. 6-7: Modeling Strategic Events

> *The important thing to know about a Strategic
> Event is that it will change your Business Model
> as opposed to stimulate it into life.*

Business Customers and Business Events

Definition of Business Customers

True Business Customers are individuals, clients, and agencies who are external to our organization over which we have no control. These Business Customers also do not regulate our organization in any way. The events that come from these customers are completely under their discretion (that is, the event does not occur within our organization).

Definition of Business Events

A Business Event is an incident that places a demand on the organization to which it responds in order to accomplish its strategic mission.

It's vital to your understanding of Re-Engineering that you have a clear understanding of Business Events (see Figure 6–8).

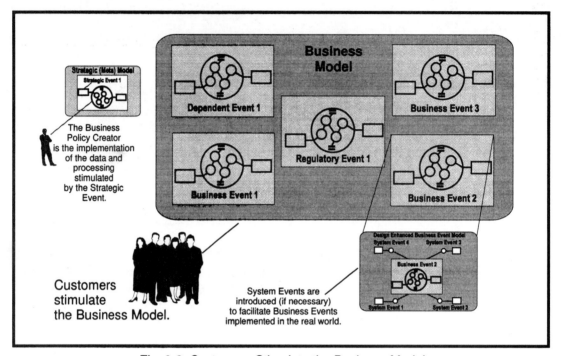

Fig. 6-8: Customers Stimulate the Business Model

Recognizing True Business Events

There's an uncountable multitude of demands that people make on the world of business and each requires a different response to satisfy it. On the other hand, any one organization responds only to some of those demands. (As an added benefit, in vertical, i.e., non-diversified, organizations we can usually obtain mass reusability in our processing and data across these demands.)

Figure 6–9 shows how something makes its way onto the Business Model.

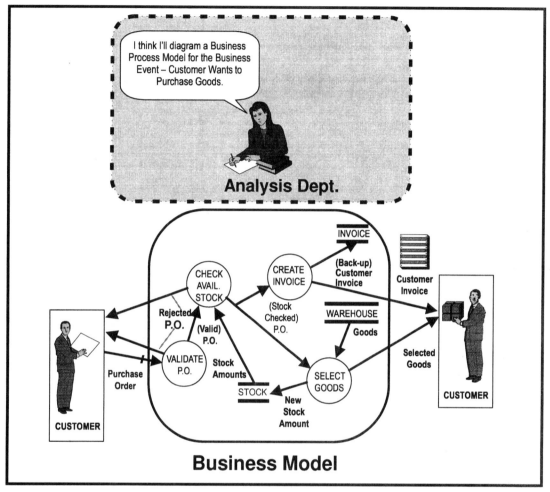

Fig. 6-9: Business Event Modeling

Even organizations that respond to the same Business Event may do so differently compared to their competitors. For example, a customer needs to have a package moved from A to B. The customer wants to make a decision of which company to use based on price and delivery time and compares two shipping companies. One uses its own fleet of aircraft and delivers quickly for a premium price, and the other company uses cargo space on slow steamships for an economical price. Even though both companies satisfy the same basic customer need, the ways they do it (i.e., their implementations of data and the processing) are different for each company. Even two airline companies may respond to a travel need Business Event (Passenger Wants to Fly from A to B) differently, even though externally, the customer (Passenger) may not notice any difference.

The above examples show that there are two factors that help us recognize a *specific* Business Event:

- the nature of the need from the external customer point of view, and

- the policy that an organization has for responding to that need (the internal organization's point of view).

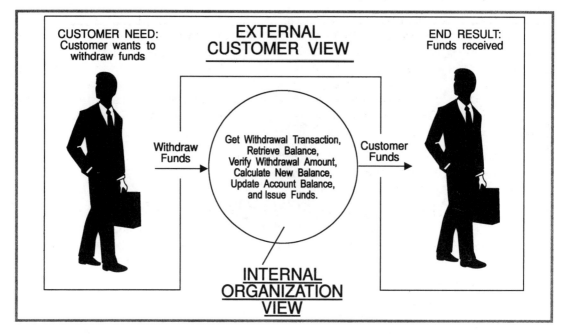

From the customers' external viewpoint we need to know what the customer expects to happen, such as walking away with products or having their service needs met. Taking the external viewpoint is where we get ahead of our customer as related to Demming's quote at the beginning of this chapter.

The particular need of the customer (outside person, other system, or external organization), plus the content of the communication is what affects the particular way our organization responds.

In a private organization, Business Events are directly associated with revenue generation. In a government organization these are the events that satisfy the laws. In either case, these events are Business Events as long as they satisfy the needs of whoever we call a customer and are documented on the Business Model (see Figure 6–8).

After years of building a methodology and giving seminars based on the Business Event concept, I believe that Business Event Partitioning is a fundamental view that unifies all the existing methods and models into a Business Re-Engineering Discipline.

Significant vs. Trivial Business Events

Business Events can be significant or trivial. What I mean by this is that varying amounts of data and processing may be involved in satisfying a Business Event. For example, in my organization, Logical Conclusions, Inc., a customer requesting a seminar stimulates many processes and involves the retrieval and updating of a substantial amount of data. A trivial event on the other hand will involve very little data and processing (and sometimes no processing). For example, we may get a call requesting the next Business Re-Engineering seminar date. This just requires a retrieval and issuance of data with no real processing.

The latter example I usually give a distinct name, Information/C.R.U.D. Event. These are events requiring a simple Create, Retrieve, Update, or Delete of an item or items of data stored in our organization.

We need to acknowledge these Information Events because they legitimize an item of data. As we'll see later in the chapter titled *The Business Event Methodology — a Synthesis*, it's important to know where the data are created or deleted even though we may not always know who our customers are for a retrieval of this data.

When I've introduced this additional definition in my seminars, I sometimes get a response that: "We might get a request for every item of data we keep in the company e.g., "How many people do you have in your seminars?" Or, "Do you have a seminar in Dallas next week?" These are perfectly valid Information Events. So, wouldn't we have an enormous number of Business Events? That is, do we need to multiply every stored data item in the organization by four because we potentially have a Create, Retrieve, Update, and Delete of each data item?" This is true and exactly why I wanted to differentiate the trivial Information/C.R.U.D. Business Events from significant Business Events. The Business Events that keep your organization in business may actually be in the minority compared to these trivial Information Events.

We will need to produce models for the significant Business Events, but we only need to identify and document trivial Information/C.R.U.D. Events for data conservation purposes, so these trivial Information Events won't result in a lot of analysis/modeling work. We'll talk more about this in the chapter: *The Business Event Methodology — a Synthesis*.

Dependent Events

This type of event is called a Dependent Event because it will be dependent on at least one other Business Event.

Dependent Events differ from Business and Regulatory Events in that we have some measure of control over them. A common example of a Dependent Event is, our organization being stimulated by an event that originates with suppliers from whom we purchase materials we need to satisfy our Business Events. For instance, we could say to a supplier: "Get me these materials by Friday or I'll go somewhere else." This causes them to stimulate us on Friday (hopefully, with a delivery). This is unlike a Business Event because we're not in control of a customer asking for an order.[1]

Definition of Dependent Events

A Dependent Event is an event that is in response to an outgoing request we have made in order to satisfy one or more Business Events.

Recognizing Dependent Events

The key idea to keep in mind is that it's a Dependent Event when we need to "go outside" our organization's span of control to satisfy one or more Business Events. It is actually what I would prefer to call a "pull" on an external organization. An example should make this clear.

If we need materials to manufacture a product to satisfy a customer (and we don't make this material ourselves), then we need to pull in those materials. When a customer asks for our product (a Business Event), we manufacture that product (within our Business Event Partition) by pulling in materials from one or more suppliers.

If we can do this dynamically within an alliance with our suppliers, then the raw materials being pulled in are actually part of our Business Event and not a separate Dependent Event. We are in semi control of these pulls. We are not in control of the customer ordering our goods, AND if we decide to buy out the supplier or produce our own raw materials, then the Dependent Event goes away and we still fully support our mission. These Dependent Events are where we're likely to find what I call the "Second Order" of improvements in a Re-Engineering project. The "First Order" of improvements is in removing old design characteristics. The second is looking beyond our organization to see how we can best totally support the Business Events — not System Events or Regulatory Events, but the ones that keep us in business.

---

1 In a government organization this may be reversed when they have legal (coercive) power to ensure that a Business Event occurs (e.g., filing taxes).

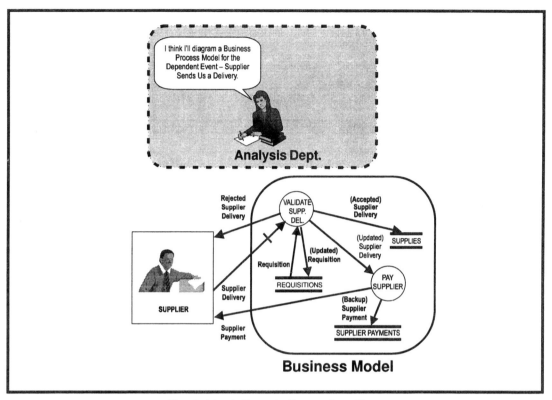

Fig. 6-10: A Sample Dependent Event

Beyond Organizational Strategic Planning

For ultimate customer satisfaction you should study the original customer's Business Event. We've talked about Business Events within an organization, why not extend the concept to include Business Events that span across organizations? This may lead you to form strategic alliances with other organizations to seamlessly accomplish what the customer ultimately needs.

Dependent Events can be a prime source for future cross-organizational alliances in a Re-Engineering effort. Dependent Events can become part of a Business Event when you form an alliance with your supplier. For example, a Dependent Event becomes part of a Business Event when you're allowed to "pull" goods directly from your supplier's warehouse as needed and reconcile payments at the time the goods are removed. I've used the word "pull" deliberately to mean "logical pull." In other words, the supplier may physically deliver the goods directly to your business customer or we may actually pick up the goods from their warehouse before giving them to the customer.

This is similar to what's happening in the banking industry. You don't have to draw out money to pay for a product you purchase. You can do a direct debit or electronic funds transfer (providing the vendor has an agreement that sets this up with the bank). In another specific example, a bank withdrawal may have been made for airline tickets. In this case the bank would benefit from forming a strategic alliance with the airline to better satisfy the customer's need to travel. From the customer's point of view, they did not want to withdraw money from the bank, they only wanted to get plane tickets. As the customer at an ATM is already built-in as part of a somewhat seamless design (their data entry is not disjointed), then why not carry on and make the rest of the system seamless? Such an alliance would obviously lead to fewer errors between each organization, fewer customer complaints, less paper handling, less shuffling of data, etc.

Please note that any aspect of satisfying a Business Event that goes on beyond your organization leads you to respond to Dependent Events (i.e., you've fragmented a Business Event). This dependence may have been caused at the inception of the organization, where the founders couldn't afford all the facilities needed to satisfy the entire Business Event. What I see happening as I write this book is that a lot of organizations are using the guise of Re-Engineering to outsource areas of satisfying their Business Events. In these cases the organizations lose the internal expertise and more importantly, the control over satisfying a complete Business Event. This is obviously acceptable when an organization does not originally have the resources to completely satisfy a Business Event. However, you should be very cautious about outsourcing something you already have the expertise in (or the facilities to provide) because of the loss of control in satisfying a complete Business Event.

Regulatory Customers and Regulatory Events

Some events are not driven by true customers, but are instead driven by laws or by external regulatory agencies. I call these Regulatory Events. An example of this is, once a year in the U.S.A., the Internal Revenue Service requires that we reconcile our tax account. The stimulus to this Regulatory Event is calendar driven (a window from January 1 through April 15). From the Internal Revenue Service's (IRS) point of view the taxpayer is the customer (*albeit at times, a reluctant one*).

Definition of Regulatory Customers

Regulatory Customers are typically external organizations with which we have to interface because of the business we are in and our location. Again, we have no control over these regulatory organizations and their events do not occur within our organization. These Regulatory Events are ones that stimulate our Business Model into life, but they are not events that change the Business Model. Strategic Events are the only type of event that change the Business Model.

Definition of Regulatory Events

A Regulatory Event is an incident that places a demand on the organization to which it responds in order to comply with legal requirements.

Recognizing Regulatory Events

Regulatory Events tend to be imposed on organizations to protect the environment, to ensure worker safety, to contribute to support the infrastructure within which the organization functions, etc.

An example of this is obviously taxes (local, state, or federal). At the end of the tax year (as set by the governing bodies or selected by the organization), an organization needs to report its tax liability. This Regulatory Event will stimulate the organization to process a certain amount of data and to disclose the results to the government body. As stated previously, individuals in the U.S. are required to reconcile their taxes stimulated by the calendar window January 1 through April 15. This is a batch Regulatory Event. The stimulus to the IRS (the 1040 Form) is actually a collection of the results of all applicable Regulatory Events that in the course of the previous year affected our tax balance.

If we take away the design from this batch system, we can say that a Regulatory Event would occur whenever we have a taxable transaction in the course of the year. Given this as a requirement in a new design, the Regulatory Event could send a stimulus, the taxable amount, to the IRS, who could put that money on deposit and make an entry in their database under my taxpayer ID. The basis for calculating the taxable amount in this transaction could be 90% of my previous year's taxes. The calendar and clock turning to one second after midnight on January 1 is the stimulus for the IRS to retrieve my account, reconcile it, and send me a refund, or a bill, by the morning of January 1st. Even the batching of the reconciliation task is a design and therefore can be changed by the IRS. This is one example of a Regulatory Event resulting from laws and regulations and hence their timing.

If your organization is a government agency, the above definitions of Business Events and Regulatory Events seem to be reversed. In a government agency the strategic mission is usually to meet legal requirements; these are their Business Events. In a private organization meeting legal requirements is a Regulatory Event. Our definition of Regulatory Events still applies to government agencies. For example, government agencies are still constrained by environmental regulations and by private organizations and individuals.

If you see any events to implement regulations, but the regulations are imposed internally, then they are really System Events and we don't want to classify them as Regulatory Events. For example, a Quality Assurance Department's regulations may trigger an internal audit, but since it is internally triggered, it's a System Event and not a Regulatory Event.

System Customers and System Events

I've found that people get so wrapped up in supporting existing systems that they lose sight of the reasons for those systems in the first place. The systems are there to support the organization — not the organization to support the systems. I'm sure that everyone reading this book has encountered organizations where it seems more important to them to perform their organization's particular system's procedures, even though it seems these make no logical sense in satisfying your needs as a customer. These organizations are actually more concerned with satisfying their system needs rather than you, the customer's, needs. These systems needs are what I call System Events.

> *As Re-Engineers we are more interested in satisfying Business Events than in supporting System Events.*

Definition of System Customers

System Customers are internal persons, departments, or systems with which we have to interface because of the existing structure of our own organization. We have control over these entities and their events occur within our organization.

Definition of System Events

An internal event created during the design of an organization's structure and systems in order to implement Business or Regulatory Events.

Figure 6–11 shows an example of a System Event.

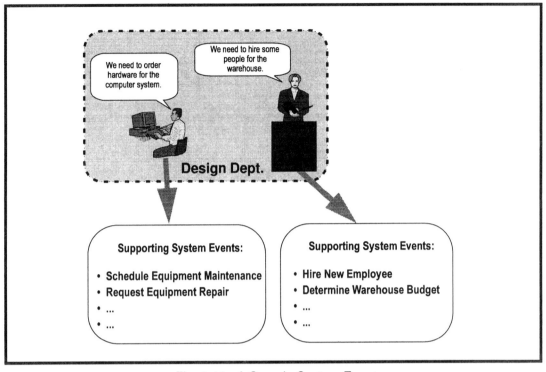

Fig. 6-11: A Sample System Event

Recognizing System Events

It's easy to get confused between Business Events (things occurring outside our organization) and System Events because we're all so involved in the existing design. I've seen material written on Event Partitioning in the past which has failed to make the important distinction between Business and System Events.

It's when we study a subset of our organization that we start to confuse System Events with fragmented Business Events. This also can happen when we break up our project into different project teams to study subsets of the organization.

If you start from the organization's true boundary (i.e., the outside) with a Business Event List, then any Business Event should be modeled in its entirety without any fragmentation. Therefore, we should not have any confusion between System Events and fragmented Business Events in an organization-wide Re-Engineering project context. Figure 6 –12) shows a complete Business Event that may be mistakenly analyzed/modeled as a fragmented Business Event in which the second fragment is triggered by a System Event.

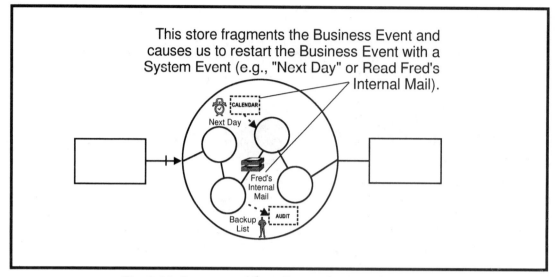

Fig. 6-12: Fragmented Bus. Events Cause a Sys. Event

I have already stated that System Events should not appear on the Business Model. Remember, we extend the Business Model at new design time (if necessary) to include System Events to make Business Events run in the real world. It's important to keep in mind the fact that System Events originate due to the needs of the system design. Figure 6–13 shows the introduction of System Events to support a Business Event.

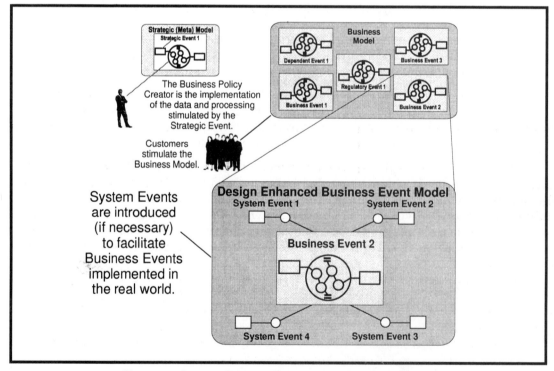

Fig. 6-13: System Events Supporting a Business Event

Of course, everything stated regarding the historical reasons for dysfunctional partitioning in the chapter on *Systems Archaeology* will help you locate and recognize System Events.

Unlike our previous example (in Figure 6–12), some System Events may be major, such as conducting a budget process once a year to support departmental/bureaucratic boundaries (see Figure 6–14).

The organization dictates when System Events occur. System Events do not directly contribute to accomplishing a customer's need. For example, hiring employees, or internal management requests, are System Events. We'll cover more on this later in the section on Business Event Traps.

System Events are tied to the issues of implementation, that is, to the particular way the organization has decided to do business. For example, an organization might decide to automate its warehouse operations. Then, the internal System Events, like employee hiring and firing, that currently support its manual warehouse operations would no longer be necessary (proving that they are not Business Events). On the other hand, if an organization decides to provide a computer-assisted system to help their warehouse staff, we would still require the System Events for hiring and firing. Please note, however, they are still System Events and can be affected by a design change. This is **not** true of a customer requesting goods from our organization. Regardless of how we implement this, it is not governed by Design Issues. It is a Business Event (i.e., we can't design it away and still accomplish the business need). We can stop selling goods as part of our business policy, but this is not just a design change, it now changes our business requirements i.e., analysis. We would have to remove the associated Business Event for selling goods.

(If you are a manager reading this and you're getting what I'm saying, this is the point where you can Re-Engineer yourself out of a "job" because you are an internal customer to the organization (i.e., an aspect of design), but please take this positively. "The way to control the future is to create it." Re-Engineering will happen, although, under a number of false starts called streamlining, right-sizing, down-sizing, etc. So, it's up to you to secure your own future by becoming a leader instead of a manager.)

The previous examples again show that System Events are a question of context of study (i.e., our organization boundary). Because of resource limits and the size of the organization, a project's context is usually restricted to the study of systems within part of an organization and therefore we are likely to find many System Events.

When we analyze just a portion of an organization, the areas that we have not analyzed (i.e., those existing implemented portions "outside" our project boundary) can now look like customers to your analyzed "inside" portion. These pseudo-outside "customers" may include department managers, other manual or automated systems, or the calendar/clock to indicate the end-of-day or Friday-batch-run processes from the old design. Now, these "designer" customers (who are internal to the organization, but external to your analyzed portion of it) can stimulate your analyzed Business Model via internal System Events. This could be a manager's requisition for more staff, or an executive issuing a budget directive to all department heads, but remember, these are not Business Events. The Re-Engineering analyst looks at System Events as a major source of change because these events may not need to stimulate their analyzed portion of the model in the first place. Or, these events may be an aspect of design that the analyst can bring before the strategic planners and ask them to look at expanding the context of the study to eliminate the System Events.

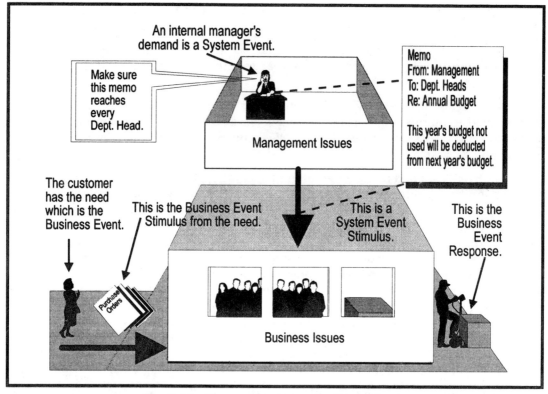

Fig. 6-14: System Events vs. Business Events

In many of my projects with the U.S. Government, the Senate and the House of Representatives show up in the context of the study as the Customer for the systems. But, if we were allowed to study a context encompassing all of government, we may "design away" the Senate and the House with, say, a government channel on an interactive TV network that citizens could use to electronically vote. The government would still accomplish its **what's**, but without the System Events from **how** it was implemented in the 1700s.[2] (The Senate and House actually are the Business Policy Creators who create Strategic Events and they are not really customers (more on this later).

> *If we have the luxury of Re-Engineering and implementing an entire organization, then modifying and removing System Events will be where we obtain the most benefits.*

---

2   By the way, that was not a political statement.

Now that we've defined a System Event, I can talk about an issue that frequently comes up in regarding old system thinking. In one of my seminars, I had a student ask, "Isn't a Business Event the same as, what in batch systems, we call a transaction?" My answer was, "Definitely maybe! But probably not. It's very likely to be a System Event."

For the Business Re-Engineering analyst it's important to keep the notion of Business Events clear of transaction issues that pertain to design and implementation. A Business Event is not a transaction. Transactions belong to the world of the designer/programmer.

Typically, what I see with "transaction thinking" is that a single Business Event is either broken down or lumped together with other kinds of Business Events to be processed in transaction batches. A dead give-away that a Business Event has been broken apart, and/or batched, is when we see "transaction type" fields. A transaction-type field is used to keep track of which data in the transaction belongs to which separate Business Event, and hence to its processing.

We call these broken apart events *Fragmented Business Events*. The important thing about a Fragmented Business Event is that it's not a true Business Event at all, but one Business Event masquerading as two or more System Events. The stimulus from a System Event (in this case a fragmented Business Event) is usually invented by some designer to accommodate a package design boundary. Figure 6–15 shows things to look out for to spot these kinds of System Events. (See the *Systems Archaeology* chapter, for why these grouped/fragmented events occur.)

So, some System Events will not just be there to support the old design, but will be formed from fragmented parts of Business Events. For example, we may have a batch process triggered by the start of the business day. This process may start at that time because that's when people show up to work in the Accounting Department. This process really should have been part of our response to a Customer Order where the flow triggers the processing in both the Order Department and the Accounting Department (ignoring the department boundaries entirely).

TYPICAL GENERIC EVENT NAME	TYPICAL CONTENT OF A FRAGMENTED EVENT
Customer Request =	Request ID + ... Business Data
Transaction =	Transaction Type + ... Business Data
System Inquiry =	Inquiry Number + ... Business Data
Midnight Batch Run =	* Scheduled Run Time for Automation of Batched Invoices *

Fig. 6-15: Sample Design Stimuli

The problem caused by Fragmented Business Events (implemented as System Events) is, data from different Fragmented Business Events require different processing. Therefore, a person or program has to interrogate the transaction type field before they or it know what type of processing needs to be executed. Unfortunately, these fragmented and lumped together Business Events make it difficult to modify procedures and/or computer code when changes are needed, because there is so much procedure and code associated with the fragmentation (design logic) in the way of the business logic. Figure 6-16 shows this unnecessary duplication of logic.

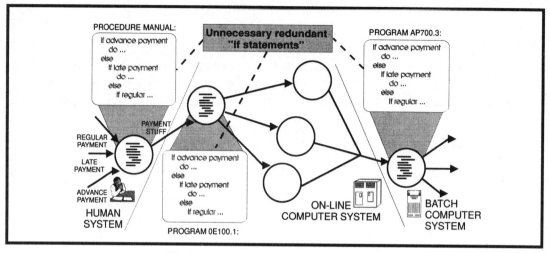

Fig. 6-16: Unnecessary Design Logic

This transaction view is one of the hardest habits to break. Most of my students who have this batch-oriented view of manual or automated systems in my seminars want to put a distribution process at the beginning of their Business Process Model (a system processing issue rather than a Business Issue). This process manifests itself in the manual system world as the Customer Service/Help Desk and in a computer system as a Transaction Center module at the beginning of the program. This distribution process is needed to separate out the lumped together Business Event Stimuli (see Figure 6–17).

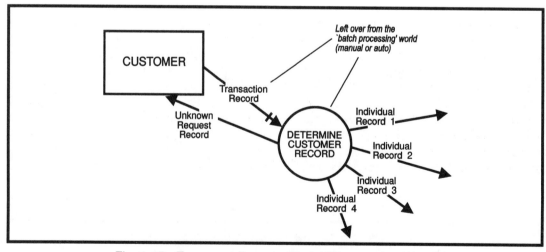

Fig. 6-17: Erroneous Process Model "Transaction Warp"

I always ask those students to try to write the *business* logic inside that distribution process — invariably a fruitless task because the logic needs a transaction type indicator that was invented by the designer, rather than requested by the business or the customer, and all of the logic is system/design oriented.

Business Event Traps

Because Business Events are so important, we must make certain we correctly identify them. Therefore, there are a number of little "traps" I'd like to talk about.

Figure 6–18 shows a design model of a hypothetical batch Order Processing computer system. This shows poor logical partitioning. This takes us right back to the D.P. Dark Ages of the monster edit, update, and print programs, or the everything-you-ever-wanted-to-know report generator.

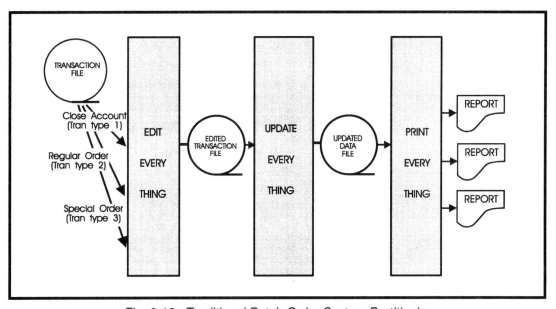

Fig. 6-18: Traditional Batch Order System Partitioning

In Figure 6–19, I have reproduced and repartitioned Figure 6–18. I have annotated it to show Business Event Stimuli, Business Event Partitions, and where data are Created, Retrieved, Updated, and Deleted. Each of the four Business Event stimuli in Figure 6–19 — Regular Order, Special Order, Open Account, and Close Account—has been indicated by a cross-bar on their Data Flows. The specific complete business policy for edit, update, and print will be assigned to the appropriate Business Event Partition. The process specification for the Business Event Partition stimulated by Special Order, for example, contains the particular edits, updates, and reporting tasks needed just for a Special Order. Note that this partitioning is based on Business Events (stimulus/response), and produces a significantly different partitioning than that shown in Figure 6–18.

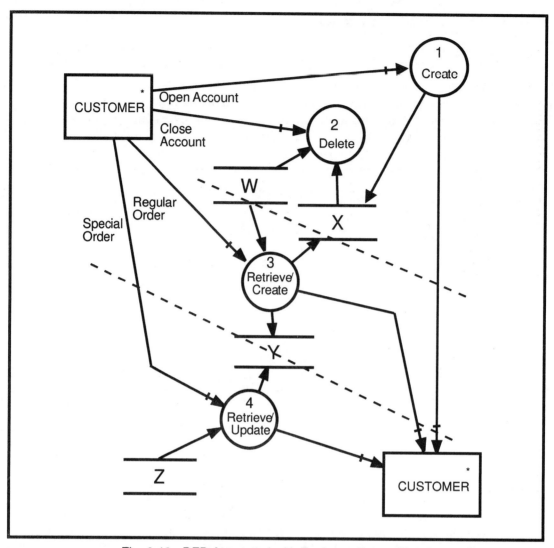

Fig. 6-19: DFD Annotated with Business Event Stimuli

Beware of Fragmented Events (Design Trap #1)

It is typical to find "design partitions" in every old system or environment that were not based on Business Event Partitioning. This is true for manual as well as automated systems (i.e., replace Edit, Update, and Print with Order Entry Department, Accounts Department, and Invoicing Department). In Figure 6–18, three Business Events were fragmented across the old design partitions of Edit, Update, and Print. So, if Special Order processing is modified or removed, for example, all three implemented partitions would have to be investigated for change. (This usually results in "commented-out," dead code, and/or inadvertent bugs in the other bundled Business Event Partitions.) This poor partitioning has already been criticized in the *Systems Archaeology* chapter.

Note that the fragmentation of Business Events will typically occur across many automated and manual boundaries. If we look upon department and computer system partitioning as vertical slices in an organization (see Figure 6–20), then Business Event Partitioning will probably take the opposite view, that is, horizontal partitioning.

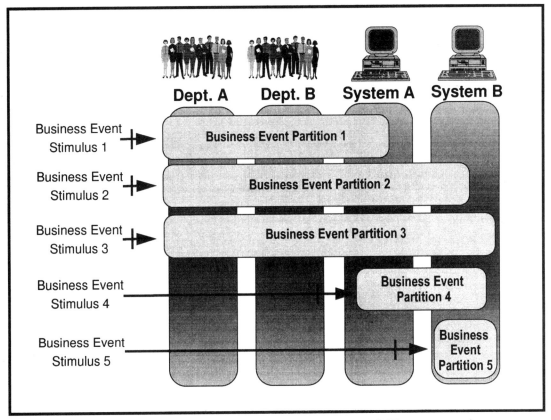

Fig. 6-20: Business Event Partitioned DFD

Notice in Figure 6–20 I've shown Business Event #5 completely subsumed within an existing designed system boundary. Hopefully, we will find some of these, but they will usually be coincidental. For example, End-of-year Tax Reporting is completely within the Accounts Department because they happen to have all of the data and the Business Event only requires financial data and processing.

There is an important issue related to the context of study that involves identifying and representing Interfaces on a Business Model.

> ***An Interface is a point at which an event is initiated or terminated (e.g., a Customer or the Outside World).***

However, in some cases, the context of the area being modeled may cause us to keep track of what I call Internal Interfaces. These are often places where a Business Event stopped in relation to our area of study (i.e., it's a point where a Business Event got fragmented). This Internal Interface may be an internal person (such as a clerk in Sales), or it could be a calendar that stimulates a batch of data to be input into our portion of the business.

When performing analysis and identifying an Interface where a Business Event occurs, we must first ask a key question. This question is whether the person or system stimulating us is external to our organization (not just to the portion under study). In other words, are they truly a customer — someone to whom we need to respond in order to satisfy our strategic mission. (Remember, this customer could be a place on Earth where lightening starts a fire, or even the calendar reaching a significant point in time for our business.) If the answer is "Yes", then this stimulus will be an External Interface. If the answer is "No", then this stimulus is an Internal Interface (i.e., it is there only because of project scope or for design reasons).

Although I am loathe to introduce new modeling symbology, there is a need to differentiate between Internal and External Interfaces on a model. If we're using a Data Flow Diagram to model our business, then an External Interface is a solid-lined rectangle. If the interface is internal, I recommend a different symbology (such as a dashed-lined rectangle). As I use a DFD as my main Business Model in this book, I recommend this extension to the DFD's symbology. However, if you are using another kind of model, then I believe it would be helpful to extend that model's symbology to address this need. For example, on an Object Oriented Model you may have Messages that are internally stimulated represented differently than externally stimulated Messages.

My reason for putting forth the idea of an Internal Interface and for recommending the introduction of new symbols is to point out where future projects need to link to other parts of a fragmented Business Event caused by the data flow terminating at an Internal Interface. In other words, at some future point, we would implement complete Business Events across the whole organization. The timing of this future point depends on the implementation of a Strategic Plan based on Business Events. After the Strategic Plan is completely implemented, there will be no Internal Interfaces on the organization's Business Model. (More on this in the *Strategic Planning via Business Events* chapter.) Also, under this unifying discipline we would not continue our old, historical error of implementing fragmented Business Events. Note that if we do Pre-Engineering (as discussed in the first chapter), we wouldn't introduce these fragmented Business Event driven Internal Interfaces in the first place.

Figure 6– 21 shows the evolution of Business Event modeling that would occur in the process of Re-Engineering an organization that was originally historically/hysterically partitioned, then partially Re-Engineered, and finally completely Re-Engineered. Note that the Internal Interfaces shown on the interim model are the result of not being able to Re-Engineer the entire organization at one time.

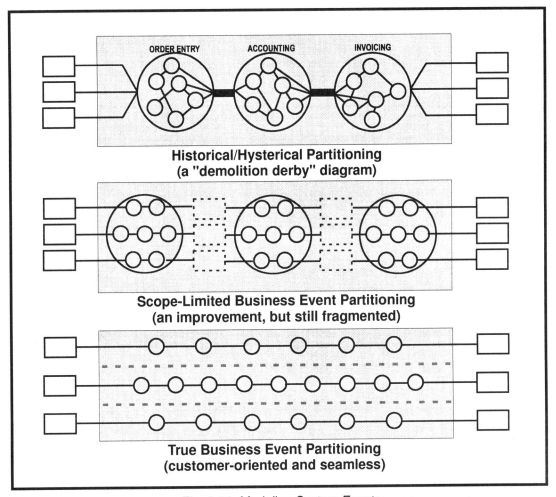

Fig. 6-21: Modeling System Events

Beware of Bundled Events (Design Trap #2)

Just as "edit-update-print" is a poor basis for partitioning because it fragments business policy, so is collecting all similar events together, such as Create, Retrieve, Update, and Delete to form monster partitions. For example, we might collect all Create events (such as Create Customer or Create Vendor) together to form a generalized Create program. This view, shown in Figure 6–22, is a "data bigot" view. This is not a specific Business Event view, and if implemented as four design partitions (programs), we would have similar maintenance problems as with the edit, update, and print partitioning.

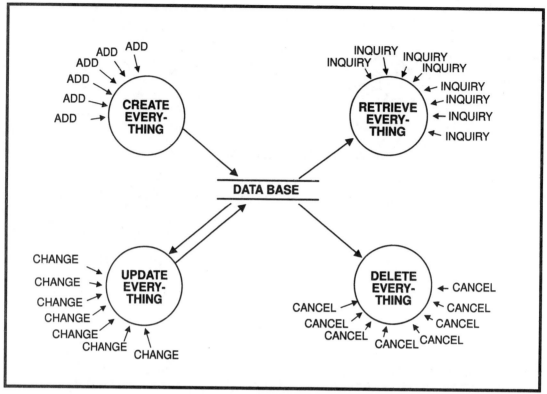

Fig. 6-22: Bundled Business Events

Beware of False Events (Design Trap #3)

We should also guard against seeing the basic manipulation tasks of Creation, Retrieval, Update, and Deletion of data as separate events. Admittedly, this may be true for very limited events such as a customer change of address or a single-deposit banking transaction — they qualify as Business Events because the business person relates to them as discrete, recognizable business activities.

If we feel a need to categorize these valid independent events, we can call them *Information/C.R.U.D. Events*, as mentioned earlier because they are usually trivial information "gets" and "puts" of data. What we should *not* do is break up, say, the Regular Order event shown in Figure 6–23 into two separate events: Retrieve Customer Information and Create Order.

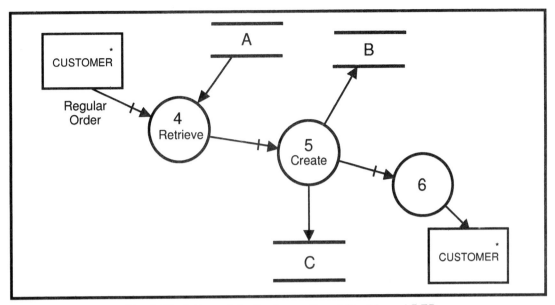

Fig. 6-23: A Complete Business Event Partitioned DFD

Carried to its extreme, we could incorrectly multiply the number of Data Elements/Fields and Entities in our business by four to incorrectly derive the total number of events in our business. (I hope that you can see that this does not represent a *business view* but rather a *data-only oriented* point of view.)

Dynamically Defined Business Events

The designers of old systems have typically not taken a customer view of system partitioning. Instead, they took the internal system view. These designers tended to look at a customer's need from the point of view of many small requests fragmented across internal systems. Rather than satisfy the customer's one request in full, they expected the customer to interact with the organization's systems to piece together fragmented requests to satisfy their needs.

Sometimes we will find that systems builders have tried to merge two or more of these small, fragmented requests into what the customer may actually want to do in one interaction with the organization. A bank deposit slip with the "less cash" option is an example of this merging. However, usually, to get a significant complete task done, the bank's customer has to perform an interactive dialogue (with either a human or an automatic teller). This dialogue is often interrupted by a number of returns to a menu screen, or there are new forms to fill out before their need is met (see Figure 6–24).

The ultimate in customer satisfaction would be for the bank to find out exactly what the customer needed to do and then to perform the entire transaction seamlessly i.e., to create customized Business Events. (In fact, I find the term, "customized" "Business Event", to be redundant.) If the Business Event isn't fulfilling one need of the customers', it's not a properly partitioned Business Event. So, we're looking to form Business Events that satisfy a specific, complete customer need.

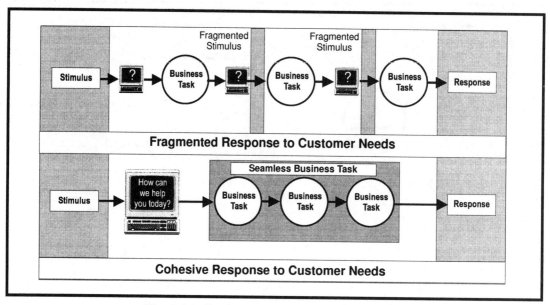

Fig. 6-24: Business-Event Driven Processing

What many designers have had to do in the past was to break a Business Event into many individual transactions based on the restrictions of batch processing, central mainframe capacity, or, from a manual point of view, on human skills and memory. An example of this latter case would be to send the customer to another department to take care of part of their request rather than have one employee empowered to service their need.

Of course, we may be lucky and find an existing design with partitions that coincide with the organization's Business Events, but this will probably be more coincidence rather than a conscious effort at having analysis govern the design.

In the Appendix on *Quality in Re-Engineering* we talk about quality as conformance to customer requirements. To obtain the ultimate customer satisfaction, we need to produce a specific model of their requirements. What I mean by this is, if we are lumping together all orders from a customer as just a customer order, we will have typically combined a set of separate events. That leads, in design, to what we find in most businesses today as the standard order form/screen and the standard processing of that order form/screen. The processing of a generic order may be implemented using human beings or an automated system. In either case, we end up with a form or screen containing data that should never be filled out for a Special Order, but which definitely needs to be filled out for a Delivery Order. Also, different parts may never have to be completed for an Advance Order while other parts may have to be filled out for a Pre-paid Order. What happens is, we end up with a global form or screen and the global processing needed to satisfy that form or screen. Often the person who fills out the form or screen has to conduct a long-winded procedure to overcome the design of the form or screen.

It appears to me that for quality customer satisfaction, we need to identify a very specific need for each customer. Each time the customer comes to us after we have initially defined any customized/dynamic events, we bring back that set of events associated with this particular customer, along with any standard events that we provide for all customers.

This might seem ridiculous to those of you reading this who have a computer orientation, because you need a transaction to process in the system and get out of the system quickly and efficiently to start the next transaction. However, for ultimate customer satisfaction, we truly want to have something at the beginnings of our systems that can form a unique Business Event Stimulus each time. Then we can bring together whatever data and processing is necessary in our organization to accomplish that Business Event.

We typically do this in a manual system because human beings can dynamically adjust to what a customer wants (and probably even recognize and remember that customer's past requests). We can bring together the necessary processes and products to satisfy that customer's specific need. So, we can do this in a new system without requiring the customer to go to other departments, or to fill out many different forms.

Any added design steps are hindrances to customer satisfaction. Let me give an example from my own business: If a customer wants me to put together a custom seminar that includes some workshops, a day of lectures, a consulting assignment in the middle of things, and then produce a production model during that workshop, then, for ultimate customer satisfaction, I can't say: "No. I can't do that. What I'll do is to teach you a seminar and then I'll do two days of consulting the following week." This is probably not what the customer is looking for. (*Of course, if I start losing seminar contracts because I don't provide this level of customization, I'd probably want to re-evaluate my policy. In fact, organizations are constantly changing to expand their services to respond to Business Events related to the ones they already respond to. That's the nature of business.*)

Now this dynamic forming of Business Events may not be realistic for implementation. You may decide to go back to a menu screen that gives a wide range of customer requests. However, for our Re-Engineering analysis effort we are chartered to produce a logical model (i.e., a Business Model) and not how we are going to ultimately implement it. Who knows? — we may decide in the implementation to use interactive television technology and put together whatever transaction the customer wants. So, in this scenario, there's no need for the form, there's no need for the customer service desk, and there's no need for the menu screen on the terminal as we know it today.

With today's technology we can be far more dynamic and interactive. In fact, there is a demand to empower employees with multiple skills, to computer assist employees, and to satisfy the customers' needs with total on-line, real-time computer processing. So, in order to provide custom Business Events, we first need to discover what Business Events are typical from the customers' point of view. Once we've identified the processing and the data required to satisfy each of these typical Business Events, then we can satisfy dynamically changing events by bringing together reusable parts of that processing and data on the fly.

Of course, if the customer requests that we embark on a new Business Event (new processing and new data), then that involves going into analysis mode. For example, if our organization is a bank and the customer wants to buy theater tickets with seat selection, then if we wish to satisfy this as yet undefined Business Event, we go into systems development mode and conduct analysis of our Business Policy for this new Business Event, etc. From a Business Policy Event point of view you could see that what I just said is, we can satisfy that customer's need providing we have the "nouns" and "verbs" within our organization's context, just as we can, as individuals, chartered with working at the Customer Information Desk, function not knowing what requests are going to be asked of us.

This is no different than you, dear reader, having the set of skills and knowledge (verbs and nouns) in a particular subject matter, and having someone requesting you to do something you've never done before in that subject. If you understand the request (i.e., it's in your knowledge base), you can satisfy that need by pulling together the procedures (the nouns and verbs) required to satisfy the demand.

> *The analysis of a Business Event becomes the act of identifying what the customer wants. The definition of the Business Event Partition becomes an issue of the collection from our organization's knowledge base of the processing and data required to satisfy the request.*

To beat this to death, let me do an example of this perfectly valid bank customer request. While talking to a customer, we find out that every other Friday the customer wants to deposit their paycheck. At the same time they want to pay their standard mortgage payment, take out an amount in "less cash" (e.g., $200.00), put an amount in their checking account (e.g., $100.00), and put the rest into their savings account. If we make that customer perform four separate transactions (either in a manual or an automated system), we have not satisfied the customers' needs. Now, the customer may accept that that's how it's supposed to be, and they may accept multiple returns to the menu screen, or fill out multiple slips of paper to make their transactions. The sum of these separated transactions are really that customer's Business Event. However, when another bank offers this type of new service, this customer may also leave and join that bank.

During my career I've done a fairly good job of defining and implementing fixed (non-dynamic) Business Events (e.g., Deposit, Withdrawal, Transfers, Inquiries, etc.). But, for ultimate customer satisfaction, we need to accommodate dynamic Business Events. In other words, we need to be able to put together custom transactions using our system knowledge base to satisfy our customer's needs.

Today we can do this bringing together of dynamic events. For those of you familiar with databases and high-level computer languages (those based on human languages such as English), this dynamic integration is currently available to us. However, this is usually on an ad-hoc basis, recreated each time (and, of course, you have to have all the data available before executing the dynamic request).

To sum up; our task when defining a Business Event and its resulting partition, is to put together that collection of nouns and verbs are understandable to the business community and can then be used for new design and implementation.

Current and New Business Events

Notice that all of the examples we've used so far seem to imply we model events that currently occur, but I hope you realize that everything we've talked about applies to new events our organization would like to fulfill in the future.

If something completely new comes along via a customer request, then we will need to go into Analysis, Design, and Implementation modes just as we would do when conducting any study in Re-Engineering. To meet the customer's needs, we may at times have to add new nouns and verbs (Data Elements and Instructions) to our knowledge base.

Figure 6–25 (based on ideas in Tom DeMarco's book[3]), shows the analysis portion of the development life cycle. We can use this to assist in developing and adding to our Business Event Model.

This diagram indicates that we can produce a model of the existing design (if one doesn't exist) for the purpose of validation and to ensure that the model is comprehensive for our project. We can then use this model to derive the true Business Model. This would be where we would extract any existing design characteristics, remove System Events, and partition by Business Events. This model, which shows all existing functionality of the business (after approval), is then used to add any new Business Events, (and Regulatory Events and/or Dependent Events) or to remove them.

This diagram also indicates two important analysis issues. The first is the one we've just mentioned (bringing in new data and processing). This is shown occurring at process 3 (Develop New Logical Specification). The other issue is that of logical and physical modeling. As stated previously in *The Model IS the Business* chapter, physical models represent Design Issues and logical models represent Analysis Issues.

As Re-Engineering analysts we're most interested in processes 2 and 3 (i.e., Develop Current Logical Specification and Develop New Logical Specification). To be able to derive a logical specification, we will probably have to understand the existing design which contains the Business Issues buried within it. The new logical specification will be used to go on to develop the new design (shown in process 4). This is where we would add design or implementation characteristics such as an "automation boundary" and any new System Events to accommodate the new design.

---

3   *Structured Analysis and System Specification* by Tom DeMarco — See Bibliography

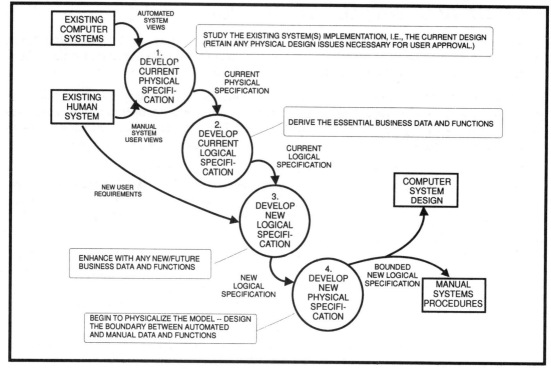

Fig. 6-25: The Stages of Analysis

Figure 6–26 shows the same portion of the life cycle in a non-DFD format. This diagram does not dictate sequential or separate analysis steps. We select the approximate number of specifications on a project-by-project basis.

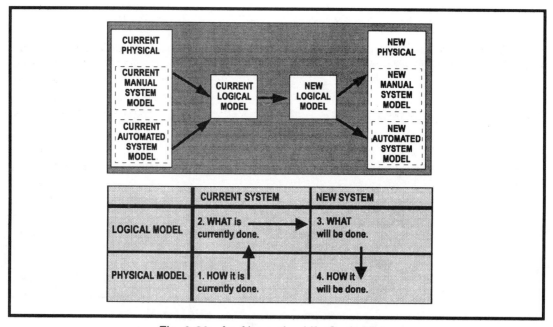

Fig. 6-26: An Alternative Life Cycle View

Summary

Even though Business Events are the most important type of event for Re-Engineering the organization, we now know that there are five types of events: Strategic Events, Business Events, Dependent Events, Regulatory Events, and System Events.

There is an order in which we filter out some types of events so they never appear in our Business Model. Additionally, there is a sequence in which we identify and categorize those events that do appear on the Business Model. This filtering and categorizing process is as follows:

- **Filter Out System Events** — The first step is to remove those events that were designed to make the old system run. These events will be of the least value to us (if they have any value) in our Re-Engineering task. However, we need to be aware that some events (those formed from fragmented Business Events), masquerade as System Events.

- **Filter Out Strategic Events** — The next step is to remove Strategic Events. These events are important for creating and modifying the Business Model, but they do not stimulate it into life. We could create a separate Meta Model for how we address the processing of Strategic Events, but they do not belong on the Business Model.

- **Identify Regulatory Events** — Regulatory Events are external to our organization and we need to model them on the Business Model, but they are probably the ones over which we have the least influence in Re-Engineering.

- **Identify Dependent Events** — These events are here to help us satisfy Business Events and they do appear on the Business Model, but they are categorized as a distinct type of event. Dependent Events will be one of the most important sources for potentially forming strategic alliances as part of a Re-Engineering effort.

- **Identify Business Events** — These are the events that keep our doors open. Therefore, they are the events we should focus upon to obtain the most improvements in our ability to satisfy our real customers.

A Business Event-driven Model captures the business rules and policy about information and processing and is the basis for Re-Engineering the business. Thus, Business Re-Engineering begins by identifying the external events that result in stimuli that trigger our organization into action. Then Business Re-Engineering makes us specify the *entire* set of business rules and data needed to formulate the correct response to each Business Event.

I believe that the recognition of Business Events and Business Event Partitioning (described in the next chapter) used with any of the existing proven methods and models allows us to do true Business Re-Engineering.

In any hierarchy of [metaphysics] classification the most important division is the first one, for this division dominates everything beneath it. If this first division is bad, there is no way you can ever build a really good system of classification around it.

Robert Pirsig
Lila

Partitioning by Business Events

I have come to realize that the ultimate *logical* view of any organization is a set of Business Objectives (i.e., its Mission Statement). For example, if our goal is simply to make money, any line of business could potentially satisfy that goal, and logical models could only show a wide and generic view. If, on the other hand, if we had a Business Objective to be the best training and consultancy organization in the field of Business Re-Engineering, then we can produce more specific Business Models of our organization. Therefore, at some point in the level of detail of our business views, we start to define what are our specific Business Events, versus those of any other organization.

In this chapter, we'll see that, based on partitioning by Business Events, we can build systems which address Business Issues (i.e., that respond to customers' needs rather than to any historical internal needs). By definition, partitioning the model of the organization by Business Events keeps Business Events *separate*, making systems much easier to modify when the business policy changes.

The discipline of Business Re-Engineering is based on partitioning each stimulus, its responses, and its process and memory together that are needed to respond to a specific customer need.

In the *Systems Archaeology* chapter we went on an archaeological dig and saw how the manual and automated systems of an organization grew up, based on a variety of factors. We also saw that these factors were issues of internal design and not Business Issues which would have taken the outside customer into account. We found that a typical organization is partitioned into departments and computer systems based on historical *(or hysterical)* reasons. Such partitions are seldom related to the way the organization needs to respond to efficiently satisfy their customers' needs in today's environment.

A major factor that affects our Business Event Partitioning is how we deal with stored data; what I call Business Event Memory. Due to its importance, this topic is covered in some detail in this chapter in the section on *Business Event Memory*.

Another important part of this chapter focuses in on what it takes to define a Business Event Partition. This process consists of identifying all of the key components of the partition and naming them. Because our task in analysis is to build models to communicate with the minds of others, it is important to use business terms and to have naming standards for Business Events and Business Event Partitions (and all of their constituent elements). Throughout this chapter, because we're dealing with *Partitioning by Business Event* (not System Events), we will only use logical names for data and processes.

In the course of identifying what each Business Event Partition element is and naming it, we also need to define what distinguishes them from all others.

Business Event Partition Defined

Now let me define what I call a natural business partition — a Business Event Partition:

A Business Event Stimulus plus all associated processing, stored memory, and outgoing responses that constitute the organization's complete reaction to a Business Event.

Whether you're Pre-Engineering a new organization or Re-Engineering an existing one, the first major step is to identify the set of single-process Business Events needed to satisfy your prospective customer's needs. Once you've reached this stage, you've already accomplished 90% of Pre-Engineering's and Re-Engineering's partitioning goals. At this point any lower level Business Event processing and data partitionings are based on rather arbitrary reasons, such as the reusability of functions or what the "customer" (in this case the implementor) decides to be an acceptable limit for grouping processing and its data.

The idea is to encapsulate the stimulus, processing, stored memory, and response for one customer's single need together without any further partitioning. This must be the ultimate logical business partitioning because we've removed any design reasons that affect the partitioning and it's based on customer/Business Issues. This entire collection is what is needed to accomplish the customer's need within the organization. This leads to what I call true *Business Functionality*.

> *The most important thing to remember regarding a Business Event Partition is that it consists of everything necessary to satisfy the Business Event from the outside agent's perspective; that is, our organization does what the customer expects of us in total within one partition.*

An organization that focuses in on technology issues, such as fast data access and high speed efficient processing, will realize only small gains if it does not formulate a cohesive Business Event Partitioned response to its customers.

When we identify Business Events, we should separate them out to a functional level. What I mean by this is, the one single need of a customer translates into one Business Event. At first this might seem ridiculous. You may think: "Our organization must have thousands of events." While that may be true depending on the diversity of your organization and the services you provide, in most organizations it will not be the case. Most organizations are what is termed "vertical." For example, my company supplies training and consulting in engineering subjects. We don't sell airline seats, bake bread, or do any banking for you.

A Business Event Partition represents the most logical view of any organization. Put another way, I'm saying that if we form any internal views (partitions) of a system that are not based on outside Business Events (no matter how minor), this will be a less functional view that restricts the business system in some way.

If we looked at any manual procedure, or a computer program's flow chart, they both show a flow of control from one instruction (verb) to the next using whatever data (nouns) are needed. This typically is linear, but it can be asynchronous. For example, while you follow a recipe when cooking (a set of sequential tasks), you may be asked to prepare the pastry while the vegetables simmer. We can look upon this set of instructions as a *control* structure consisting of these non-divisible tasks and their data.

As stated previously, when conducting initial analysis and defining Business Events, the analyst must be cognizant of the broader ability to satisfy customer needs. Ultimately, our task is to bring together the set of needed nouns and verbs in a control structure (linear tasks) to satisfy the customer's needs. This set of nouns and verbs will make up the Business Event Partition.

We can use any model that shows data and processing to capture these nouns and verbs within a Business Event. For example, Figure 7–1 shows a process view using a DFD of the information we need to gather about a Business Event during analysis.

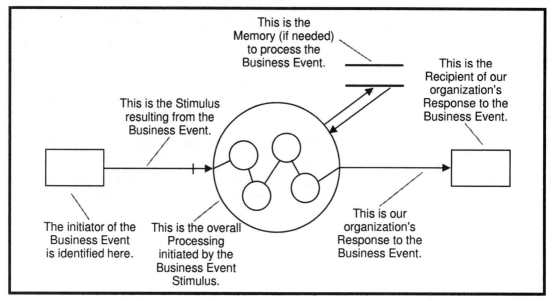

Fig. 7-1: What Data to Gather about a Business Event

When a customer stimulus arrives at the boundary of our organization, one or more processes are stimulated to perform whatever logic is needed (with whatever data are needed) to satisfy that stimulus, or, in other words, to execute the business policy associated with that stimulus. Using a Dependent Event as an example, if a Delivery comes in from a Supplier, we should do everything necessary to deal with the Delivery, such as verifying the Delivery against the original Purchase Order, Restocking material, and storing Accepted Delivery data (for a future inquiry, or when the Supplier's Invoice arrives). We may immediately pay the supplier based on what we accepted. All the processing we do and all the data we access is in response to the external need (Business Event) of the customer (Supplier) wanting us to accept their Delivery (Business Event Stimulus).

It is this collection of data and processing associated with an event that we should logically package together in a Business Event Partition. Notice that in this case, the Supplier is a customer in the model. They generate a Dependent Event — not a Regulatory Event (because they are not regulating us) and not a System Event (because the Supplier is not a Design Issue). This is not classified as a Business Event because we have some control over the Supplier. If you take the event away, you remove an aspect of the business, not the old design.

Now is a good time to reiterate the statement that Business Event Partitions are based on *business policy*, not on any technology or data processing designer's view. In the example in Figure 7–2 we may find in the current system that the Customer Payment is separated from the Customer Order. This may be because the Customer Payment processing was part of the Accounting system and the Customer Order was part of the Order Entry system. However, the real company policy may have been to always try to collect payment and orders together. Payment and order processing should not have been separated. That is, the Business Event: "Customer wants to Purchase Goods" requires Customer Payment to be received and processed before the Business Event is complete.

In the correct Business Model (as shown in Figure 7–2), our Business Event Partition would consist of the two processes and data combined into one process, with associated input and output data flows. Please note that the data store Customer Invoices would not be needed (unless used by some other Business Event Partition), but would become a transient data flow. Also note that the stimulating data flow Customer Payment would become a *response data flow* (a "pull"). The high-level single process (and any lower-level sub-processes) for this Business Event would obviously also reflect this combination.

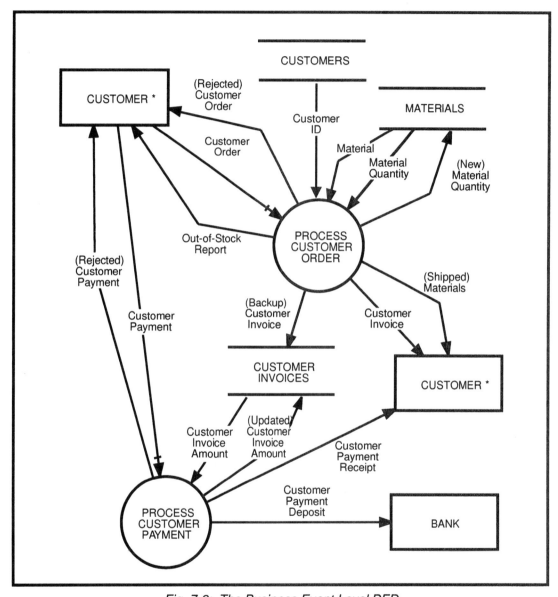

Fig. 7-2: The Business Event Level DFD

What Constitutes a Total Business Event

Having identified a Business Event, the elements of the Business Event Partition are:

- *The Business Event Source (the Need)*
- *The Business Event Stimulus*
- *The Business Event Processing*
- *The Business Event Memory*
- *The Business Event Response*
- *The Business Event Recipient*

Let me elaborate on each of these elements, but before talking about each of these, we need to talk about naming Business Events.

Business Event Naming

I recommend a Business Event Name consisting of a whole sentence. I think that it's ridiculous to limit ourselves to only a verb-object name, or worse, to eight characters for our naming standard. (We can invent an additional cryptic identifier during design if necessary.)

For accurate management of our models, the Business Event Name must be unique and associated with only one Business Event.

We should try to name a Business Event from the perspective of *what the customer expects of the organization as opposed to what we do in response to the stimulus.* For example, if a customer wants to buy our product(s), pay for it now, and take it away, then I would name the event:

"Customer wants to buy our product(s), pay for it, and take it away."

The Business Event Stimulus for this may be named: "Regular Order."

We may also have a Business Event in which a customer wants to buy our product(s), pay for it now, but have us deliver it. Again, I would produce a meaningful name:

"Customer wants to buy our product(s), pay for it now, and have it delivered."

The Business Event Stimulus for this may be named: "Delivery Order."

This naming may seem simplistic to you, but I have found one of the hardest tasks in analysis is to separate out specific Business Events before starting our Business Model. Also, as we've said, the purpose of producing models is to get approval from someone other than ourselves, so meaningful names are essential for stand-alone models.

Our naming conventions can be the same as those used for English Language sentence structures (i.e., Subject, Verb, and Object) especially as our Business Model is intended for a non-technical audience.

Business Event Naming Examples

Let me define some Business Events using some examples that are close to home. As a person who is in business I can respond to my customers providing they use (or get close to using) the nouns and verbs that I use in my organization's context.

Suppose one of my customers calls me and states that they would like to set up two "kickoff" seminars (one for business people and one for data processing people) on analysis issues:

- First, I ask the customer if they want to study their business processing and/or their data needs. My thought processes behind asking the question are that they may be asking for two different types of seminars (a Business Process Analysis Seminar or a Business Information Analysis Seminar). They respond then with: "Both are needed." The customer then tells me that they want to support their project team with regular consulting visits to help them with the project and its deliverables. When they tell me this, I translate their statement into a request for on-going consulting.

- Next, the customer mentions that they need to get any new members of the project team who join after the initial seminars trained individually. This leads me to think that I need to possibly reserve these new team members some seats in public, or open in-house seminars.

- The customer concludes the conversation by asking if I can provide these services and if so, can I write up a contract with a cost estimate. My answer is: "Sure!"

Now, because I as a business person can do this in my brain, then if an analyst was to study my operation, they should certainly be able to model these business requests and in this case put together a Business Model that I, the Business Policy Creator, can understand.

The Business Event Source

This is a customer — an external individual, agency, organization, system, or other impetus that creates a stimulus to our organization. For example, this could be a flood occurring on a piece of land, or the closing of a foreign stock exchange. The non-shaded area in Figure 7–3 represents the Business Event Source.

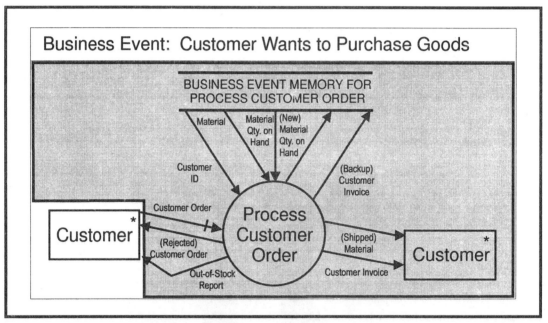

Fig. 7-3: The Business Event Source

Naming the Business Event Source

The source would always be an animate entity as opposed to inanimate. For example, processing beyond our organization stimulates us into life. Typically, the source will be a person, system, agency, or organization, but the naming of this source should be in singular form and in non implementation terms (e.g., Bank instead of Joe at the Bank). The source, remember, can be any system. This can include the ecosystem (e.g., events occurring in the environment that affect the land like an earthquake). It could also be the system of measuring time (i.e., a clock/calendar), or an external device (e.g., an elevator).

The Business Event Stimulus

A process does not start up on its own — it needs to be stimulated into life by a data flow or control flow. Without such a stimulus, the process would lie idle even though data was waiting to be "pulled" into it.

Remember, we can extend the Data Flow Diagram (DFD) and even the State Transition Diagram (STD) symbology to indicate the stimulating data flow or control flow with a cross-bar across the flow. The cross-bar is helpful because there are other data flows that are not active, such as those that are pulled in from stores. Figure 7–4 shows the symbology used to show Stimulating Data Flows and Stimulating Control Flows.

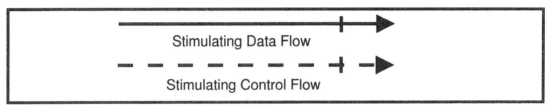

Fig. 7-4: Stimulus Flow Symbology Extensions

You can see that a Business Event Stimulus is a demand (input data, control trigger, or material) resulting from a Business Event that activates part of the organization. This could be a period of 90 days elapsing since we sent an invoice, or unused goods returning from a customer. The Business Event Stimulus is the first thing we see about a Business Event from within our organization. Because of the importance of the first division (as Pirsig said), it's vital to identify autonomous stimuli. Therefore, I need to elaborate on this element of a Business Event more than the others. The non-shaded area in Figure 7–5 represents the Business Event Stimulus.

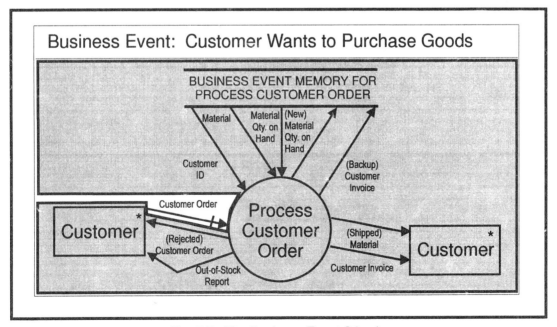

Fig. 7-5: The Business Event Stimulus

Once we have defined a Business Event itself, we realize that the stimulus is completely dependent on the Business Event. In other words, the contents of the stimulus (the nouns) will mostly be dependent on what the customer needs (and not on what the systems people think the customer should fill out on a form or on a screen).

When analyzing a Business Event Stimulus, it's important to know which of the three types of Business Event Stimuli it is: whether it's Data Triggered, Control Triggered, or Material Triggered.

Data-triggered Stimuli

These consist of what I call a cohesive set of data necessary for processing the event. For example, when a customer wants to purchase some of our goods, he/she has an order in their head. The order stimulates the system to provide those goods. The order contains data that is essential for generating the response — which goods, for whom, by when, and so on. The data in the order makes up our cohesive data stimulus.

Figure 7–6 shows some examples of Business Events with Data-triggered Stimuli.

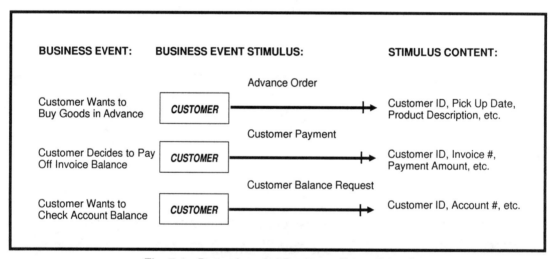

Fig. 7-6: Data-triggered Business Event Stimuli

For a data stimulus we need enough information in the stimulus to understand the requirements of the need. For example, if a customer wants to send their package from A to B, we'll need a cohesive set of data before we can satisfy that Business Event. For one organization that delivers door to door to respond to this Business Event correctly, the stimulus may contain:

- the container's size,
- the container's weight,
- the container's contents,
- the container's pick-up location, and
- the container's ultimate destination.

For another organization that picks up from one depot and delivers to another of their depots for you to pick up, the stimulus for the same Business Event may contain:

- the customer name,
- the container weight, and
- the destination zip code.

When an event occurs outside my company, such as, an organization needs training, I need to know certain things to be able to respond. If a customer calls us to set up a seminar at their site, I need to know more than just their name before I can respond to that request. To satisfy their basic need, I need to know:

- the customer ID,
- the seminar subject,
- the required date,
- the seminar location, and
- the number of students.

This set of data forms the Data-triggered Stimulus to Logical Conclusions, Inc. It is the set of data the customer knows to supply us, but there may be additional data we at LCI need. To satisfy our business policy, we need certain information, like whether they would allow outside students in their seminar and do they wish to take care of hotel, car reservations, etc. So, this cohesive stimulus set of data may also contain data that the organization needs in order to satisfy the Business Event.

Another event outside my organization might be that someone wants to train one or more individuals in a particular subject at an open public seminar.

In this example, I'd need to know:

- the number of individuals who need this training,
- where their students are willing to travel, and
- the student names.

This need results in a different stimulus and policy in my company. Some of the information I need will be the same as for the previous caller, but this is a different Business Event and at least some part of the response and/or some of the data needed to make that response will be different. For example, in the latter case, LCI dictates the date and location. This information is no longer part of the stimulus — it is part of my response. If a third caller wants a fully catered seminar, I would tell her that I'd be happy to do the seminar part, but she would need to arrange catering herself. Responding to requests for catering is not part of my present business policy.

Naming the Data-triggered Stimuli

I have already given some samples of data-triggered Business Event Stimuli names with their corresponding Business Event names. Here I would like to add that the Data-triggered Business Event Stimuli Names will often be aggregate names. A Data-triggered Stimuli, for example, would have a name that contains a cohesive set of Data Elements that make up the stimuli. For example, the stimuli "Delivery Order" will be made up of things such as "Delivery Location", "Delivery Payment Type", "Delivery Date", etc.

Material-triggered Stimuli

These are actual products or items that are part of the business (for example, goods) that arrive at our organization. However, for a governmental disaster relief agency, the Material-triggered stimuli could be water overflowing its banks when a river floods. (Note, I find that Data Processing people have a hard time associating with Material-triggered Stimuli on a Business Model because they tend to want to turn everything into data.) My example to deter this is to use an example of a warehouse where incoming goods must make it to the actual inventory (not just a quantity field stored in a database). These goods must be shown on the Business Model because they are not an aspect of design, they are an aspect of the business. Figure 7–7 shows some examples of Business Events with Material-triggered Stimuli.

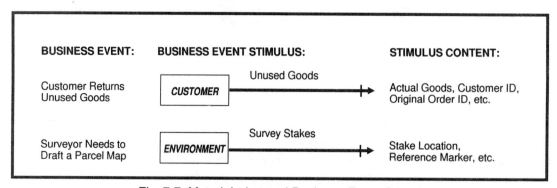

Fig. 7-7: Material-triggered Business Event Stimuli

Naming the Material-triggered Stimuli

Material-triggered stimuli names may or may not contain data, but they will always contain a description of what is in the stimulus flow of the actual material. This may be money, products, or legal documents, for example.

Control-triggered Stimuli

These merely prompt the system to do something and have no data. The arrival of the end of the fiscal year, for example, merely *triggers* part of the organization into action. The appearance of "April 15" on the calendar doesn't provide data to be processed, but merely stimulates a system into action. It is a control stimulus and contains no data. The event that produces this stimulus is, in fact, the calendar or clock reaching a predetermined point in time. Figure 7–8 shows some examples of Business Events with Control-triggered Stimuli.

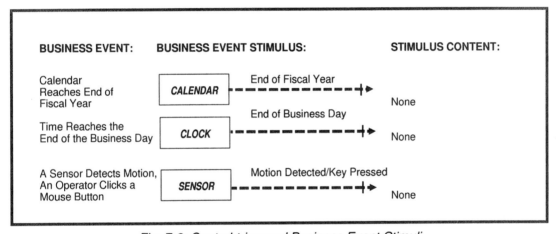

Fig. 7-8: Control-triggered Business Event Stimuli

Not all Business Event Stimuli are so straight forward. For example, one stimulus might be, if funds are not collected in 30, 60, or 90 days after an item is purchased from you on credit, this may stimulate your system to produce an overdue notice.

Your first analysis task, of course, would be to question the 30, 60, or 90 day periods as a design issue. Always question control issues in business systems, as control is primarily a design issue. However, control can also be a requirements issue, especially in real-time systems. If this is found to be essential business policy, then what we have is a Control triggered type of stimulus (e.g., Review Invoice Time) that makes us review every invoice looking for an over 30, 60, or 90 day difference between the invoice's date and today's date. It sounds strange, but in these kinds of Business Events, the calendar is the customer because it is the passing of time indicated by the calendar that produces the stimulus.

Be cautious to identify the correct stimulus. For example, the marketing staff of an organization may dream up ways of trying to get people outside the organization to initiate Business Events, as when a phone company advertises its services with "Have you called your mother lately?" But we should not look upon the marketing drive as a Business Event Stimulus itself. (In fact, the marketing drive is a response to another event, and the stimulus that initiates a marketing drive may be poor sales figures, a scheduled time of the year such as Christmas, and so on.) The stimulus in this case is the customer who happens to respond to the ad.

Naming the Control-triggered Stimuli

Control-triggered stimuli names do not contain any data, so their names will be associated with what is happening, or what has happened, or a threshold that has been reached. For example, the name may indicate that a temperature has exceeded acceptable limits, it's time to restock, or that we've reached the "End of the Fiscal Year."

Business Event Processing

Business Event Processing is all of the business logic and its transient data required to produce a Business Event Response. This is put in place by our organization. For example, we could have processing to deduct 10% from the final invoice for special customers, or to close a flow valve when the temperature gets above 100 degrees. The non-shaded area in Figure 7–9 represents the Business Event Processing.

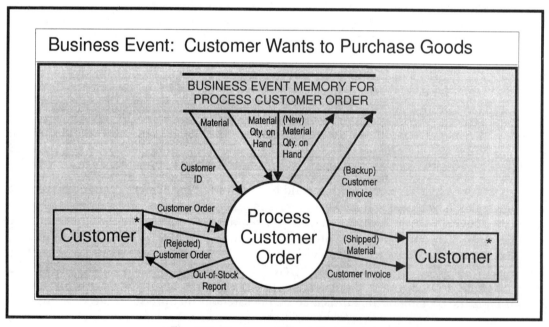

Fig. 7-9: Business Event Processing

Naming the Business Event Processing

Unlike the Business Event name, we want the Business Event Processing name to be relatively cryptic because it will always be supported by more detail in either the form of a lower-level diagram/model, or a detailed process specification/procedure. So, we like to use a verb-object name to sum up the process. For example, Order Goods, Process Customer Order, etc. The names may be more descriptive such as Calculate Special Customer Product Discount. The important thing to note here is that we're not looking for generic names such as Process Stuff, Handle Data, Do Everything Else, etc. Rather, we're looking for quite specific names that truly sum up what's going on in the process.

The Business Event Memory

This book is aimed at the business person, so I do not pre-suppose that the reader already knows Information Engineering Techniques or such methods as normalizing data structures. Therefore, I have found it useful to teach the concept of grouping data via a logical collection of Data Elements that I call Business Event Memory.

The *Business Event Memory* is defined as:

> **"The collection of all the stored (i.e., non-transient) Data Elements necessary to accomplish the processing contained in one Business Event Partition."**

Beware of System Stores

Before explaining Business Event Memory, we need to identify the current physical source of our data for producing these logical cohesive sets of data, and we need to identify things we should beware of so we don't get corrupted by the old environment.

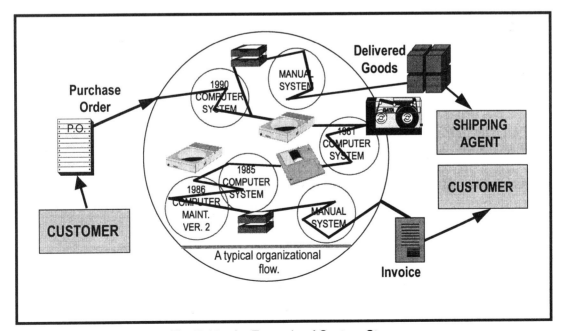

Fig. 7-10: An Example of System Stores

The big problem we have when looking at stores is that a significant number of the stores in the existing design should not be stores at all. They are what we call System Stores (see Figure 7–10) and they are there to support the existing design. These stores will turn out to be transient data flows on our Business Model. Also note that any System Store will make us form an Internal Interface and its stimulus to restart the flow of data for the fragmented Business Event.

As stated in the *Systems Archaeology* chapter, we have a problem when we try to form a cohesive data store (Entity) because its Data Elements will be typically scattered or bundled across old design stores. (I call these "convenience" or "designer" stores because they are created as a matter of human or computer access convenience.) For example, information on a Customer could be scattered across Sales files, Accounts Receivable and Payable, and Invoicing files. We'll also find stores of data between old system boundaries that shouldn't be stores.

Unfortunately, these bundled and fragmented stores contain the source of our input for repartitioned stores in our Business Model. The analyst needs to identify essential stored data needs and then gather associated Data Elements from all of the above old data stores and bring them together into a cohesive unit.

The Need for Stored Data

We need to store data from one Business Event Partition to await retrieval by another Business Event Partition. In fact, this is the reason why stored data exists — to respond to external Business Events occurring independently.

The non-shaded area in Figure 7–11 represents the Business Event Memory.

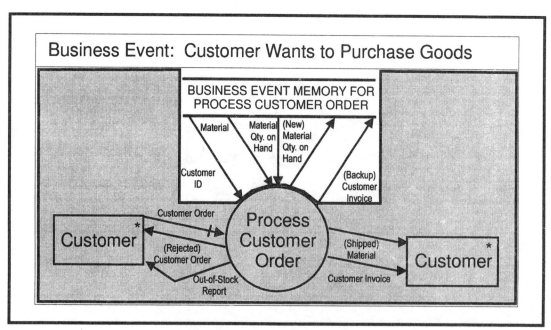

Fig. 7-11: Business Event Memory

Unfortunately, in many existing, non-Re-Engineered environments, we will find designer stores between divisions, departments, etc. in manual systems and between systems, subsystems, and programs in automated systems (see Figure 7–12).

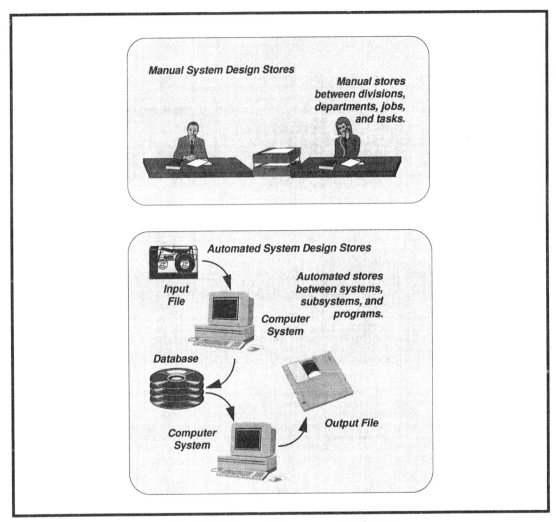

Fig. 7-12: Sample Non-essential Stores

Now we can identify the need for *business data stores*. With Business Event Partitioning, we can see the true business need for data stores and state a fundamental rule of Business Event Partitioning:

Stores are only necessary when information needs to be shared across two or more Business Event Partitions or across two occurrences of the same Business Event Partition. All data other than those used across Business Events are transient data that "burn up" after completion of the Business Event processing.

This means that stored data will only exist on the boundaries of Business Event Partitions (see the Essential Stores in Figure 7–13).

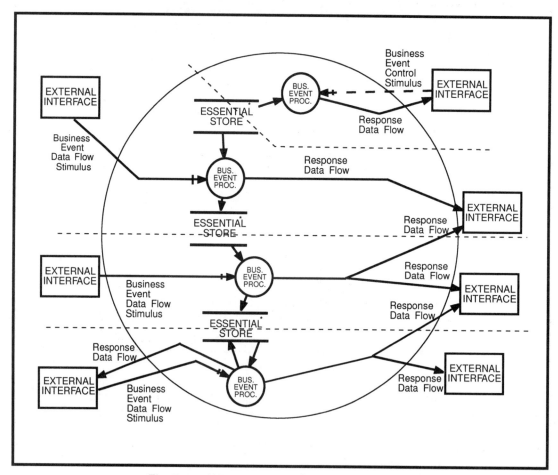

Fig. 7-13: Where Essential Stores are Needed

This "ESSENTIAL STORE" of data is shown as a data store on our Business Model because it is an essential element of the business. We will support it using a data model (ERD) and associated specifications and each store should be data conserved. Figure 7–14 shows a model where stores W, Y, and Z are not *fully data-conserved*. In the case of store Y, what goes in doesn't come out (it's a "black hole") and in the case of stores W and Z, what comes out doesn't go in (they're created by "magic").

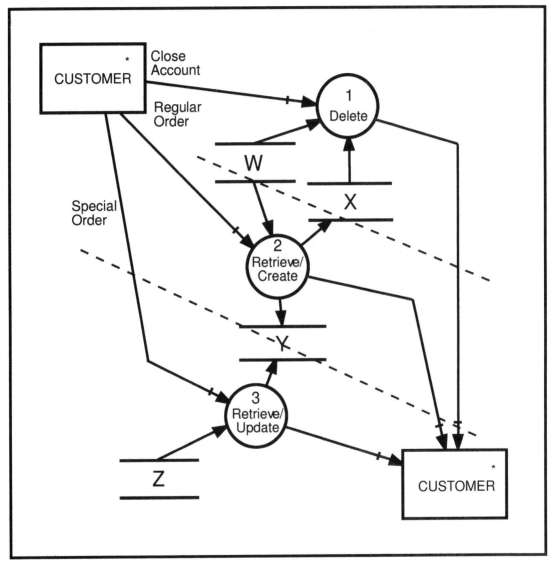

Fig. 7-14: Black Hole and Magic Stores

Our interest here is how we partition stored data because the data groupings of the existing world will probably be based on the old design as stated in the *Systems Archaeology* chapter.

Stored Data Traps

Just like we have old design traps for data flow and processing, we have design traps for *stored data*.

Beware of Fragmented Stores

Just as we can find fragmented Business Events due to old Design Issues, it is typical to find fragmented "data sets" (i.e., data Entities) across old designer stores. For example, information on a Customer could be scattered across Sales files, Purchased Products files, and Service Agreement files as in Figure 7–15. If a Customer sends in a change of address, all three files would need to be updated. The analyst must bring these Data Elements together into a cohesive data grouping (i.e., an Entity) when repartitioning stores.

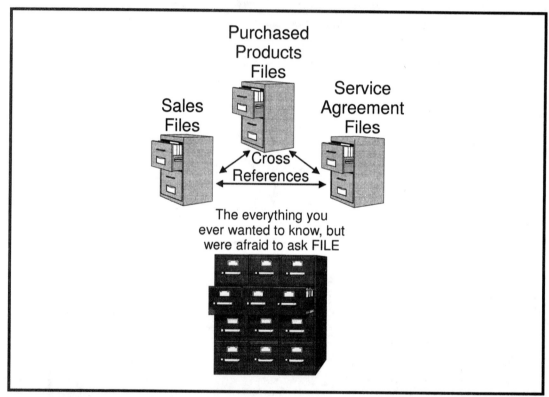

Fig. 7-15: An Example of Fragmented Manual Stores

Beware of Bundled Data

As we saw in the chapter *System Archaeology*, bundled stores arise when the previous designer grouped separate sets of data together, possibly for the sake of efficiency. This is very common of the files used in "edit-update-print" computer systems, because this data partitioning was based on process bundling for technology and efficiency. The analyst must break up these bundled stores (typified on the left side of Figure 7–16), and assign their Data Elements to cohesive data groupings or Entities (typified on the right side of Figure 7–16) when repartitioning stores.

A Typical Bundled Store	Partitioned Cohesive Stores

Customer Name
Customer Address
Customer City/State/Zip
Account Number
Account Balance
Account Creation Date
Product Number
Product Cost
Product Lease Number
Credit Account Number
Credit Account Limit
Customer Old Address
Product Service Agreement
	Customer Data
	   Customer Name
	   Customer Address
	   Customer City/State/Zip
	   Customer Old Address
	   Customer Old City/State/Zip
	
	Products Data
	   Product Number
	   Product Cost
	   Product Lease Number
	   Product Service Agreement
	
	Customer Account Data
	   Customer Account Number
	   Customer Account Balance
	   Customer Account Creation Date
	   Customer Account Credit Number
	   Customer Account Credit Limit

Fig. 7-16: Bundled vs. Cohesive Stores

Beware of Convenience Stores

Figure 7–17 is a generic model showing a convenience store — Orders. The designer had to create this so that the Order Department could accumulate orders, waiting until the scheduled time for the Accounting Department to pick them up. Note that whenever the data in one Business Event Partition crossed an old design boundary (Order Department to Accounting Department), a convenience store would have been created. Or, put another way, between each and every old design boundaries there will be some kind of store. This store is usually unnecessary in the business world, and the analyst must remove these during analysis.

If the analyst does not recognize this old design characteristic, the old store is very likely to become part of the requirements for a new file/database. This will perpetuate unnecessary stored data and the housekeeping processes associated with it, such as Creating, Deleting, and Updating data.

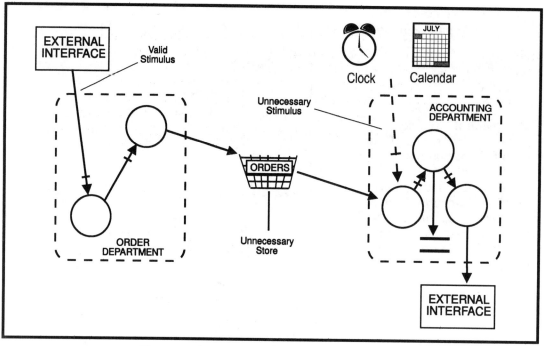

Fig. 7-17: An Example of Convenience Stores

Looking back at our Order Processing system (Figure 7–18), we see at least two convenience stores: the Transaction File input to the batch run and the Edited Transaction File. The updated data file shown may actually be a valid file if needed across two or more Business Events. The *convenience stores* were needed only because of the batch design partitioning into three programs.

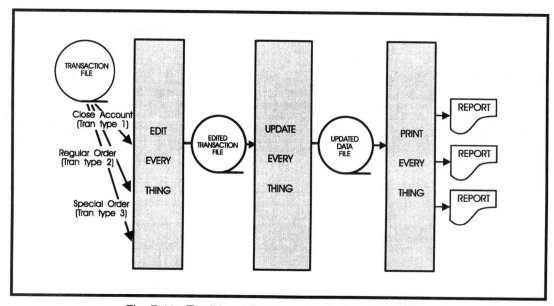

Fig. 7-18: Traditional Batch Order System Partitioning

Logical Stores

When we think about stored data logically, we could think about part of the human brain being a data store. The human brain seems to work by dynamically linking global Data Elements. For example, if I asked you to think of all your friends who had red hair, you would create two mental sets — friends and red heads — and identify those falling into the intersection of the two sets. The brain does this so quickly and effortlessly that we don't usually stop to think how we did it. It's as though we don't have any pre-conceived groupings, just a *Data Element pool*, that is, a large set of facts (i.e., each Data Element is a separate fact).

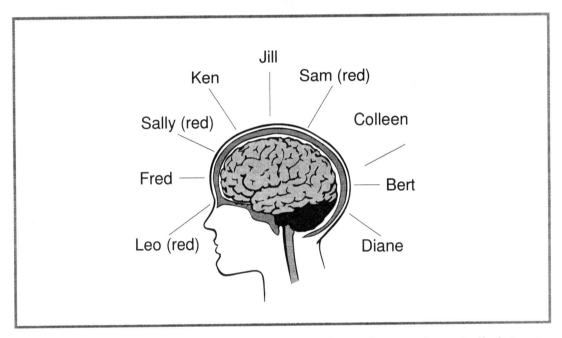

Unfortunately, we do not yet have business machines that can dynamically bring together a Data Element pool efficiently in the implemented world, but this doesn't stop us from modeling the concept of a Data Element pool.

If we understand the concept of Business Events as portrayed in this book, then we could look upon the groupings of Data Elements needed for each Business Event Partition's stored data needs as the most logical grouping (i.e., mini Data Element pools — one for each Business Event Partition).

Forming Data Element Pools

We can identify potential Data Elements using either Process Analysis or Information Analysis (see Figure 7–19).

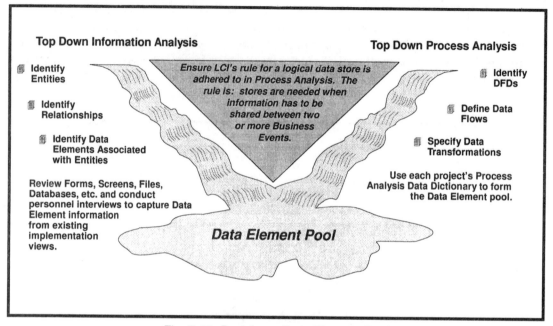

Top Down Information Analysis

- Identify Entities
- Identify Relationships
- Identify Data Elements Associated with Entities

Review Forms, Screens, Files, Databases, etc. and conduct personnel interviews to capture Data Element information from existing implementation views.

Ensure LCI's rule for a logical data store is adhered to in Process Analysis. The rule is: stores are needed when information has to be shared between two or more Business Events.

Data Element Pool

Top Down Process Analysis

- Identify DFDs
- Define Data Flows
- Specify Data Transformations

Use each project's Process Analysis Data Dictionary to form the Data Element pool.

Fig. 7-19: Deriving a Data Element Pool

Obviously data would be duplicated across Business Event Memory (because stores are only necessary across these mini Data Element pools), but as with the concept of reusable processing, data really doesn't appear twice. Each Business Event Partition can "point" to the actual data it needs. For example, a parts list can be documented once, put in a library, and referenced by many people/programs.

Of course, it's very likely that, for any Business Event other than those that just Create, Retrieve, Update, or Delete a specific set of data, the Business Event Memory will contain a diverse set of Data Elements. For example, in Figure 7–20, we see a Business Event, "Customer wants to Purchase Goods", resulting in the stimulus Customer Order. This Business Event Partition requires a Business Event Memory store which contains information about a Customer, a Customer Invoice, and Material.

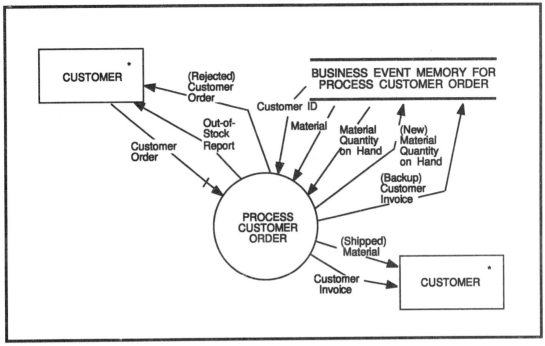

Fig. 7-20: Example Business Event Memory Store

If we add another Business Event Process Model for "Customer Pays Our Invoice" resulting in the stimulus Customer Payment to Figure 7–20, the result is as shown in Figure 7–21.

Note that we now see the redundancy between the stored data of the two Business Events: "Customer Pays Our Invoice" and "Customer wants to Purchase Goods." The two stores both contain identical data (Customer Information and Customer Invoice information). This is, however, only "modeling" redundancy, and when we apply correct Data Element naming standards, there is no logical redundancy. In the next chapter, we will bring these Business Event Memory stores together to form our Entity Relationship Diagram which would contain no redundancy of data.

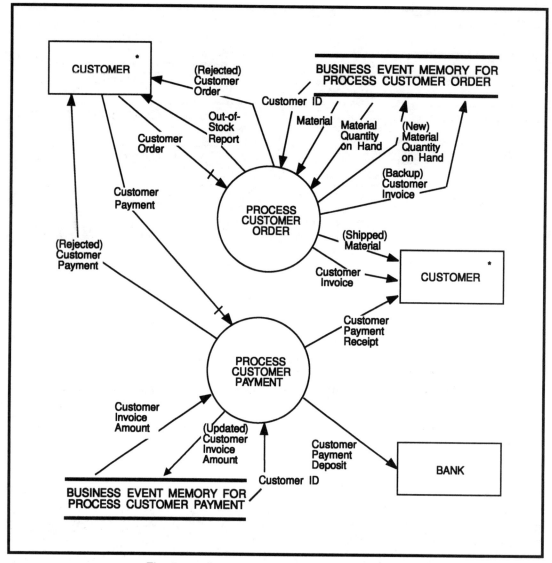

Fig. 7-21: Business Event Process & Memory

Naming the Business Event Memory

Notice the naming for the Business Event Memory can simply be based on the summary process name for the Business Event. This is because the store is only ever going to be used by this one Business Event. Remember, these names will go away when we produce our data model for our project's portion of our organization (see Figure 7–21 for store names).

The Business Event Response

This is any output consisting of data, control, products, or services produced from our organization for this one specific event. For example, this might be delivered products, or the switching on of some equipment. The non-shaded area in Figure 7–22 represents the Business Event Response.

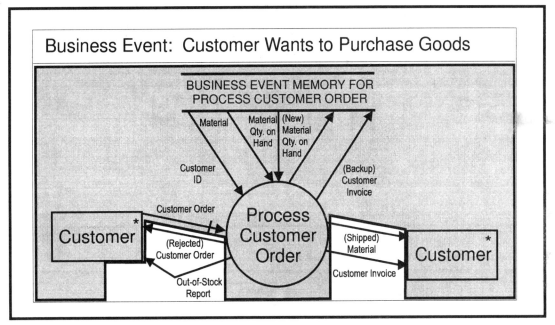

Fig. 7-22: Business Event Response

Naming the Business Event Response

These names use the same naming convention as used for Business Event Stimulus names.

The Business Event Recipient

This is who (or what) is the recipient of our organization's response. This may be exactly the same as the original customer, but it doesn't have to be. For example, when I initiate a charitable contribution, I may not expect an acknowledgment, but the recipient gets the benefit of my contribution. There may also be little or no output from the system in some Business Event Partitions. For example, an airline customer may expect no actual data, only an acknowledgment of some kind of their flight reservation request from the airline's reservation system. The non-shaded area in Figure 7–23 represents the Business Event Recipient.

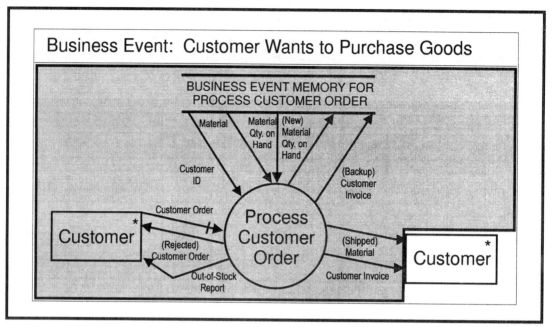

Fig. 7-23: Business Event Recipient

Naming the Business Event Recipient

These names use the same naming convention as used for Business Event Source names.

The Business Event List

The first major deliverable of identifying all of the Business Events in the organization (or that part of it under study) is a Business Event List. A Business Event List is simply a list of all the Business Events (as well as Dependent and Regulatory Events) to which our organization responds, along with their associated stimuli.

The main point to keep in mind while creating this list is to err on the side of having too many events. Too many is better than too few because a finer granularity list makes it easier to spot opportunities for reusability, and you will satisfy the customer's needs better than when you rely on generic/merged together Business Events.

A Business Event List would allow one to quickly and easily understand an organization, even if they were unfamiliar with it. Someone new to banking Business Events would understand their environment easier with a Business Event List containing meaningful names such as: "Customer wants to know their savings account balance," "Customer wants to withdraw funds from their checking account," or "Customer wants to transfer funds from their checking to their savings account."

For a small, vertical organization (limited products or services), we may have only tens of Business Events in our list. For a diverse organization, the list may have thousands. Please note, also, that it's usual at the beginning of a study to underestimate the Business Event count and to discover more Business Events during detailed analysis. What I have found in over ten years of working with Business Events is that the number of events first identified will almost invariably grow throughout the project. This may grow out of our tendency to use one order form for many different kinds of orders, or thinking at too high a level and stating: "Our organization just sells materials and that's it." However the resulting Business Events will be more specific, more easily understood, and will be truly more functional.

The Beginnings of the Business Event Library

The result of producing the high-level specifications, as recommended in this chapter, will be the beginnings of a Business Event Library. This library *is* a model of the business (the Organizational Repository). That is, it is the description of the business — what the organization currently does, or will do, in the future from a functionally partitioned (Business Event) point of view. Figure 7–24 shows what we would gather for each Business Event at this level to start our Business Event Library.

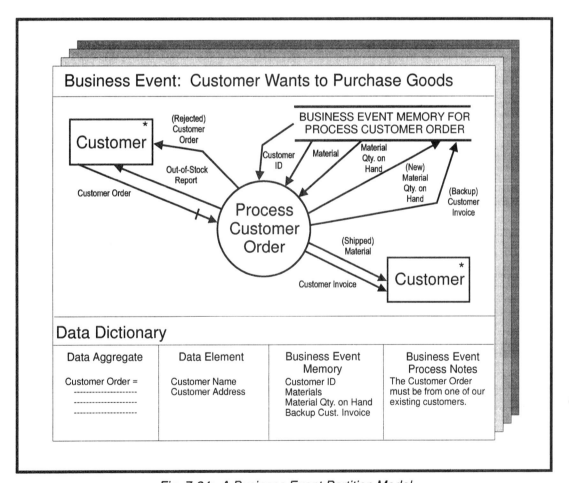

Fig. 7-24: A Business Event Partition Model

Summary

Understanding Business Events is the most important part of Business Re-Engineering. It's the System Issues that we have to remove before we can Re-Engineer any system.

The analyst's task is to be able to identify and pigeon-hole the six aspects of a Business Event Partition (Source, Stimulus, Processing, Memory, Response, and Recipient). Any other basis for partitioning will reflect some aspect of design and will therefore not be a functional Business Event Partitioning as I've defined it.

The result of identifying and documenting our Business Events is the foundation of the beginnings of our Business Event Library, which is the only way you're going to see the real business and not its implementation.

The remainder of the analysis portion of Re-Engineering is to flesh out the Business Event Library in more detail which is the subject of the next chapter.

Men who wish to know about the world must learn about it in its particular details.

Heraclitus

The Detailed Business Event Specification

Now that we've talked about models and their purposes, Business Events with Business Event Partitioning (and how they're the ultimate view of the business), we can talk about how we actually document a detailed Business Event Specification. This is where the "tire meets the road" within each Business Event Partition.

We use the term Business Event in this chapter, but the same concepts of subpartitioning apply to Dependent Events and Regulatory Events. Note, however, that although these concepts also apply to Strategic Events, we would put these events on a different model.

As stated in the title of a previous chapter, I believe the Logical Model IS the Business (or the only way we're going to see the true business). Therefore, in this chapter we will bring together a set of models to specify each Business Event and the library of these specifications will form the view of the actual business.

Later, in the *Designing and Implementing Business Event Systems* chapter we'll extend the specification to include the design (physical) point of view. With these two views we can see what the business is and how it is/will be implemented.

Our task here is to model our organization's total response to each Business Event. We've already defined this in our term *Business Event Partition*. So, returning to the previous chapter's definition of a Business Event Partition:

A Business Event Stimulus plus all associated processing, stored memory, and outgoing responses that constitute the organization's complete reaction to a Business Event.

Given this definition, we need to produce analysis models of the Business Event Partition by capturing the business *Stimulus*, *Processing*, stored *Memory*, and *Response* in one partition. We can then use this analysis model to invent the design of this portion of our organization.

In analysis, individual Process Specifications are used to declare the Business Policy (as opposed to a solution procedure) governing the transformation of Input Data Flow(s) to Output Data Flow(s) for each lowest level process (functional primitive) on a Data Flow Diagram.

The one-page specification should be written to enable SOMEONE ELSE to carry out the Process' policy without your assistance. That is, the specification should be a stand-alone maintainable product. The Business Event Specification needs to be able to represent our organization from an analysis (logical) point of view. Figure 8–1 shows how a non-Re-Engineered organization's historically/hysterically derived partitions would appear when leveled for both its manual and automated systems.

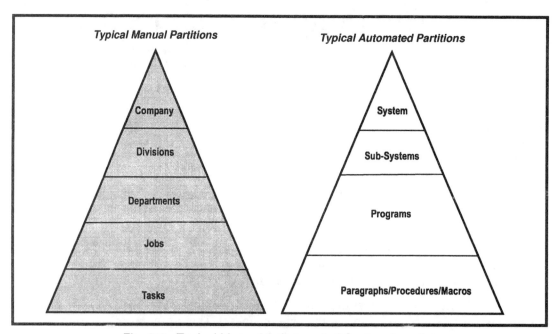

Fig. 8-1: Typical Manual & Automated System Leveling

For areas of our project that require us to validate the current Physical environment, before deriving the equivalent Logical Model, we can use the existing Physical partitions for our leveled partitions.

Notice that we've already been using the tried and tested models and symbology of process and information modeling as our means of depicting Business Event Partitions. So, for consistency we'll build on these. However, in this chapter we'll use the extended symbology to indicate a stimulus to accommodate Business Event Issues. (Remember, it's not the type of model that's important, but rather the logical view it provides and the Business Event Partitioning of the model.)

Subpartitioning of Processing and Memory

Up to this point we've replaced old partitioning based on systems, departments, divisions, etc. with one based on a truly functional Business Event Partitioning. Another milestone of our progress is that we have each Business Event Partition represented as a single process and data model. If the single-process Business Event Partitions are small (i.e., they are understandable and comprehensible by anyone in the organization), then any further subpartitioning is not necessary. If the single-process Business Event is complex, voluminous, or unwieldy in human terms, then we need to partition within a Business Event.

Just as it's beneficial to sub-partition the old design into sub-procedures within a task and fields within a file, it's helpful to do a further subpartitioning within a major Business Event. These further partitions may be of help, especially where this subpartitioning would identify reusable processes and stored data and hence save repetition and redundancy in future procedures, programs, and files. But it also helps us deal with the complexity and volume of a Business Event Specification, so we can use the idea of "leveling" to progress from a high-level abstract to a low-level detailed specification. Figure 8–2 shows an example of decomposition and leveling of processes on a DFD until we reach what we call a Functional Primitive level.

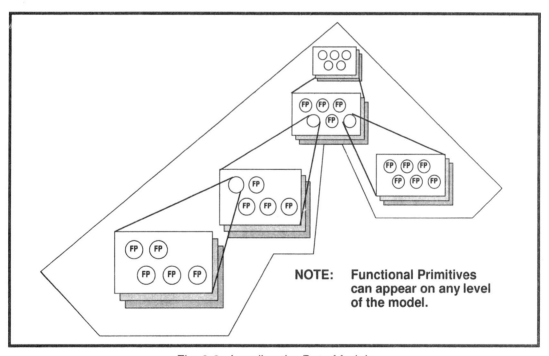

NOTE: Functional Primitives can appear on any level of the model.

Fig. 8-2: Leveling the Data Models

You may have noticed that in my previous examples, I typically show one process within the Business Event Partition and that some processes use data stores (and some do not). Before creating a fully-partitioned Business Event Specification, we need to talk about how we partition processing and memory within the organization's response to a Business Event. This chapter explains the reasons for subpartitioning and how we conduct this further process partitioning and data (memory) partitioning.

Subpartitioning Processing

A valid Business Event level, logical process model would show one process for one Business Event. If we decompose this process into sub-partitions (also known as leveling), we continue to show the stimulating flow to each and every process. So, when a Business Event Stimuli arrives from the outside world, it triggers **all** the processing and data required to respond to that event. Figure 8–3 shows the partition for "Customer Wants to Purchase Goods" in which the arrival of a stimulating Customer Order Data Flow from the Customer triggers three consecutive processes.

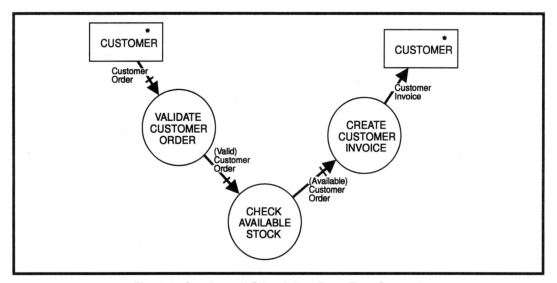

Fig. 8-3: Continuous Stimulating Data Flow Scenario

For each Business Event, there can be *one, and only one*, Business Event Stimulus from the outside world, but that doesn't mean we can't have more than one stimulus for the sub-processes for that Business Event. In fact, in a business environment, it is obviously possible to have two concurrent sub-processes feed another. (*As the real world is not sequential, our modeling tool must not be limited to sequential views.*)

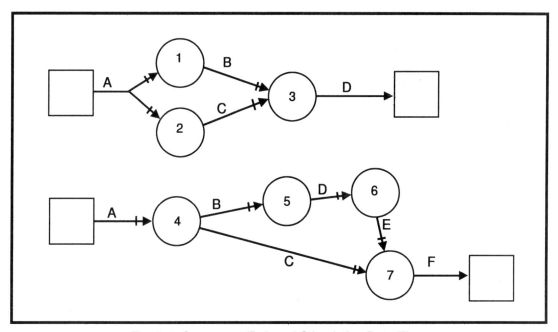

Fig. 8-4: Concurrent/Delayed Stimulating Data Flows

In the upper model of Figure 8–4, we see that process 3 cannot begin until stimulating Data Flows B and C arrive. Note that the business policy for process 3 will dictate whether B *and* C are both needed before it can begin its work, or whether only B *or* C is needed.

In the lower example in Figure 8–4, we see that process 7 is stimulated by two Data Flows, C and E. If process 7 requires both Data Flows C and E to start up, then either Data Flow C or E will have to wait in their data-flow pipeline until the other one is available. We do not make Data Flow C or E into a data store on our Business Model because they are transient within one Business Event.

A stimulating flow can be data- or control-oriented as indicated in the modeling chapter. Figure 8–5 shows the symbology used to indicate a Stimulating Data Flow and a Stimulating Control Flow.

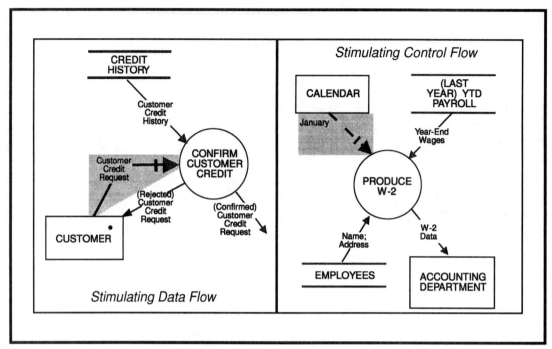

Fig. 8-5: Sample Stimulating Data & Control Flows

The Reasons for Subpartitioning Processing

When we conduct process subpartitioning, we could say that the ultimate partitioning is, of course, a single instruction (i.e., a verb-object). But this isn't a realistic business partitioning (i.e., all business functions don't partition down to one instruction). Obviously a better partition would be a process that does one complete, specific task. So, we sub-partition (and hence stop partitioning) for reasons such as:

- Reusability (i.e., a process can be re-used across Business Events). The reasons for partitioning for reusability tend to be internally driven.

- The Business Policy Creator sees the process as a single function. The reasons for the Business Policy Creator determining partitioning may also be internally driven, but are based on how they see the customer interacting with the organization's systems

- The process needs to be partitioned down into manageable units for human complexity reasons. This last rationale for partitioning is obviously a physical limitation because people have to build and maintain complex systems.

The Business Event (outside the organization) determines the set of data that must come in or out in order to fully accomplish that event. That is, the difference between "Customer Wants to Purchase Goods" through a Regular Order stimulus being one Business Event or multiple Business Events is based on what the outside customer expects to complete their transaction (or, what the Business Policy dictates).

For example, processing the Business Event, "Customer Wants to Purchase Goods," resulting in the stimulus, "Regular Order," can include three distinct activities:

- Customer Requests Goods
- Take Payment
- Customer Takes Goods

Or, Regular Order can include five distinct tasks:

- Customer Requests Goods
- Confirm Material Quantity
- Take Customer Description
- Take Payment
- Customer Takes Goods

Or, Regular Order can even be split into two Business Events:

- "Customer Wants to Order Goods" and
- "Customer Wants to Pay for Goods Previously Ordered"

The banking-based example of using an ATM near the end of the previous chapter does this partitioning of one Business Event. For example, if you want to deposit money, the system asks for many separate inputs to accomplish the event. However, it could have made you perform separate events to accomplish the deposit.

The Customer (External Interface) has expectations and our organization decides what part of these expectations to which to respond. For example, at LCI, our customer's expectations may be for a Business Event to include:

- Conduct Seminar
- Provide Food

At LCI, we only conduct seminars. We could provide the food, but we have decided not to. We could outsource the food service to a caterer, but we decided that wasn't part of our Business Policy. So, the Business Policy Creator at LCI has decided not to provide food, even though the customer may request it.

So, we don't just perform an analysis of our existing systems, we also analyze the current Business Policy.

Note that we may encounter a problem though, when subpartitioning based on the Business Policy Creator's view of the business, because there's more than one way to do business. Keep in mind that, depending on who we speak to, we may also find a different policy being stated by different detailed policy representatives within the same organization.

Figure 8–6 shows four views of the same Business Event: "Customer Wants to Purchase Goods." View (1) appears to be high-level, but the business person may not see the need to decompose it. That is, it could be a perfectly valid detailed process from a business point of view and it can be supported by a process specification. (This view indicates that the Customer Order includes the Payment.)

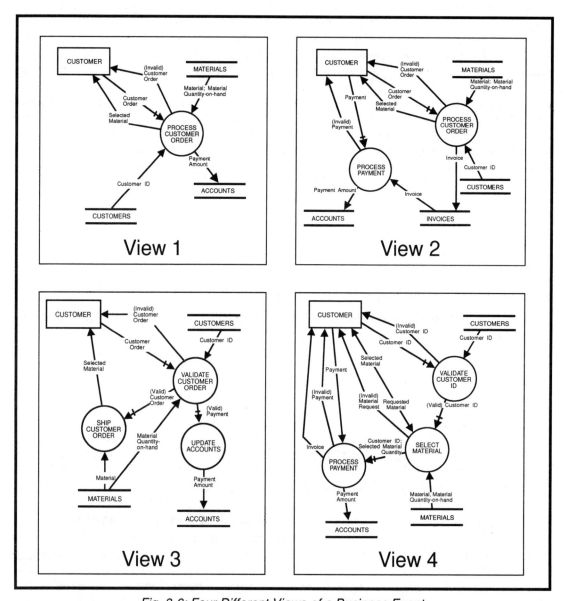

Fig. 8-6: Four Different Views of a Business Event

View (2) is from a business person who sees the same Business Event as two distinct Business Events. The first is the processing of the Customer Order information itself and the second is the processing of the Payment for that order.

View (3) comes from a business person who sees one Business Event, but decomposed into three distinct processes (the second and third processes triggered by transient data resulting from the first process).

View (4) comes from a business person who sees one Business Event decomposed into even more detail, especially from a data point of view. That is, processes get only as much data as they need to do their job. Notice that in this view the second and third processes are not stimulated from the outside world, but by transient data even though new data are "pulled" in from the outside world (the Customer).

All four of the above views are valid for our Business Event. The difference between them is what I call the distinction between *data cohesion* and *data conservation*. In views (1) and (3) all the Customer Order information comes in at once, so our Business Event Stimulus would be termed a *cohesive* set of data. View 2 has at least partitioned the incoming stimulus into Customer Order and Payment, but this results in forming two Business Events from a single event. This may not be a good thing to do if the customer wants to accomplish everything at once. View (4) fragments the Business Event Stimulus even more (*fully data conserved*), and produces a potentially more reusable set of processes that are easier to develop and modify. (But please note, dear reader, that in my experience, building fully data conserved models can get quite complex and time-consuming. In this case, an organizational goal for system reusability and maintainability should be in place before we invest in fully data-conserved models.)

Subpartitioning Logical Processes

From an individual logical process point of view, we show a specific process on a logical model because:

- We create new data (e.g., Invoice Total given the Item Quantity and Price).

- We change the value of data (e.g., Old Customer Balance to New Customer Balance updated with Deposit Amount).

- We change the status of data (e.g., *approved* Loan Amount given *requested* Loan Amount and Credit Rating).

Of course in a control-oriented process we can also produce additional control output (e.g., a human approaching triggers the door to open). All of the above would also be reasons for partitioning processes.

Figure 8–7 shows two *functional* Business Event Partitions. These two Business Events are separated by a dashed line. Each Business Event Partition consists only of business policy responses. The business policy responses consist of processing, any intermediate data, interactions with data stores, and issuance's of outbound data.

These are the two Business Event examples from the previous chapter, "Customer Wants to Purchase Goods" and "Customer Pays Our Invoice." In them we can see an example of subpartitioning. The Business Event, "Customer Wants to Purchase Goods", results in the stimulus, Customer Order, which stimulates processing that is shown subpartitioned into four sub-processes. The first of these is to "Validate Customer Order." This process performs a data status change from *Raw* Customer Order to *Valid* or *Rejected* Customer Order. The *Valid* Customer Order stimulates another process (Check Material Availability) that changes the data status from *Valid* to *Available* Customer Order. The (Available) Customer Order can then stimulate two processes — Create Customer Invoice which creates new data (this will probably be reusable in other Business Events) and Ship Materials which changes the status of materials from *Stored* to *Shipped*.

Remember that this is a Business Model, so we are not interested in whether Ship Materials is manual or automated — the model just shows the processing and data that are triggered by a Customer Order coming into the business. (This process may have been separated out because the Business Policy Creator sees it as a significant separate task.) Note that not all processes relate to a stored data. Some may simply perform calculations to generate data that is transient to the system. The Business Event Partition stimulated by Customer Payment is also sub-partitioned into three lower-level processes as shown in Figure 8–7.

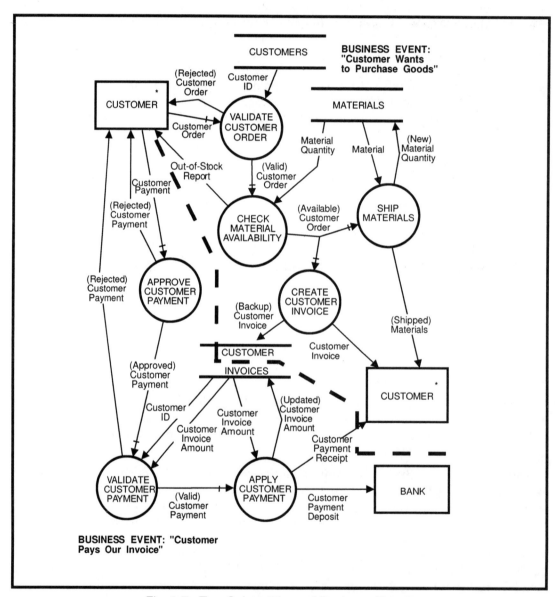

Fig. 8-7: Two Subpartitions of Business Events

Notice that given one Business Event Stimulus, we follow it through any and all business processing until it terminates in a data store or an external interface. (These are the only two terminations of data that can occur in a logical model.)

In this case the payment is transformed in the first two processes from Customer Payment to *Approved* Customer Payment, and then to *Valid* Customer Payment. These are again *status changes* because they have not changed any data content, just the status of Customer Payment — from *Raw* to *Approved* to *Valid*. However, the third process (i.e., Apply Customer Payment) does change the data content. The Valid Customer Payment and the existing Customer Invoice Amount are used to form an Updated Customer Invoice Amount, a Bank Deposit, and a Customer Payment Receipt.

The result of the decomposition of these two Business Events leads us to what I call *seamless business systems* — an approach in which we do not see any design seams in a Business Model. The response to a stimulus flows naturally from beginning to end, with no artificial design boundaries or stores. We will see later that these Business Event Partitions are also very effective partitions for implementation.

So, not only does the Re-Engineering analyst need to bring together all processing and data for a Business Event, but he or she must also partition them into cohesive sets. If a decomposition of a Business Event Partition itself is still complex, we may want to further partition another level. Again, we would do this to help us manage complexity. For example, we could decompose Calculate Taxes into Calculate Federal Taxes, Calculate State Taxes, and Calculate Local Taxes if we see the need for this further level. We don't want to get too concerned with any intermediate levels or spend too much time on their production. We do, however, want to be quite concerned (picky) with the correctness and completeness of the lowest-level model.

Figure 8–8 reflects this idea of the important levels via the process model. The three important levels of Figure 8–8 are the Business Event Context Diagram level, the Business Event level, and the Detailed (Functional Primitive) level. Any other levels are only presentation levels and do not need to be rigorously validated because, from a logical model's point of view, they are never implemented. The details of how we perform this method of subpartitioning is the subject of Business Process Analysis (covered in greater detail in Book III of the series).

The process model will be supported with:

- Data Dictionary entries for all Data Flows.

- Process Specifications for the lowest-level processes.

- Optional process notes for any intermediate-level processes to help clarify these processes when we return to document them in detail.

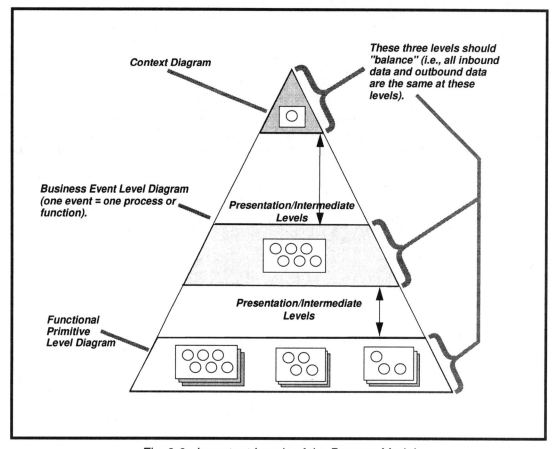

Fig. 8-8: Important Levels of the Process Model

Subpartitioning Memory

The Business Event level of our process model will be the first level at which genuine Business Event Memory (stores) need to be shown (based on our rule that stores are only essential when data are shared between two or more Business Events).

The ultimate partition of stored data is a single field (Data Element), but in most cases this isn't a realistic business partitioning (i.e., all business sets of data don't partition down to one Data Element). A better partitioning would be a grouping together of only strongly related data (what I like to call a cohesive set of stored data).

The Reasons for Subpartitioning Memory

Similar to process subpartitioning, we would like this subpartitioning of data to be because of:

- Reusability (i.e., the subpartitioned memory store can be re-used across many Business Events).

- The Business Policy Creator may see the set of stored data as being cohesive.

- All the Data Elements within a cohesive unit are accessed by the same business key (i.e., Product ID to access Product Price, Product Quantity on Hand, Product Weight, Product Quantity Discount, etc.).

Subpartitioning Business Event Memory

One of the physical/logical issues that must be cleaned up by the Re-Engineering analyst is that of extracting the data from old file boundaries and transforming them into logical entities. For this the old stores form one of our inputs. A better source though would be the Business Event Memory stores as introduced in the previous chapter. This is because these stores should only contain the *essential* stored data needed for the Business Event Partition (as opposed to using what happens to be in the existing stores). As stated before, any Data Element in one store must be duplicated in at least one other Business Event Memory store. (If not, it indicates what we called a non-conserved "black hole" or "magic" store issue.) Also, the recommended naming standard will be of help here because our task is to assemble all of the data names (Data Elements), with the same qualifier, that are duplicated across Business Event Memory stores into a collection of reusable, non-redundant, cohesive data sets (see Figure 8–9).

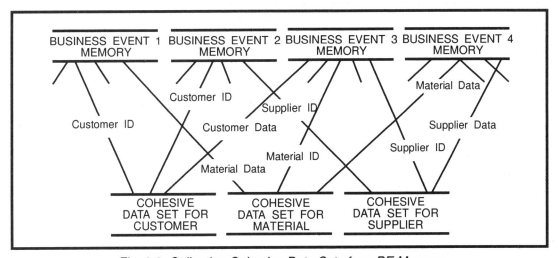

Fig. 8-9: Collecting Cohesive Data Sets from BE Memory

Figure 8–10 shows the seamless system that would result from a truly functional partitioning. The dashed lines in the figure separate the Business Events. Note that stores only
occur at the intersection of the Business Events.

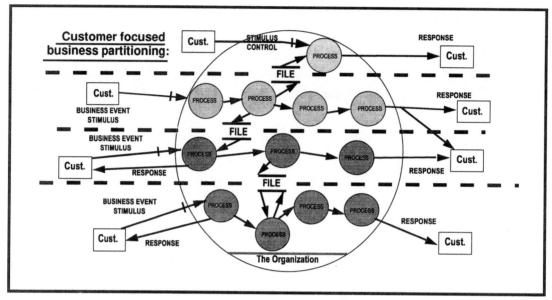

Fig. 8-10: A Seamless Business Event Partitioning

Please realize that depending on the number of Business Events in our organization,
identifying and specifying them may be a non-trivial task because we'll have one Business
Event Memory store for each Business Event, and each Business Event Memory store can
contain a diverse set of data. This task will be helped greatly, if during the development of
our models, we created and maintained an adequate Data Dictionary that defines each
term as we discovered it in its context.

The result will be the sets of cohesive stored data. Note, however, that we must not lose
the relationships between these sets of stored data. In other words, we must not lose how
the processing relates one set of data to another (e.g., Customer *Orders Many* Products.
Other examples would be: Supplier *Supplies Many* Products and a Product is *Supplied* by
Many Suppliers).

From a data point of view we have some techniques from the D.P. world that allow us
to arrive at a reusable, cohesive set of stored data. One of these techniques is that of Data
Normalization, which involves producing sets of data where every Data Element in the set
can only be dependent upon a specific identifying key for that set of data. This key can be
a "compound key." For example, we may need Product ID and Warehouse ID to determine the Product Quantity on Hand because, each warehouse may have a different
product quantity for the same product depending on the size of the warehouse.

This is where we can use an Entity Relationship Diagram to take care of the stored memory in our Business Event Partition definition. We don't need any modifications to the symbology already recommended for ERDs. We will, however, make a modification to how we partition the ERD. Whereas Entity Relationship Diagrams have been proposed as a means of representing a complete enterprise (organization) with further design partitioning of this model, we will use the Business Event to provide an additional business-oriented partitioning. I recommend producing partitioned ERDs (or an equivalent data model), one for each Business Event Partition.

In the partitioning of our process model (DFD) we may end up with little or no duplication of logic or transient data across Business Events. This is not true for stored memory. As stated earlier, each Data Element of memory will be used in the processing of at least two Business Events, otherwise we wouldn't be storing the data.

If we take the Business Event Partition, ("Customer Wants to Purchase Goods"), shown on the top part of the process model in Figure 8-11, we see it contains information in its Data Flows about Customers, Materials, and Customer Invoices.

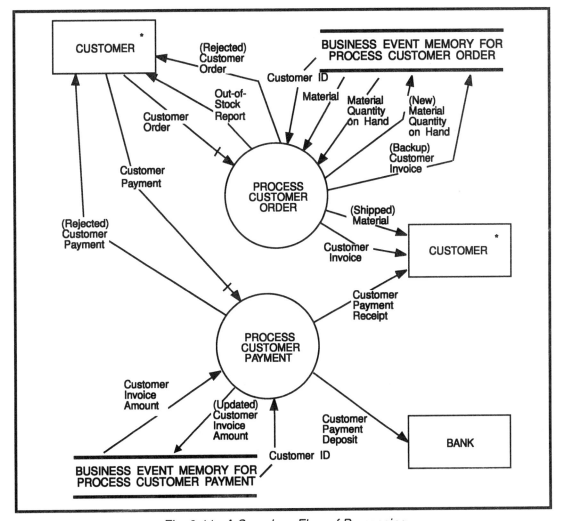

Fig. 8-11: A Seamless Flow of Processing

If we look inside of Process Customer Order, the logic tells us that *Many* Materials are sold to *One* Customer via *One* Customer Invoice. So, we will produce a partitioned data model for this Business Event Partition (as shown in Figure 8–12). (I have used a Chen-style Entity Relationship Diagram.)

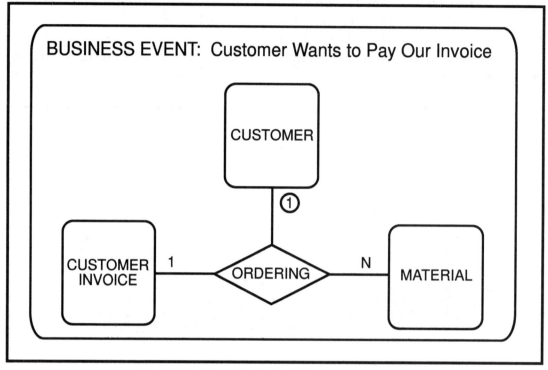

Fig. 8-12: A Sample Entity Relationship Diagram

Doing the same process on the "Customer Pays Our Invoice" Business Event results in the diagram in Figure 8–13. This ERD states that *One* Customer is involved in a *Paying* relationship with *Many* Invoices.

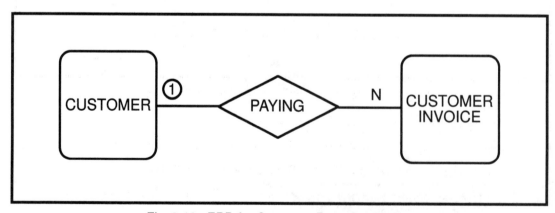

Fig. 8-13: ERD for Customer Pays Our Invoice

For the ERD to show this 1-to-N relationship, the logical process specifications for this Business Event will have stated that *One* Customer can pay off *Many* Invoices. Notice that the Customer and Customer Invoice Entities are repeated between the two Business Event Partitioned ERDs. Again, this is only a modeling redundancy (i.e., the Customer and Customer Invoice Entities are the same on each model). If we wish to bring all of the resultant sets of Business Event Partitioned ERDs together, we can form the Organizational ERD where these Entities would be shown only once (see Figure 8-14).

Once we have our Cohesive Entities partitioned on our Business Event Partitioned ERD, we may want to return to our process model and replace our Business Event Memory store with these Cohesive Entities.

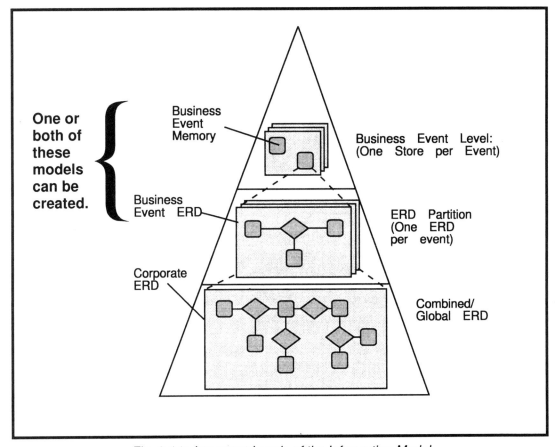

Fig. 8-14: Important Levels of the Information Model

We will support this ERD model with the following:

• Entity Specifications — one for each Entity in our ERD

• Relationship Specification — for the Relationship in our ERD

• Data Element Specifications — one for each Data Element in each Entity in our ERD

The details of how we perform this method of subpartitioning entities is the subject of *Business Information Analysis* (covered in greater detail in Book III in this series).

The Business Event Library — Documenting the Analysis Business Event Specification

Now we can bring together the data and process models for each Business Event. (As I've already stated, they should never have been split apart in the first place.) I recommend that we produce a set of models for each Business Event. Together, these sets constitute what I call the Business Event Library. This library contains all of the models and the names and their definitions for each Business Event. Figure 8–15 shows a sample of an entry in a Business Event Library. It shows the analysis documentation for our previous Business Event, "Customer Wants to Purchase Goods." We see, in this figure the two analysis models we decided to use for our Business Event Specification — a Business Event Partitioned DFD and a Business Event Partitioned ERD (although other models are equally valid). These are also supported with textual specifications in the Data Dictionary.

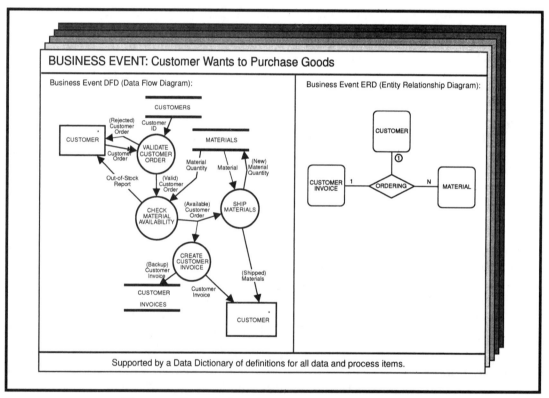

Fig. 8-15: Sample Bus. Event Library Entry (Analysis)

Managing the Library via the Business Event Conservator

If our business responds to a hundred different Business Event stimuli, then we will have one hundred of these Business Event Specifications. I propose that each organization have one or more "Business Event Conservators" to maintain the consistency and the integrity of the Organizational Business Event Library. For example, if another system we are developing requires retrieval of occurrences of Material data, the Business Event Conservator ensures that some other Business Event has already created them and ensures that a project doesn't reinvent the wheel and write Data Definitions or Process Specifications (and hence, procedures or software) that already exist and can be re-used.

This library could be part of what's known as a repository/encyclopedia where we keep not only the models, but all support documentation/specifications. The analysis portion of the Business Event Specification would consist of such entries as:

- Business Event Models (e.g., DFD, ERD, Object Oriented Model, etc.)
- External Interface Specifications
- Process Specifications
- Data Elements Specifications
- Entity Specifications
- Relationship Specifications
- Object/Class Specifications

Summary

Now we can see the detailed documentation needed for the analysis stage of Business Re-Engineering. The most important thing I can say here is that Business Events can be treated as individual portions of the business (i.e., each entry in the Business Event Library can be treated as a mini-project for Strategic Planning and Implementation. The data stores across Business Events are the only items with which we'll have to be concerned. If we decide to implement Business Events separately, then we may have to create intermediate steps in our Implementation Plan for "out of sync" stored data.

To return to my house-building analogy, when a client's requirements completely match the specifications of another house (verified by looking at such models as blueprints), then the client can buy the already existing models, or even buy the pre-built house from the factory. By applying engineering principles to systems, there is every reason to exercise the same option, that is, to buy existing models and systems from an organization's Business Event Library. This assumes that our specifications are worth buying (i.e., they are engineered). [1]

---

1   I wouldn't dream of buying a new house without its engineered blue-print, and similarly, I would recommend not buying a new system package without seeing its engineered specifications.

9

We build up whole cultural intellectual patterns based on past "facts" which are extremely selective. When a new fact comes in that does not fit the pattern[,] we don't throw out the pattern. We throw out the fact. A contradictory fact has to keep hammering and hammering, sometimes for centuries, before maybe one or two people will see it. And then these one or two have to start hammering on others for a long time before they see it too.

Robert Pirsig
Lila

The Business Event Methodology — a Synthesis

Now that we understand the concept of Business Events, have produced Business Specifications partitioned by Business Events, and we have created our Business Event Library, we can realize the significant benefits of Re-Engineering across the Business Event Library. By using the Business Event Methodology, we don't just gain a better implementation of a Business Event; we also gain:

- Process Integrity (Reusability)
- Data Integrity (Conservation)
- Substantial Savings of System Development Time/Investment

One dictionary defines "synthesis" as:

A process of reasoning in which the conclusion is reached directly from given propositions and established or assumed principles. [1]

---

1   *Webster's Encyclopedic Unabridged Dictionary of the English Language* — see Bibliography

I have subtitled this chapter *a Synthesis* because of the fact that these additional advantages are obviously available only when using the previously discussed methods of Business Re-Engineering.

Maintaining the Business Model's Integrity

As I mentioned earlier, I believe we need to have one or more Business Event Conservators to manage our Business Event Library. The task of the Business Event Conservator is to take care of the first two bullet items in the list above. Each system's Development Manager would take care of the third item.

In our capacity as the Business Event Conservator, we maintain and conserve our organization's data and processing. We do this:

- Across Business Events in our organization, whether implemented as human-based or computer-based systems.

- Within all computer databases and manual files.

- During the development of new systems.

We use a set of Business Event Matrices for this conservation task. Using these matrices will yield positive results in terms of managing business or system changes, re-using data and processing, and allowing our organization to easily identify and remove dead data and processing. This chapter's primary focus is on Business Events and these various matrices. Please note, however, that everything we say regarding Business Events can be applied to Dependent Events and Regulatory Events, since these types of events also belong in the Business Model.

Before going further, it's important to realize that the main role of the Business Event Conservator is to be concerned with "data about our organization's data." In other words, they maintain the information about the various Data Elements themselves as opposed to being responsible for the contents of those Data Elements. *(Business Event Conservators take care of the radio, not the music.)* In a small organization, the Business Event Conservator may also "wear other hats" such as Data Administrator, but it's important to keep the conservator role distinct and separate.

Obtaining Process Integrity (Reusability)

Process Integrity is a feature of a single-function process indicating that all data input into it is utilized and that all data output from it is derived only from its input. Process Integrity is an important point when we want to re-use processing across Business Events and hence across applications. Each process that is re-used must not be corrupted by haphazard changes and it must be used in a consistent manner. For example, if a modification is applied to a process, the modification needs to be immediately applied everywhere the process is used. If a proposed modification to a process will affect its reusability across Business Events or applications, the Business Policy Creator must make the decision to either: ensure that the proposed change is acceptable in every Business Event that uses the process, create another reusable process and leave the original process unchanged, or sacrifice the advantage of having the process re-used.

Re-using processing and data is one way we can increase productivity during system development as well as during global maintenance/modification changes. We need an organizational objective and incentives in place for reusability to gain the full benefits of reusability.

As I said in a previous chapter, we should emphasize the reusability of both data and processing during the modeling stages of Re-Engineering (i.e., during analysis and design). We can spot reusability at the analysis level and at the design level by having a consistent, organization-wide naming standard and a Data Dictionary.

Again, reusability is one of the major reasons for performing sub-partitioning of Business Event Partitions in the first place. Without it, we re-invent the wheel and may end up with monstrous programs and procedures.

Determining the Potential for Reusability

The one example that we're probably most familiar with where we see reusability is in the automotive world. When a brand new automobile is introduced, it's never completely new from the point of view of its design. In this industry we can see large scale and small scale reusability. For example, we see engines and maybe even chassis re-used across models. But the most reusability we see is when we look at the smallest components. It's very unlikely that the designers of a new vehicle invented their own nuts, bolts, washers, etc. and had them specially machined.

Notice that the reason for ceasing to subdivide components for reusability would be the functionality of the component. Take for example, the case of an automobile battery. Even though it does have components, there's no point in breaking it down into smaller components, at least from a customer's point of view. Another example of this component functionality is in such items as spark plugs and wiper blades. The customer is interested in being able to replace a spark plug rather than an entire engine, or the wiper blade, as opposed to the complete wiper assembly. These items are typically reusable even across manufacturers.

The acid test of whether someone will use a component is how much extra work is necessary to re-use a unit of processing or how much extra baggage is associated with re-using a unit of data. The 10,000 line program or the three inch thick procedure manual is reusable in a sense, but usually with massive wastage. We are looking for process and data units that give a one-for-one match between the functionality of content needed, and the functionality of content provided.

> *The cornerstone of what makes any component reusable is the fact that it is a quality engineered product.*

Figure 9–1 shows what I see as a *Pyramid of Reusability*. This diagram shows where the Business Event level fits. Notice that it's possible to re-use a Business Event Partition's specification as a whole. For example, the Business Event Partition "Customer Pays Our Invoice" would also be subsumed within the Business Event Partition for "Customer Wants to Purchase Our Goods and Pay for them Now."

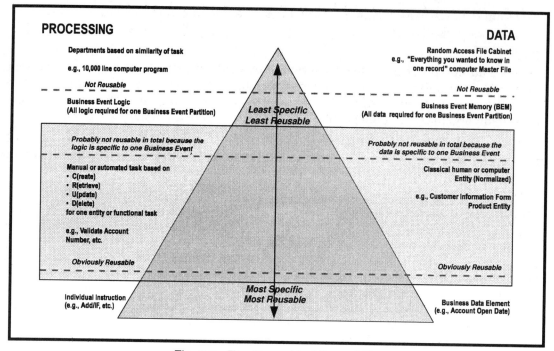

Fig. 9-1: The Pyramid of Reusability

Another example may be that our organization decides to introduce A Special Order Business Event that is similar to a Regular Order except for needing a longer lead-time, an extra stocking charge, or a smaller discount. In this case we may be able to completely re-use Regular Order processing within Special Order processing. Of course, we would still document the new Business Event in the Business Event Library showing any modifications and specifying areas in which Special Order processing or data differed from that for a Regular Order.

The left side of Figure 9–1 refers to processing and the right to data description. At the bottom of the pyramid we see a single instruction and a single Data Element. These are reusable, but they are not too useful for our purposes. Just above this, we see the primitive process and the data aggregate level. This level is very reusable. Above that, we see the specific customer data (e.g., Customer Account) and the Create, Retrieve, Update, and Delete (C.R.U.D.) logic that is specific to the entity. This level, too, is reusable, though an entity may contain too much data for a single procedure or module. The lowest levels of reusability are at the top — the traditional 10,000 line program and "kitchen sink" master file.

The Business Event/Reusable Process Matrix

In our role as Business Event Conservator, we use a Business Event/Reusable Process Matrix to obtain process integrity by keeping track of reusable processes as they are created, modified, or deleted. This matrix would include all potentially reusable processes, even if they are currently used but once. This matrix shows all of the places where a reusable process is used. If the last Business Event where a reusable process is used gets canceled, the process itself could be eliminated or flagged as inactive.

The Business Event Conservator ensures that reusable processes are used and not corrupted, catalogs new processes, and enforces a naming standard for all process and their implementations. This is done via the Business Event/Reusable Process Matrix as shown in Figure 9–2.

Just as we have a hierarchy of data (e.g., Customer Address contains the customer's street, city, state, and zip), we can also have a hierarchy of reusable processing. The Business Event/Reusable Process Matrix diagram can be used to show this relationship between the subordinate and superordinate processes. For example, the reusable process, "Calculate Invoice", may rely on two reusable subordinate processes: "Calculate Commission" and "Calculate Sales Tax." Changes to any of these three processes will affect how our organization creates its invoices. This integrity issue can be taken care of using the third dimension of the Business Event/Reusable Process Matrix. That is, we may have notes or pointers to dependent processes. This could be a bi-directional pointer between subordinate and super-ordinate processes.

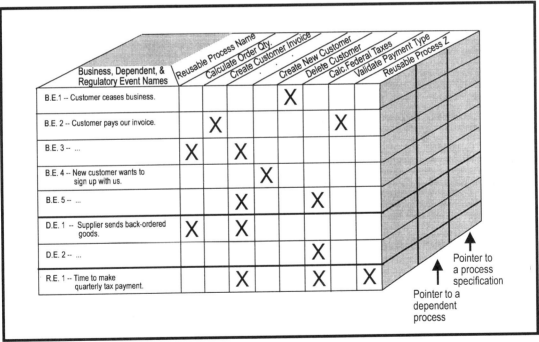

Fig. 9-2: The Business Event/Reusable Process Matrix

If using Object Oriented technology, this matrix is where "objects" are correlated to their Business Events.

The Business Event/Reusable Process Matrix would list on one axis all the Business Events, Dependent Events, and Regulatory Events to which our organization must respond. So the size of this axis obviously depends on the scope of the business we're modeling. For example, an organization that specializes in shipping packages would need to respond to fewer Business Events than a conglomerate in the airline, pharmaceutical, and restaurant markets. The other axis would list every reusable process required by every Business, Dependent, and Regulatory Event listed on the other axis.

It's largely from the Business Event/Reusable Process Matrix Library that we determine productivity. One way we can gauge our organization's productivity is by how many Business Events use each reusable process. I feel that an organization should be averaging 60% – 70% reusability, that is, about two-thirds of a Business Event Partition should be made up of reusable processes or processes that can be re-used in the future. (This percentage is an aggregate of reusable components discovered through analysis, design, and implementation.) This means that if your organization is not using a Reusable Library, then each new system development is wasting up to two thirds of its budget. Preparing an engineered component for reusability should cost no more than one which will not be re-used.

When a process developed for one Business Event is used in another Business Event, I advocate using a symbol such as an asterisk to mark both occurrences of the process on the Business Events' model (e.g., DFD). This tells the developer or maintenance person not to write this procedure more than once and that it will be located in the Reusable Library.

Reusability Incentives

I urge organizations to consider introducing some or all of the following measures to encourage reusability:

- *Introduce Reusability Standards* — To promote reusability and discourage the "Not-Invented-Here" syndrome, organizational standards should be set for: procedure writing, consistent human interfaces to computer users and between departments, interfaces for data and control flow, internal module structuring aimed at easy modification and the separation of business issues and technology issues, technical environments aimed at portability, and the level and quality of all documentation.

- *Introduce Centralized Naming* — A central function should assign names for business terms, files (entities), processes (functional modules), and technology interfaces.

- *Set up a "Reusable Library"* — A well-indexed and cross-referenced, on-line automated repository of off-the-shelf components and procedures will do much to alleviate the complaints that finding a reusable procedure or software component is more trouble than starting from scratch.

- *Launch an Incentive Program* — Introduce some form of recognition for the producers of reusable software, such as posting reusability figures, like the number of reusable modules created by project and even by employee. Offer an incentive for people to use reusable components, for example, a percentage of time saved on a project can be rewarded as time off.

Reusability Is All in the Name

Data Elements, stored data sets (Entities), relationships, and processes must be meaningfully named. Ensuring unique and standardized names is one of the responsibilities of the Business Event Conservator. Standardized naming is essential for reusability. Without it, the function and purpose of a data file, a piece of software, or a human-based procedure may be so obscure and difficult to locate that it defies any hope of reusability. We should avoid using generic names in favor of specific names which will allow us to find a reusable component in the future.

Limiting the number of reusable verbs that are used in a verb-object process name will help searching later, but we don't want the definitions to overlap. The object naming in the process can be the unique identifier. In Table 9–1 I offer examples of names for processes and procedures using process verbs (and the synonymous terms they absorb) for use in our specification. Add to this list verbs that are applicable to your business. At the detail level, we should avoid high-level verbs such as Process, Produce, Analyze, Match, and Execute. When naming logical processes, we should also avoid verbs that suggest getting and putting of data, such as Collect, Gather, Determine, Assign, Identify, Issue, Package, Communicate, Respond, Distribute, Access, Formalize, Record, and Submit. These may well be used as verbs for reusable components (e.g., modules) identified during design.

Sample Verb	Replaces ...
Create	Define, Build, Propose, Generate, Develop, Establish, Derive, or any other verb that involves producing something that did not exist before.
Validate	Calibrate, Check, Verify, Inspect, Edit, or any other verb to do with detecting potential errors.
Confirm	Any verb to do with asking whether data are there or not.
Compare	Any verb to do with the association of two or more pieces of data or processing.
Update	Any verb that uses existing data, modifies it, and replaces it.
Delete	Destroy, Eliminate, Cancel, or any verb implying removal of data.

Table 9–1: A Sample List of Possible Process Name Verbs

Similarly, as a convention for giving unique names to all Data Elements (attributes), I suggest a scheme of names made up of three parts: a Qualifier, an Adjective, and a Reserved Word. In Table 9–2 I offer a taxonomy for data naming.

Sample Qualifier (Mandatory)	Sample Adjective (Optional)	Sample Reserved Word – Data Types (Mandatory)
Supplier	Daily	Name
Part	Weekly	Description
Customer	Monthly	Number
Order	Yearly	Amount
Seminar	Minimum	Quantity
Student	Maximum	Count
Product	Average	Price
Account	Federal	Identification
	State	Date
	Standard	Deduction
	Special	Item
		Indicator
		Code

Table 9–2: A Sample List of Possible Data Names

Again, we should try to limit the number of reusable data type names without overlaying their definitions. Let the qualifier and adjective(s) be the unique identifier.

Obtaining Data Integrity (Conservation)

Stores must be *data conserved* across Business Event Partitions. When we, as customers, deposit money into our account at the bank (a Business Event to the bank), we expect the bank to keep our new balance on file. When we withdraw our money from the bank (a second Business Event to the bank), the bank uses the last balance to verify that our withdrawal amount is valid. If it is valid, the second Business Event updates the balance again. Thus the store is data conserved from a Business Event point of view (stuff goes in and out across two Business Events). Now, we may make a third withdrawal. This time the balance may be too low, so the processing issues a withdrawal reject. This latter example shows the need for the data stored across *occurrences* of the same Business Event type. Note that the second and third withdrawals were not different types of Business Event (a "valid" withdrawal and an "invalid" withdrawal), because the bank does not have control over whether we make a valid or invalid request. (The bank's business policy, of course, includes checking the balance within the Business Event Partition because it has no control over the customer.)

Notice that this data integrity checking across Business Events is not intended to guard against the imperfections of the outside world — we cannot prevent a customer from trying to pay an invoice which does not exist, or from entering bad data. Such imperfections require us to build the usual edits into our Business Event Responses. The Business Policy Creator ensures that these edits, etc. are included in the business. As Business Event Conservators, it is our task to ensure completeness within the total Business Model (i.e., across Business Events).

Data Ownership

I've read many technical books that talk about identifying "who owns" data. You probably already know what I'm going to say, but here goes. People or job titles don't own data any more than computer programs do — Business Events own data. Having said this, it's important to realize that the organization is the ultimate owner of its data. Figure 9–3 shows that at the Business Event level, Business Events own the data and at the system level, it may be helpful to identify the systems as the users of data via Business Events that have had a design placed on them. It is important to recognize that Business Events own data because when a business change occurs, we need to go back to the Business Event(s) that own(s) the data before looking at the implemented systems.

Fig. 9-3: The Progression of Data Ownership

Managing Data Elements vs. their Contents

At this point I need to re-introduce the concept and use of the term "Meta Model." We need this term to separate the issue of "data values" verses "data about data." I mention this here because the following matrices are data-oriented. When describing these matrices, the issues that we, as Business Event Conservators, will concern ourselves with center on identifying what needs to go into the matrices' cells as opposed to the actual data values that will populate the contents of the cells.

You folks who are familiar with spreadsheets are already aware of the difference between setting up the rows and columns of a spreadsheet versus populating the cells of the spreadsheet with data. The Business Event Conservator maintains the Meta Model (the cells) while the Business Events themselves running in a production system (i.e., the real world) perform the actions that Create, Retrieve, Update, and Delete the <u>contents</u> of the cells (see Figure 9–4).

So, when relating to one of the matrices in this chapter, a Delete operation noted in a cell indicates a deletion of the contents of the cell and NOT the cell itself. The deletion of the cell itself would be requested by the Business Policy Creator via a Strategic Event and would constitute a change to the Meta Model and therefore a change to the design of the matrices. The actual value (along with the Data Dictionary definition) is the responsibility of the applications that use the Data Element, Entity, or other cell contents. So, as the Business Event Conservator, we're not concerned with "data value conservation", but with "Data Element conservation." For example, when a customer goes out of business, an application process should use the Customer ID (the value of the field) to look up any outstanding invoices to see what should be done to retrieve the outstanding money due us. This is data value conservation.

Our dichotomy here is between the Meta Model and the Implementation of the Meta Model. It is the same one we had between Business Events and Policy Events as stated in the *Business Events — The Key to Ultimate Customer Satisfaction* chapter. The Meta Model, affects and is affected by the Business Policy and is crucial to the Business Event Conservator to maintain the integrity of Data Elements. The Implemented Model, is crucial to our organization's files, databases, or its applications or where the contents of the Data Element or Data Entity "cells" are important.

For example, if a business decision is made to no longer do Advanced Orders ("Customer Wants to Order Goods and Pay when Picking them up Later"), then the Business Event Conservator can look up the one row of the Business Event/Data Element Matrix that shows all of the Data Elements that this Business Event uses. Each column will also show all Business Events that use the same Data Elements. In this case we would change the matrix itself (i.e., eliminate the Data Elements applicable to Advanced Orders in the table).

The Business Event Conservator is now responsible during the life of our organization to ensure that no violations of integrity within and across Business Events can occur when aspects of the business change.

This conservation process points out the additional Business Events and their implementations that need to be changed to accommodate any Business Event that is being modified. The requester of the business change can then be told the ramifications of a requested change. If the impacts of the change are acceptable, we can make changes to the computer code, the procedure manuals, forms, screens, etc. knowing that we have covered all of the bases. This procedure eliminates dead data and dead processing in our manual and/or automated systems. It also eliminates any potential system "down time" that would result from inadvertently deleting something that was used in other Business Events.

Fig. 9-4: Managing Data Elements vs. their Contents

A business change may require us to remove any other solely dependent Business Events or individual Data Elements affected by this change from the matrix. Therefore, in this case the Business Event Conservator's job is to Create, Retrieve, Update, and Delete the matrix itself. In other words, they deal with the Meta C.R.U.D. *(excuse my French)*.

The Business Event/Data Element Matrix

The most important matrix to be maintained by the Business Event Conservator is the Business Event/Data Element Matrix. Creating and maintaining this matrix is vital to support the Re-Engineering effort and to maintain the on-going quality of any Re-Engineered systems. An important by-product of using this matrix is that it allows the Business Event Conservator to identify reusable data and it ensures data conservation throughout our organization.

Data conservation for processing is the practice of ensuring that data entering and leaving a process, procedure, or system is conserved (i.e., all data are used to derive the outputs and all outputs could be derived from their inputs). Data conservation for memory is the practice of ensuring that any data that is Created (captured) by a process, procedure, or system must be Retrieved (and optionally Deleted) by at least one other process, procedure, or system. Conversely, any data that is Retrieved, Updated, or Deleted must have been Created by at least one other process, procedure, or system.

The Business Event/Data Element Matrix (see Figure 9–5) lists on one axis all the Business Events, Dependent Events, and Regulatory Events to which our organization must respond.

On the other axis, the matrix lists all the Data Elements identified in our organization. This matrix may have several thousand columns and its organization and storage would probably require computer assistance. At each intersection of a Business Event and a Data Element, we would indicate whether an occurrence of the Business Event **Creates**, **Retrieves**, **Updates** or **Deletes** (**C.R.U.D.s**) the data in this Data Element. The third dimension of the matrix could show pointers to Data Element Specifications, to dependent Data Elements, and to processes that use a particular Data Element.

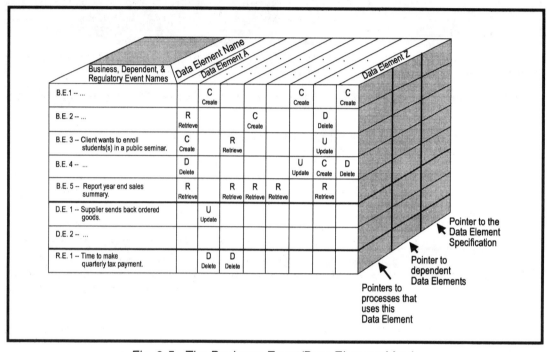

Fig. 9-5: The Business Event/Data Element Matrix

For this matrix the Business Event Conservator would:

- Perform the initial set up of the Business Event/Data Element Matrix. (This task includes identifying all of the Data Elements and all of our organization's Business Events.) This is also known as setting up a data Meta Model.

- Identify where the Data Elements are Created, Retrieved, Updated, and Deleted by each and every Business Event in the matrix.

- Maintain the integrity of the Business Event/Data Element Matrix during production changes or new systems development.

The Business Event/Data Element matrix is used to track how all of the data in your organization are used to support all of the defined Business Events.

The Business Event Conservator maintains the data conservation of our organization via these matrices. For any given Data Element, there should be a collection of Business Events that cover the Create, Retrieve, and Delete actions for that element. Updates to Data Elements are optional.

Ideally, each column in the matrix would have a Delete to ensure that implemented data files don't grow forever. Even a seven-year tax file should have a Business Event that Deletes (e.g., archives) the data after the statute of limitations has expired. This deletion of data may be done via a Regulatory or System Event. However, we may find some data that is only deleted at the demise of our organization (such as the organization's address or its Fiscal Year End Date).

The following two rules illustrate the minimum Create, Retrieve, Update, and Delete (C.R.U.D.) Business Events required to recognize a conserved Data Element:

- Data that is Retrieved, Updated, or Deleted must have been Created in another Business Event.

- Data that is Created in a Business Event must be Retrieved in another Business Event.

In some cases the creation of certain Data Elements may be accomplished in a one-time conversion procedure. In these cases there may not be any Business Event that creates these elements in the course of our organization's normal operations (for example, Fiscal Year End Date, the Organization's Name or, the Incorporation Data). If the Business Event that Creates the Data Element is implemented by a one-time conversion/data entry (i.e., there is no Business Event that allows you to Create the Data Element again), then a valid Data Element may have only a Retrieve and a Delete or a Retrieve, Update, and Delete. In other cases where no initial conversion occurs, these would not be valid (conserved) Data Elements.

The first use of this matrix will be to identify a "Where Used" List of Business Events. If, based on our above "serious" business change, a Data Element is removed (e.g., Advance Order Quantity) all other Business Events that use that Data Element will need modification.

The second use of the matrix is in the identification of which Data Elements are Created, Retrieved, Updated, or Deleted by this Business Event and to maintain the data conservation of each Data Element associated with it.

If this Business Event is the only place a particular Data Element is Retrieved (i.e., the Business Event uses the Data Element for derivation of other data or for reporting outside the Business Event), then all other places where the Data Element is Created, Updated, or Deleted will have to be modified. In other words, to obtain data conservation (i.e., no "dead" data and no "magic" data) as stated before, each column of the Business Event/Data Element Matrix must have at least one Create, one Retrieve, and one Delete.

The "Where Used" List of Business Events will also be of help when a design change occurs (e.g., when the format of a Data Element changes).

So, the Business Event Conservator at times may have to adjust the Business Model accordingly or bring to the attention of the Business Policy Creator (the person requesting the change) any Business Event integrity problems caused by the Business Event's deletion.

Transient Data (Data Flows between processes) on our process model does not need integrity as it "burns up" after a Business Event has finished doing its job (similar to a manual "scratch pad" or working storage within a program). But we should still note that Transient Data needs to be defined in our organization's Data Dictionary for format and content reasons. Stored Data, on the other hand, requires integrity because it is being used across Business Events and is therefore capable of perpetuating its errors across other processing. For these reasons, the Business Event/Data Element Matrix is for Stored Data only.

The Business Event/Data Entity Matrix

We can also generate a Business Event/Data Entity Matrix as in Figure 9–6 from our Business Event/Data Element Matrix.

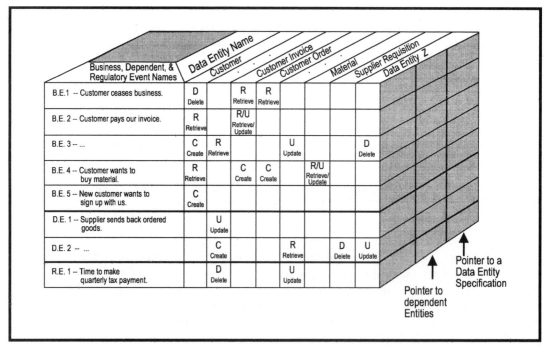

Fig. 9-6: The Business Event/Data Entity Matrix

The Business Event/Data Entity Matrix (see Figure 9–6) would list on one axis all the Business Events, Dependent Events, and Regulatory Events to which our organization must respond. On the other axis we would list the entire set of the Cohesive Data Entities (groups of Data Elements).

The third dimension of the matrix could show pointers to Data Entity Specifications or pointers to dependent Entities.

In some Business Events we will Create and Delete complete Data Entities as opposed to individual Data Elements (also, most databases work at the entity level), so this matrix will be more helpful in these situations. In our example for the Business Policy decision to become a "Cash and Carry" operation, we may no longer store Customer Invoices or Customer Orders. We will then use the matrix to see all places where these Entities are used.

Please note that this Business Event/Data Entity Matrix is quite redundant with the Business Event/Data Element Matrix. The Business Event/Data Element Matrix is more important and is where we show the actual Create, Retrieve, Update, and Delete activities. We may Create and Delete whole entities and possibly use all of an entity's Data Elements in a Retrieve. However, we don't really Update whole Entities — we Update the Data Elements within Entities.

In Figure 9–6 we can see that we must be missing some Dependent Events. For example, how do we create a new Supplier Requisition? The matrix in Figure 9–6 only shows a Delete for the Data Entity, Supplier Requisition. Also note that if we only Created, Updated, and Deleted entities, there would be no point in having them.

The Business Event/Relationship Matrix

The Business Event/Relationship Matrix (see Figure 9–7) is used to track and conserve the Relationships between the Entities listed on the Business Event/Data Entity Matrix. When a Relationship is established between two Entities (or two occurrences of the same Entity), this is reflected with a Connect in this matrix. When a Relationship is severed, this is indicated by a Disconnect in this matrix. Of course, this could also be related to the creation or deletion on an Entity. This matrix allows us to ensure the conservation of Relationships (i.e., a Disconnect must previously have had a Connection with associated it). Also, when we see a Connect we must ask if there should be a Disconnect in some event to sever this Relationship.

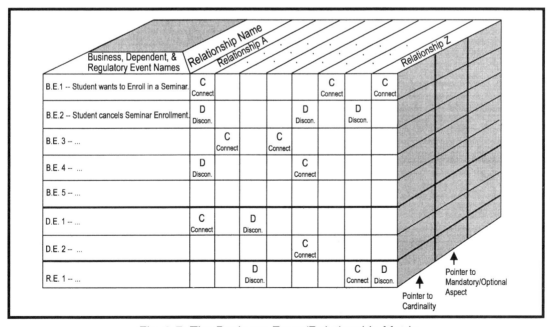

Fig. 9-7: The Business Event/Relationship Matrix

The Business Event/Engineered System Matrix

When we come to the implementation phase of a Re-Engineering project, we can produce a Business Event/Engineered System Matrix.

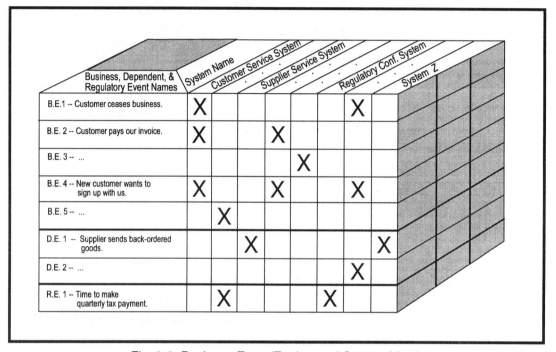

Fig. 9-8: Business Event/Engineered System Matrix

As we will discuss in the *Designing and Implementing Business Event Systems* chapter, we try not to fragment Business Events across systems. However, we may form cohesive collections of related, complete Business Events within one system. If we did this, we may want to keep track of these systems in a matrix (see Figure 9–8). In other words, we can use this matrix to keep track of the designs for how we implemented our Business Events.

The Business Event/Engineered System Matrix would list on one axis all the Business Events, Dependent Events, and Regulatory Events to which our organization must respond. On the other axis we would list the systems we have engineered to satisfy these events. This matrix will be helpful in the modification of production systems because it points to the implementation of a Business Event.

Saving System Development Time/Investment

Most system development projects have a deadline as their main constraint. If our project is using a standard dependency "Waterfall Methodology" of analysis, design, implementation, and installation. This means, for example, that we don't start on design until we finish analysis. All of these activities are on the "critical path", so that a slip in one phase automatically produces an equivalent slip in the succeeding phases. This is acceptable if we have no easy way of partitioning the analysis activity itself (i.e., the system cannot be partitioned and is considered a whole unit). But with Business Event Partitioning we can treat each Business Event as a "mini-project" because they naturally stand alone — connected only by stores. If we have multiple project members, we can assign each individual one or more Business Events. This won't cause any interface problems; especially if we're using a Reusable Library and a Data Dictionary with the recommended naming standards.

Figure 9–9 shows how we can use Business Events to significantly compress the development life cycle and meet a deadline without any disruption to the final system or sacrifices in quality.

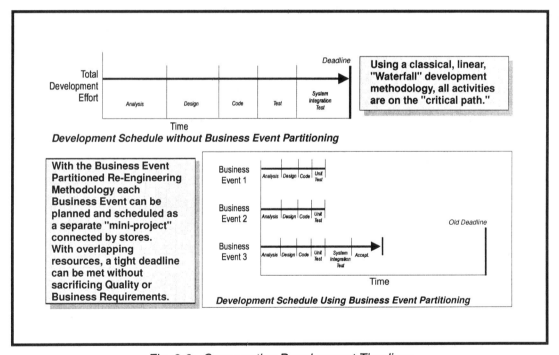

Fig. 9-9: Comparative Development Timelines

Summary

The matrices described in this chapter will allow the Business Event Conservator to verify that the Business Models partitioned by Business Events are completely reconciled and consistent across the whole enterprise.

With these matrices we can readily assess the impact on the whole business of a new Business Event Partition (i.e., a new line of business), or a change to an existing Business Event Partition. Such matrices would also readily show the availability of reusable data and processes, and so avoid, if not eliminate, many re-inventions of the wheel. This would enable us to respond more quickly to business changes.

I haven't found a single organization in over 30 years that would take me up on the bet that I can't find dead data and dead processing in their systems. I hope you can see that by using this Business Re-Engineering Methodology, this elimination of dead data and processing is not only possible, but quite attainable. [2]

---

2   At the time of the writing of this book, LCI is in the process of building a Business Re-Engineering Automated Tool (BRAT) that will take care of most of the systematic cross checking in the matrices. Also, using BRAT, the enforcement and maintenance of the matrices will be fully computer assisted to greatly ease the workload of the Business Event Conservator.

In a time of drastic change it is the learners who inherit the future. The learned usually find themselves equipped to live in a world that no longer exists.

Eric Hoffer

Reflections on the Human Condition

Designing and Implementing Business Event Systems

This is where we take our Business Model and turn it into a system model by adding design features. Now, we put our "designer hats on" and we can concern ourselves with using the best and appropriate technology that we have today to implement the business. (Remember that people are a technology issue, just as are computers.)

We have a major benefit at this point — we do not need to concern ourselves with any issues to do with business correctness. Issues of correctness have been taken care of during the analysis stage. When a new house is being constructed, the brick layer or a carpenter does not need to worry about whether the door is in the right place or if the room is the correct size.

By the end of this chapter, we will see a Business Event Specification containing models from analysis, through design, to implementation. We will also see a scenario showing the old design and the new design of a typical Business Event.

It's during this new design stage that we introduce any System Events necessary to make the new implementation work. Consequently, we'll introduce any associated System Event memory stores (e.g., file cabinets between departments or computer files between computer systems). Given this, we can use the same concepts as those that underlie the Business Event/Data Element and other matrices to maintain the data conservation across our System Events (during the time that those System Events are implemented).

As far as possible, we must carry the business view (i.e., our Business Event Partitions) into the design and implementation of systems. This may be a little more difficult in a manual implementation than in an automated, computer implementation.

We obviously have many options to choose from when designing and implementing a Business Event Partition, such as:

- Empower individual employees, who interface with customers, with the many skills plus the responsibilities and authority (and with the support systems) needed to completely satisfy a customer's needs and therefore to obtain ultimate customer satisfaction.

- Empower teams of single-skill employees to bring together the resources needed to best meet the customer's needs.

- Create an environment that integrates the empowered employees with the computer support and other system technology to satisfy the customer's needs.

- Design and implement a fully automated system to meet the customer's needs.

We will address these options in this chapter.

Business Event-Driven Systems Design

If we have the opportunity to implement our new system in accordance with the Business Events it supports, then each implemented Business Event Partition should endure as long as its associated business does (that is, as long as the organization is in that line of business), rather than for the duration of the technology (hardware or support software) used to implement it.

If we are to restructure manual areas, then Business Event Partitioning will also yield an ideal manual implementation partitioning. For example, we may find that having one employee call upon "subject area experts" when needed, putting together a team of people, or empowering one employee with the necessary skills to accomplish one Business Event Partition produces a higher quality product than a production line where each person sees only a small part of every end-product. In the past, we have tended, partly for economy of scale and because of historical models of human efficiency (based on Frederick Winslow Taylor's ideas of management from the 1920s) to design departments and programs according to similarity of tasks as described in *Systems Archaeology*. As we can see, looking back at Figure 6–16, Business Event Partitioning will yield an almost opposite view, with a Business Event Partition typically spanning many old design partitions.

Re-Engineering Human Systems — Design

Allow me to begin this section with a quote I sometimes use in my seminars. Groucho Marx once said:

"I don't care to belong to a club that will have me as a member."

I call this the "Groucho syndrome," and I see it manifested in the lack of management support for their employees in many organizations. One of the "buzz" words in Re-Engineering is "empowerment." To implement empowerment we have to abolish the Groucho syndrome especially as it is interpreted as: "If you were good, you wouldn't be working here." When an organization does not give its employees the opportunity of being true engineers and fails to provide adequate training and a supportive environment, this leads to the employees themselves not feeling their products are worthy or needing high quality. Therefore, quality is preempted by the managers not having an engineering vision and not being leaders.

I realize that within an organization, human beings (employees), just like computer systems, are implementation devices for business systems. So, we should look on the human world of Re-Engineering just like we can on the computer world of Re-Engineering (i.e., from a "zero defect" system point of view).

How do we achieve zero defects in human-based systems? We may have to accept that a system implemented with human beings can have the potential for more errors than a computer system that has been Re-Engineered because unlike in a human environment, a computer system (once in place) will perform exactly the same each time it's invoked. But this does not mean that we can't apply the same ideas to Re-Engineering the role of human beings by empowering them with the correct skills, training, procedures, and equipment to do their jobs more effectively and by providing a work environment that promotes productivity (even if that work environment is at home).

By using ideas such as *Partitioning by Business Events*, we can simplify the forms and procedures for human beings to eliminate (or at least minimize) potential errors and omissions in their jobs. And, of course, the introduction of technology, such as assisting the human being with powerful Personal Computers (PCs) and links to on-line databases can ensure minimum errors in data by eliminating redundancy, synchronizing data, and providing easily accessible data. There is no difference between partitioning software systems and partitioning the procedures in a human-based system.

The Benefits of Re-Engineering Human-based Systems

An added bonus with human-based systems is their ability to take advantage of the fact that humans can learn "on the fly" to dynamically adjust to the changing needs of a customer. In other words, humans can modify the system design when it's not working well and still stay within the organization's business requirements. Obviously, they can adapt to exception conditions far more readily than computer systems. Most importantly, when customers interact with our systems, a human-being interface is usually looked upon as a far more personable environment than a computer system or other technology. They also make certain customers feel more valued and are less intimidating than technology to customers who are not computer literate.

Some Design Scenarios

I find design to be the easy/fun part of Re-Engineering providing I have a comprehensive Business Specification as input. This is where we can implement the concept of an empowered employee or team of employees by giving them the responsibility and authority to conduct many diverse tasks. In the past organizations that have tried to (or had to) respond to a customer's need immediately have tended to empower employees. For example, the emergency operator can take calls, allocate resources, dispatch rescue units, etc. We can use this same empowerment idea even in systems that aren't time critical. We obviously should still want to satisfy the customer's needs with an efficient design.

When we implement each Business Event, it doesn't have to be implemented with one person. A localized team can be used also for Business Events requiring many complex skills. A hybrid of computer assistance and manual operations may also be effective. Using our Business Event example from the previous chapters, "Customer Wants to Purchase Goods", we can use a hybrid implementation as shown in Figure 10–1.

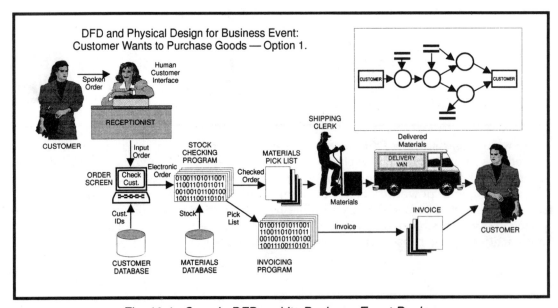

Fig. 10-1: Sample DFD and Its Business Event Design

In this figure I've annotated the analysis DFD to show the design characteristics of how the data and processes are implemented. Notice that there are many designs that can be used here. Considering that I believe that **Systems Should Last as Long as the Organization**, we may want to propose a significantly new design (see Figure 10–2).

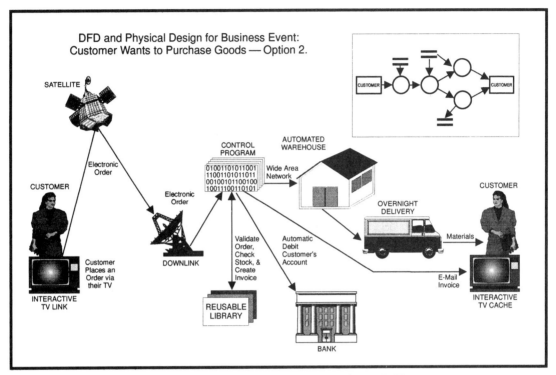

Fig. 10-2: Another Design for the Same DFD

This design, overlaid on the analysis DFD, shows an interactive TV link from the customer to our organization. Our organization processes their electronic order on-line by dynamically calling upon the set of modules needed to process this particular order. Simultaneously our implemented system triggers three things:

- It causes the nearest or most appropriate automated warehouse (which may be our vendor's warehouse) to ship the order directly to the customer.

- We send an electronic receipt to the customer's interactive TV's cache (internal storage).

- We obtain an automatic transfer of funds from the customer's bank account into our organization's account.

As you can see at this point, there are many designs we can place on our Business Event Partition.

Three Implementations of a Business Event

As mentioned previously, we tend to believe that an existing design is the basis for future designs and as a result, we get stuck in perpetuating this same design (remember the QWERTY keyboard example). Let me show three implementations of an industry as an example of breaking this pattern.

The following sections show a worst case, current case, and future case example of customer service. I have used the airline industry as the basis for the scenarios because the joys and frustrations of air travel are something to which many people can relate.

The worst case scenario shows how intolerable air travel would be if the airlines followed what many organizations mistakenly call a "functional partitioning." This worst case scenario may have resulted from a designer focusing only on satisfying their organization's internal departmental managers' goals.

The current case scenario briefly outlines the processes involved in air travel today. The designer of this scenario obviously focused on satisfying both internal and external (customer) goals.

The future case scenario shows one new design for air travel, if we were allowed to Re-Engineer the entire system. As designers of the future case scenario we need to keep the focus exclusively on satisfying the external (customer) goals.

The Worst Case — I'd Rather Walk

If the airline operations designer had come from an all too typical old mentality environment, their check-in operations design could require that all passengers allow one full day to take care of customer administration tasks (as shown in Figure 10–3 with matching step numbers) and documented in the following steps:

1. Set up an account with the airline at their New Accounts Department, get a credit check and, on approval, have an account number allocated with a pre-approved credit amount.

2. Find the Help Desk and research the flight's equipment catalog number for your particular flight.

3. Go to the Order Department and set up and document your flight.

4. Be prepared to get put on back order if the flight is full. If so, go to the Help Desk to see when the next available flight leaves.

5. Go to the Accounts Receivable Department to pay for your flight.

6. Then go to the Special Services Department to register your frequent-flier ID. Of course, if you don't have a frequent-flier ID, you'll need to return to the Order Department.

7. Your next stop will be at the Catering Department where you'll need to make your meal request. If you have no meal request, you only need to fill out the "short form."

8. If you've made it this far (and still have time before the airline closes for the day), you now go to the Help Desk to turn over all of the assorted paperwork given to you by all the other departments. After the clerk gets around to inspecting all of your paperwork, they type all of the same information into a computer terminal ready for their batch-process computer system. The computer batch process runs at 5:00 P.M. every evening. (The airline is currently making a significant investment in a new "modern" system to capture data at each department so that your wait time at each counter will be reduced!)

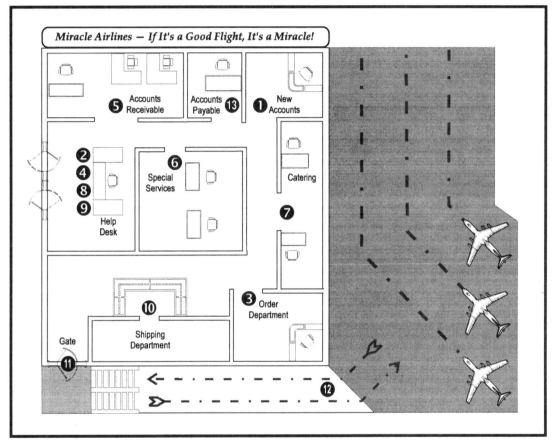

Fig. 10-3: The Worst Case Scenario

9. You then show up the following morning at the Help Desk to see the printout which may contain an error message for your account/reservation number. If so, you start the entire procedure again. If the plane you originally intended to board is full by this time, the Help Desk clerk may be able to direct you to another flight. If so, you may have to repeat some or all of the previous steps with another airline in another terminal! If no errors are found or typed in wrong on your mountain of paperwork, you get a printed invoice that you use for boarding. The Help Desk clerk tells you your departure Gate number (and, if they're not too busy, where there are restaurants and passenger lounges).

10. Before going to the Gate, your next stop will be at the Shipping Department where you'll leave all of the luggage you've toted around in exchange for more paperwork in the form of baggage claim tags.

11. Now you go to the Gate where you turn over your boarding documents to the clerk who promptly tears them in half.

12. The Gate leads you to a path across the complex to the tarmac where the planes sit in a row in ascending order by catalog number. Unfortunately, when you finally board the plane, due to one or two minor "bugs" in the computer program, you might end up sitting on someone's lap. That's just part of traveling — you have to expect some bugs because flying is a complex task.

13. If you give up in despair or you simply can't get a flight, the airline's modern daily batch computer system feeds a monthly batch system run to take care of credits, refunds, etc. In this case you can go to Accounts Payable to file a refund claim. Then return to the scene of the crime at the end of the month and go to the Accounts Department to receive your refund check. It's that simple!

The Current Case — Why's My Luggage in Paris when I'm in LA?

Looking at the current airline industry as a contrasting example, we see that even with its imperfections, it is externally (customer) oriented in a way that puts most other operations to shame. If I show up at the airport wanting to take a flight home as soon as possible, the check-in clerk will do whatever is necessary (within their Business Policy Rules) to get me on my flight. This one person is empowered to take on the roles of Computer Operator, Baggage Handler, Cashier, Caterer, and Information Desk representative — all in order to get my business. They will find a flight or series of flights (even on another airline) on their computer terminal, tag and lift my luggage over to the baggage conveyer, take my food and seating preference, and direct me to a specific location (usually in a large, complex airport). They will even help me with questions about the location of airport lounges, concessions, restaurants, etc. All of this takes place in just a few minutes of elapsed time (see Figure 10–4).

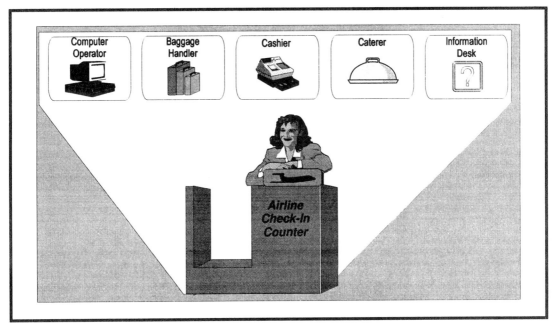

Fig. 10-4: An Empowered Employee

The customer-oriented design of this operation is not reflected in all of the designs in the airline industry. For example, the baggage handling design leaves much to be desired. The problem with poor baggage handling is so endemic in fact (and unfortunately accepted), that almost every experienced air traveler takes on board with them some carry-on luggage with their toiletries, valuables, and important documents (this is even recommended by the airlines themselves).

The Future Case — The Way You Want it Airline

As this is the design section of this book, I find myself concentrating on how to address the design of the baggage system mentioned in the preceding scenario. Baggage is part of my Business Event with the airline, so it should NOT be separated.

Let me practice what I preach and do an analysis of this Business Event first and then create a new design. The Data Flow Diagram in Figure 10–5 (which I have already annotated with design features) depicts what is needed to satisfy our requirements for air travel.

Given this Business Event Partitioned model, we can now put on our designer hats and come up with a design based upon what we encompass in the manual and automated environments. The DFD shows a "Carte Blanche" design that is only one of many possible designs. The dashed line on the DFD represents the automation boundary. A basic rule is that wherever our automation boundary cuts across any data flow, we need to utilize some technology.

So, now let me describe the new design for a Business Event Partition that was created with the customer's ultimate satisfaction in mind. You could create variations of this DFD for Business Travelers, Occasional/Holiday Travelers, First Class Travelers, or Economy Class Travelers. Each type of customers' Business Event would result in variations on this same design. Let me preempt any comments regarding the cost of the new design. Remember that the initial setup of an ATM network was very costly, but after ATMs were in use, it cost banks less to use the ATM network than to use the manual teller-based design. Therefore, it may be that Economy Class Travelers eventually are the ones who pay for a new implemented airline system based on their sheer numbers.

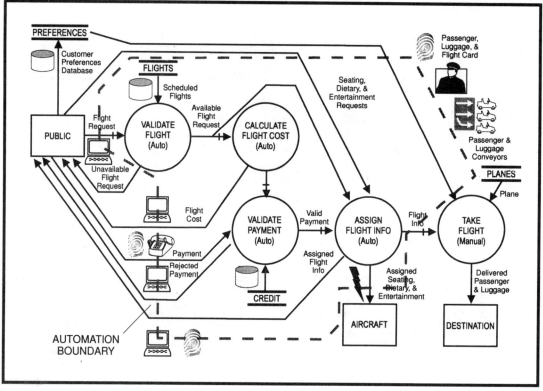

Fig. 10-5: The Future Case Scenario Design DFD

Depending on the scope of what we are allowed to Re-Engineer, we could redesign the entire terminal to create a seamless system where your luggage is never separated from you. After all, you were capable enough to make it to the airport with your luggage, you can surely make it a few yards further.

In this new design (see Figure 10–6) as you enter the airport, you place your thumb on a thumbprint reader. If you have traveled before with the airline and have made a reservation in advance, the thumbprint reader retrieves a cohesive set of data from a database including your flight information (destination and gate), seating and meal preferences, frequent flier discount, etc. You don't even need to know a flight number in this design as this is the airline's internal flight ID and not something you care about. If you have not made previous arrangements, the thumbprint reader has a means for you to make your needs known to the system at the entry to the terminal.

At this point the system knows who you are, which flight you are taking, and everything else required to satisfy your needs in this Business Event. To simplify your travel, the thumbprint reader has a direction indicator that points out which gondola-style conveyor to board to take you and your luggage to the correct gate.

The conveyor has a seat for you and a detachable baggage cart for your luggage. At this point a Sky Cap helps those passengers who need assistance to board the correct conveyor gondola with their luggage. This empowered employee is not a behind-the-scenes service agent. In this design there is no longer any "pre-boarding" for those needing special assistance because helping those in need is part of the Sky Cap's job. They also take care of oversized luggage and help foreign travelers with the use of computer-assisted translators.

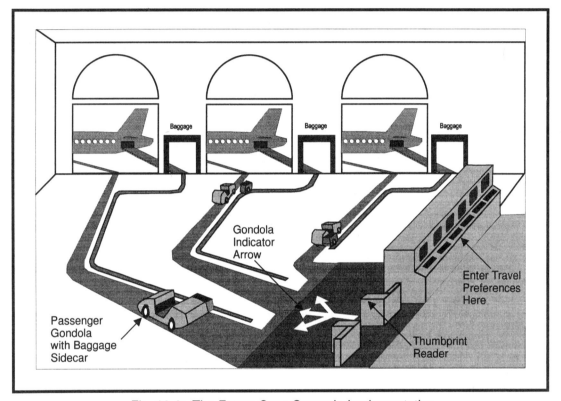

Fig. 10-6: The Future Case Scenario Implementation

When the conveyor reaches the correct gate, the luggage carts split off and goes directly into the plane's cargo hold (if we're not allowed to redesign the airplane, that is). As you board the plane, your name is displayed above the seat you selected. In this system your portion of the luggage compartment in the airplane's hold and your seat assignment are directly linked, so that as you exit the plane, your luggage is shuttled off of the plane to meet your conveyor gondola (even on flights with transfers). You don't need any bits of paper such as luggage tags or boarding passes for other people to collect from you later.

When you arrive at your destination, the baggage compartment re-connects with the conveyor cart you board upon leaving the plane. Then, you and your baggage are whisked to a selected destination in the terminal that you previously entered (e.g., hotel shuttle, taxi stand, car rental, etc.).

From an implementation point of view, any subset of this seamless, ticketless, paperless journey could be phased in. For example, the first phase may be to create an Airline Travel Card instead of a thumbprint reader that debits your bank account for the flight's cost (minus your frequent-flier discount, of course) and has your seating and dietary preferences encoded. These advantages could be provided in stages where First Class Travelers get the benefits in the system's release 1.1, the Business Class Travelers get included in release 1.2, and Economy Class Travelers get them in release 1.3. Release 2.0 could introduce the thumbprint reader system to eliminate the card entirely.

Re-Engineering Computer Systems — Design

If we look at the last 30 years of computer's technological advances, we see an orders of magnitude growth of capability and capacity. For example, today we get a lot more machine power for our dollar. Because of the advances from the early days of vacuum tube machines, something with the power of the IBM System 370 mainframe machine that used to fill a large air-conditioned room now fits on my lap, and maybe in the palm of my hand. These kinds of improvements match what we strive for in a Re-Engineering project.

The Benefits of Re-Engineering Computer Systems

Since an automated product (software) contains no material resources, it can be replicated at practically no cost once it has been created.

A building, for example, may cost millions of dollars and take years to build. To build another identical building will cost almost the same and take equally as long. By contrast, an air traffic control system or an operating system for a personal computer may cost millions and take many person years to develop. However, once built the system can be replicated for the cost of the magnetic medium and of copying the procedures documentation. The implications of this are that the computer software industry can benefit a large market quickly.

A benefit of implementing computer-based systems using an engineering discipline is that any modifications are made everywhere instantly with no need for retraining. Of course the capacity and speed of computers exceed that of human beings when implementing a systematic process. In addition, there is a growing market segment that prefers to interface with computer systems. Obviously, any external computer systems linking to our organization would be prime targets for linking to another computer system within our organization.

When we come to implement, with new computer systems, the new design from our Business Event-partitioned model, we should "package" as much as possible by Business Event Partitions, and not replicate the old physical system partitions that we saw in *Systems Archaeology*. In Figure 10–7, we see five Business Event Partitions packaged into four computer partitions. The top two on-line computer partitions mirror their Business Event Partitions. The middle part of the diagram shows one Business Event partitioned by time into batch daily and batch weekly packages for today's *design* reasons, and the partitions interface with a design tape store. If this whole Business Event Partition later became implemented totally on-line or totally as daily batch runs, we would remove this connecting design store. The lower portion of the diagram shows two Business Events packaged into one ad hoc reporting system. All these design packages are functional (i.e., they have not fragmented any Business Events).

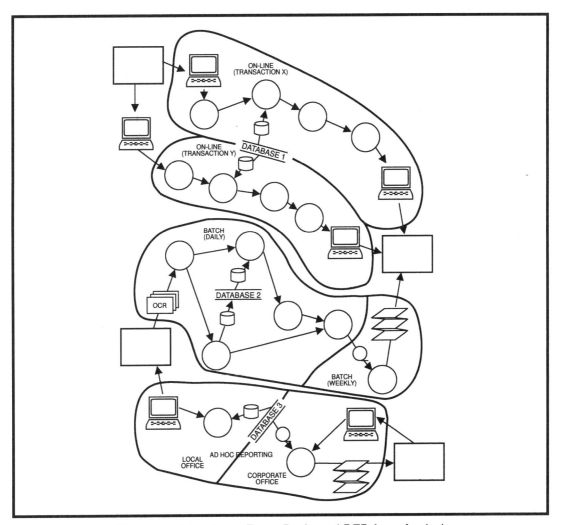

Fig. 10-7: A Business Event Packaged DFD from Analysis

During the design phase of computer systems, one problem in the past, even with modern methods, has been deciding what constitutes a program and subsystem boundary. We can see now that the best program or subsystem partitioning is by Business Event Partitions. From a computer system implementation point of view, we have many design methods to choose from.

Now, as I've already said, my background is in Software Engineering. Therefore, I'll show an example using Structured Design for the design of the automated part of a Business Event Specification.

When we partition our automated designs by Business Event Partitions, we should keep *business* processing and data separate from *computer* processing (e.g., control logic) and data. Both of these must also be kept separate from *technology* support logic and data. We can separate each of these issues by showing these as separate modules in the design model (see Figure 10–8).

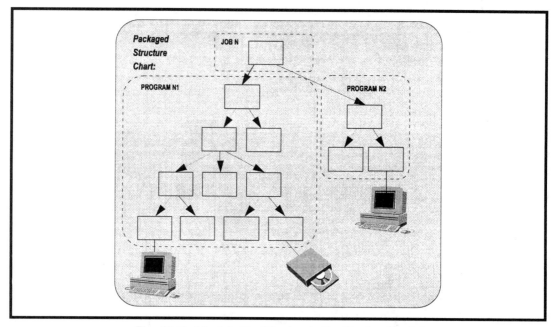

Fig. 10-8: Module Partitioning in the Design Model

Figure 10–8 shows a generic Structure Chart indicating how we separate:

- *Technology modules*, supporting logic for hardware, database management systems, support software, etc.

- *Control modules*, supporting logic for batched processing loops, N-to-one and one-to-N structures, managing initiation, termination and design error processing, etc.

- *Business modules*, supporting logic which comes directly from the business processing on the DFDs and is specified in the analysis Process Specifications.

This separation is a major step to achieving the design goals of system maintainability and flexibility. When a change occurs in production, it should be easy to isolate the required modification to specific modules. The separation will also reduce, if not solve, the "ripple effect" through other modules (i.e., one modification ripples through many system programs).

Using Structured Design techniques[1], we use the Business Event partitioned DFD and ERD of analysis in Figures 10–9 and 10–10 to produce the system/program design chart of Figure 10–11.[2]

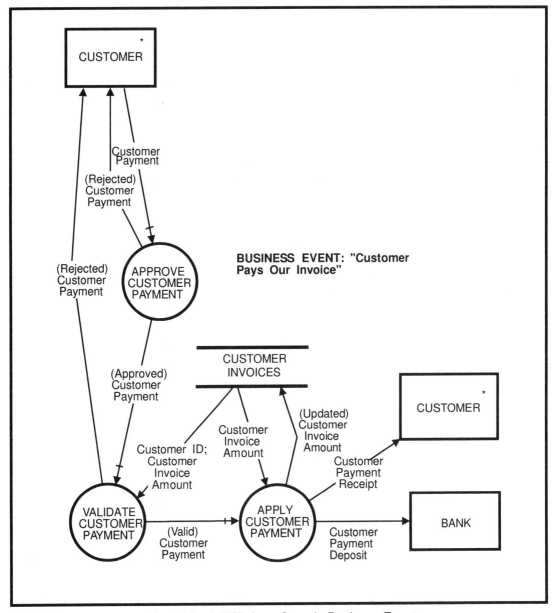

Fig. 10-9: A DFD for a Sample Business Event

1 Yourdon/Constantine and Page-Jones style Structure Chart — see Bibliography

2 I showed a systematic *Seven-step Transform Analysis* procedure in my previous book "Developing Quality Systems," and used this approach to derive this design Structure Chart from the Customer Payment Business Event-partitioned DFD. Don't ask me why bubbles change to boxes. By convention, design modules are shown as boxes, and processes are shown as bubbles. If we used an Object Oriented Model, then we wouldn't go from circles to rectangles. Think of this stage as just adding control processes instead of circles.

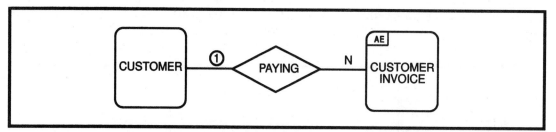

Fig. 10-10: An ERD for a Sample Business Event

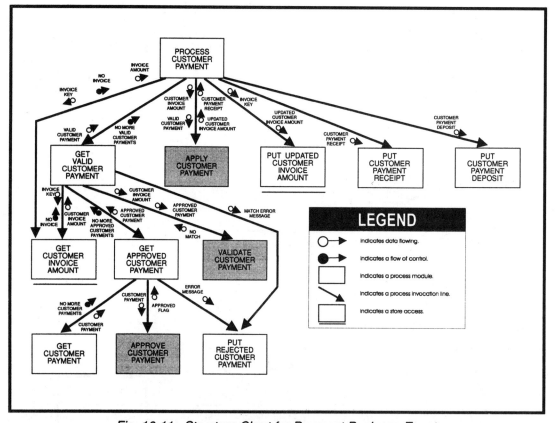

Fig. 10-11: Structure Chart for Payment Business Event

The shaded modules on this Structure Chart come directly from the business processes on the DFD. Just as we may isolate management tasks in a manual design, we introduce control modules in design to isolate the implementation control needs. Similarly, in a manual design, we may have members of a team who are skilled in Shipping and Receiving. So, here we introduce the technology modules to isolate the edges of the business processing (i.e., the external interfaces and their devices). We must support these additional modules with some form or "write up" such as pseudocode. And, if we need to make any design modifications to the business Process Specifications to support the new design, then we must produce the documentation to also support these. The Structure Chart will assist the implementor of the system by showing the internal partitioning of a system into modules, and the interaction between, and structure of, those modules.

Using the Business Event DFD and the entities in the Business Event ERD, we can generate the Business Event Access Path Diagram shown in Figure 10–12 to show how the processing will navigate through our Business Event portion of the organization's ERD shown in Figure 10–10. This is the beginning of design of the data memory part of our Business Specification.

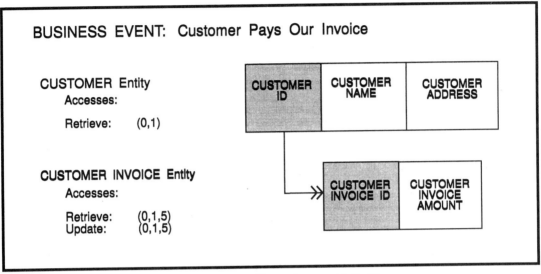

Fig. 10-12: Business Event Access Path Diagram

Each Business Event Access Path Diagram (APD) represents one Business Event's data access needs. This model is derived by using the detailed business logic in the Business Event Partition's process specification(s), and tracing the data and their access needs through the ERD.

For each Business Event, one Access Path Diagram shows:

- The entry point.
- Key Data Elements (fields).
- Specific Data Elements required from each entity.
- Data usage type (Create, Retrieve, Update, Delete).
- Minimum, average, and maximum accesses of each entity by data usage type.
- Direction of access of entities.

The Access Path Diagram will assist the implementor of the data by showing the necessary connection, frequency, and specific Data Element needs that the data design should support.[3] We'll use the diagrams to implement a physical data design (e.g., hierarchical,

---

3   Even though the APD is a computer-oriented model, it is also helpful for showing the navigation through data in manual systems. This is because the APD is still relatively logical at this point — so it's an LAPD *(great acronym, eh?).*

network, and relational structures), just as we'll use the Structure Chart for implementing physical data processing (consisting of programs and subsystems written in a specific computer language).

The Complete Business Event Specification — An Example

At this point in the book you may be tired of my generic examples, so now let me use another example — one that's more realistic and closer to my heart. At Logical Conclusions one critical Business Event is when a client wants to enroll one or more students in a public seminar. Let's study the set of models that we can use to completely specify this Business Event Partition, "Client wants to register student(s) in a public seminar." I will concentrate only on the detailed level for this example.

Sample Business Event Analysis Specification: Data on the Move

First, we can produce a Logical Data Flow Diagram stimulated by a "Seminar Enrollment Request." If we had an Organizational Entity Relationship Diagram already available for LCI, we would probably already have identified the three entities shown as data stores on the DFD. Otherwise we can produce a single Business Event Entity as one data store, and repartition it into the three stores after we produce the detailed ERD.

The DFD of Figure 10–13 should speak for itself, but would obviously have to be supported with an associated Data Dictionary and Process Specifications.

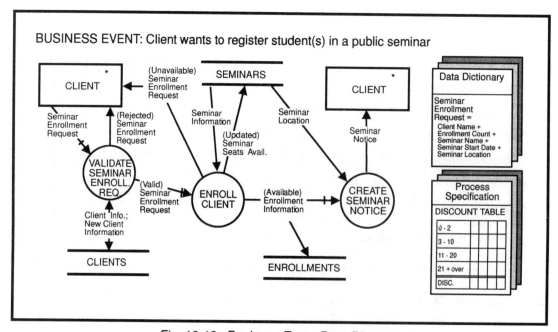

Fig. 10-13: Business Event Data Diagram

Sample Business Event Analysis Specification: Data at Rest

For the details on the static data side, we can produce an Entity Relationship Diagram indicating that this Business Event associates three entities together in an "Enrolling" relationship. LCI's policy is to form one enrollment per Seminar Enrollment request. We don't create separate student entries in this Business Event, so we have a 1:1 cardinality between the entities in this model. (Note that this is for one Business Event, and that after many occurrences of this Business Event, we may have many enrollments associated with a seminar, and even many enrollments for the same Client on that Seminar.) The "Enrolling" Relationship Specification can specify this for this Business Event and we can remove the cardinality on the combined Organizational ERD as this cardinality will not be applicable in the total organization-wide view.

Again, we would support the ERD model of Figure 10–14 with Entity, Relationship, and Data Element Specifications.

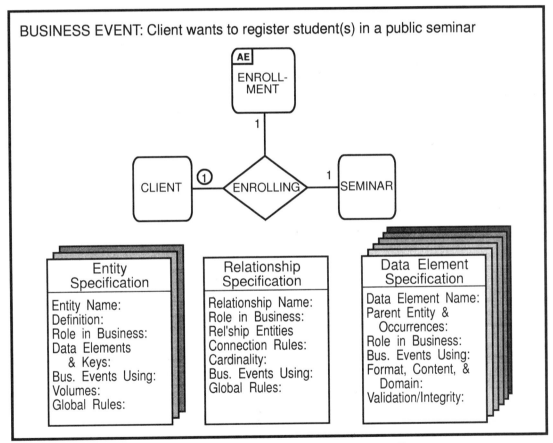

Fig. 10-14: Business Event ERD & Supporting Specs.

The Beginnings of Design: Data on the Move

We can now use the logical DFD to show physical characteristics of our New Design. For example, we can overlay an automation boundary on the Analysis Model. We may also decide to further package our Business Event DFD into two subsystems: an on-line Registration system and a batch Seminar Notification system. *(You already know that I do not recommend fragmenting a Business Event in this way, but I want to show you one example of the repercussions of this fragmentation.)* This will result in one Business Event Partition spanning two systems. Notice that if we do this, we must create a design store between the two subsystems with a second stimulus for "Time" to trigger the batch processing system.

We would support the bounded and packaged DFD model of Figure 10–15 with specifications such as screen and record layouts for the physical boundary flows. (Again, note that wherever a data flow intersects a boundary, some device or media is required to move the data between the automated and manual environments.)

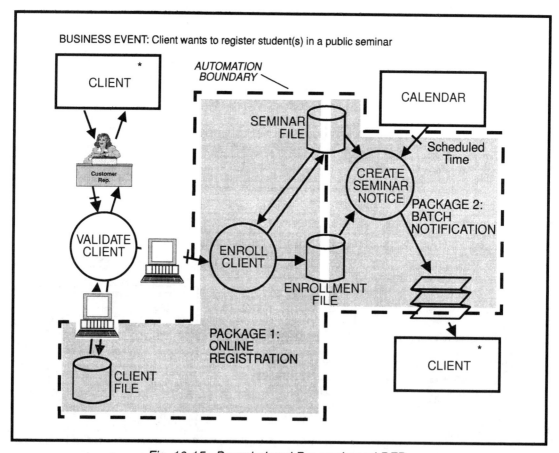

Fig. 10-15: Bounded and Pre-packaged DFD

The Beginnings of Design: Data at Rest

We can take the first step of design on the static data side of our Business Event Partition by using a Logical Access Path Diagram (LAPD) to identify how we need to access the entities on our ERD. As there may be many data accesses for one Business Event Partition, the LAPD may be disjointed as shown in Figure 10–16. We limit the Data Elements shown on the LAPD to those necessary for this Business Event Partition, as opposed to all the Data Elements in the Entity Specification. Also, we can indicate the frequency of accesses for this Business Event next to each entity.

At this time, we would also identify the data to be implemented manually (using file cabinets, Rolodex files, and so on), and the automated system data to be implemented using databases, sequential files, and so on.

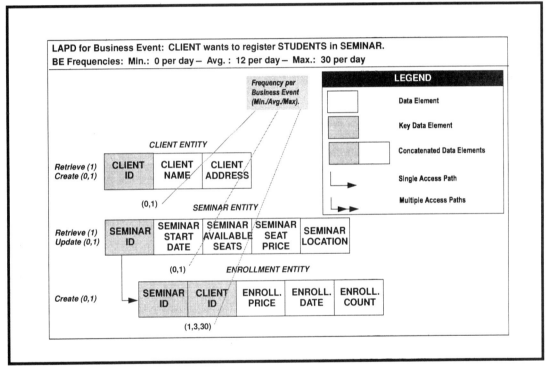

Fig. 10-16: Business Event LAPD

The Business Event Detailed Design Specification: Data on the Move

If we decide to use Structured Design to derive our detailed system architecture, we can produce Structure Charts for each Business Event Partition fragment. Applying a strategy in Structured Design called Transform Analysis, we would produce two Structure Charts, as shown in Figures 10–17 and 10–18.

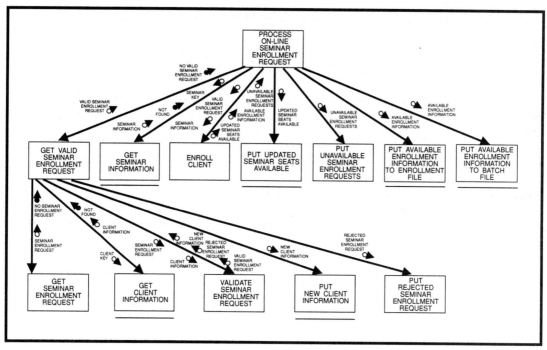

Fig. 10-17: Structure Chart for On-Line Packaged System

At this point, we would introduce control and technology modules, as well as transform Business Process Specifications into business modules. We support these modules with pseudocode and the Data Dictionary embellished with design formats and value ranges (if these are not already defined in the Organizational Data Dictionary).

We next use the Packaged Structure Chart as input to the Implementation phase.

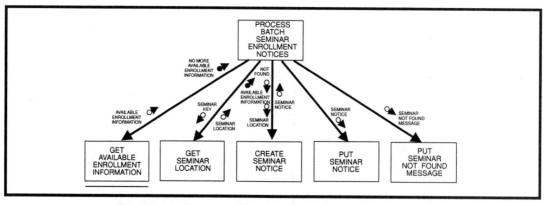

Fig. 10-18: Structure Chart for Batch Packaged System

The Business Event Detailed Design Specification: Data at Rest

Using the information on the ERD, LAPD, and supporting specifications, we produce the Detailed Design for the data structure. For example, we might implement our data in relational tables as shown in Figure 10–19. We use the resulting structure as input for implementation in a particular database management system or manual filing system. Of course, because data are global, there will be some redundancy (in the model only) between this and other Business Event Specifications. So we may replace this model by a reference to the organization's data structure.

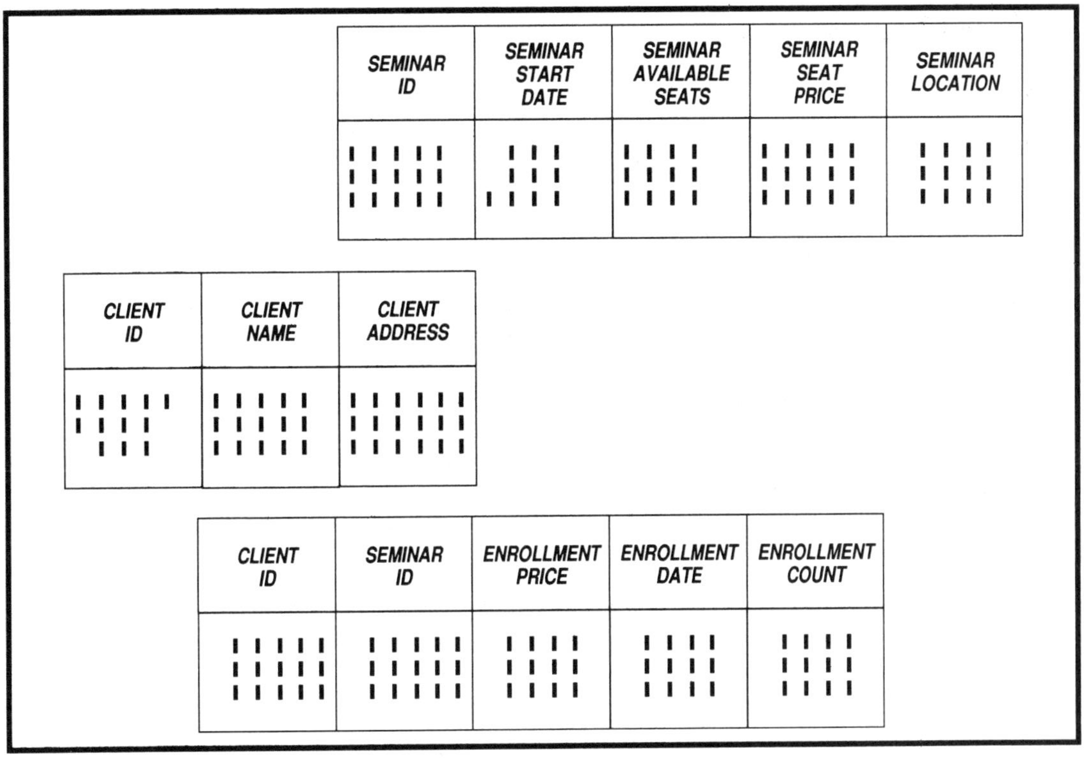

SEMINAR ID	SEMINAR START DATE	SEMINAR AVAILABLE SEATS	SEMINAR SEAT PRICE	SEMINAR LOCATION

CLIENT ID	CLIENT NAME	CLIENT ADDRESS

CLIENT ID	SEMINAR ID	ENROLLMENT PRICE	ENROLLMENT DATE	ENROLLMENT COUNT

Fig. 10-19: Database Structure

Figure 10–20 shows all these models and supporting specifications brought together to form one Business Event Specification entry in the Business Event Library. This Business Event Specification consists of:

- The detailed Data Flow Diagram (DFD).

- The detailed Entity Relationship Diagram (ERD).

- Bounding and packaging of the DFD into manual and automated portions.

- Access Path Diagram (APD).

- Design Structure Chart(s).

- Database/file structure(s).

- All supporting specifications for the above models.

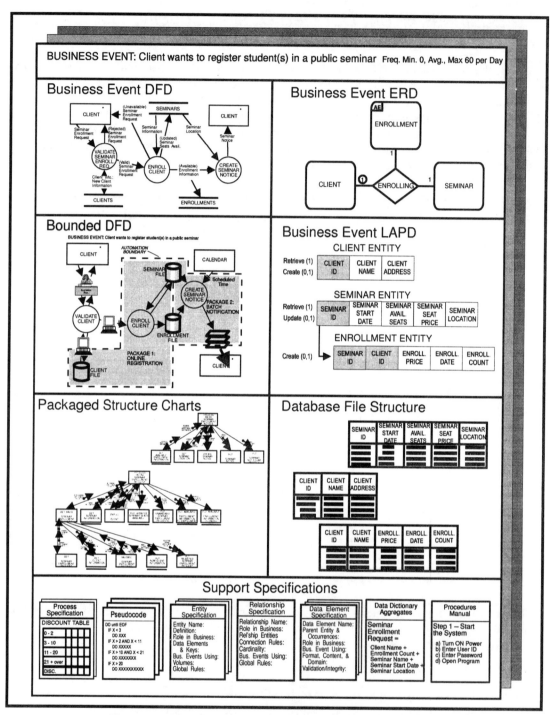

Fig. 10-20: Sample Complete Analysis & Design BE Spec.

The comprehensive diagram of Figure 10–20 is the final result of using the Business Event Methodology through the stages of analysis and design. (Note that in real-time systems, we may also add models such as Control Flow Diagrams and State Transition Diagrams.) We can add procedure manuals, computer code, databases, and file layouts to this Business Event Library entry.

As I've already said, the complete set of Business Event Specifications *is* the business, but at a detailed level. We must take other aggregate models into consideration, such as system- and organization-level models. Remember that systems are arbitrary collections of Business Event Partitions over which we already have control, but we, as Re-Engineers will have much less control over the organization's collections of Business Event Partitions. The methodology in Book II addresses these aggregate models, along with a more detailed Business Event Model.

In my judgment, this complete set of Business Event Specifications *is* the Organizational Repository, that is, it is the total description of the business — what it does and how it is currently implemented.

Summary

Given the complete set of Business Event entries in the Business Event Library, the Business Event Conservator can fully assist with any future changes of business and its implementation by having a link from the Business Models to the Design Models as they are implemented today. With the Business Event Library and the Business Event Matrices we can see that any change to the business will be an engineered change (i.e., no dead data, dead processing, or crossing our fingers to hope that nothing is going to get "messed up" by a simple change).

With our organization Re-Engineered, we can focus on introducing new Business Issues instead of putting out internal "fires."

With engineered systems we can take advantage of any new technology in the future because we have separated Business Issues from Technology/Implementation Issues.

Many people don't plan to fail, but they do fail to plan.

Unknown

Strategic Planning via Business Events

At the beginning of this book we talked about *Re-Engineering and Strategic Planning*. I had to bite my tongue in that chapter because I needed you to understand the concepts of Business Events, Business Event Partitioning, etc. to truly put over my view of Strategic Planning. In that chapter I had to use terms like "line of business" and "customer need" when I was really talking about what we now know as Business Events. My concern in that chapter was that your understanding of the critical issues of Strategic Planning would have been corrupted by your "design-oriented" glasses. So let me now mirror and rectify the wording in part of that chapter and use the correct terms to convey Strategic Planning issues.

The Strategic Business Planning I advocate here differs from classical Strategic Planning by focusing on Business Events and the resources needed to respond to those events. It produces a strategic plan for both the information and processing needs of the enterprise.

The Strategic Plan is presented in terms of:

- An agreed upon set of organizational goals.
- A organizational Business Event List.
- A Business Model devoid of any implementation characteristics.
- Matrices of relationships between Business Events and Data Elements, Entities, Processes, and Relationships.
- Lists of obstacles to achieving the organization's goals.
- A transition plan for Re-Engineering the organization.

Note that you would not need a transition plan when creating a Pre-Engineering project's Strategic Plan.

Even if you're a management major straight out of college and you're starting off fresh, you must be careful to avoid the trap of creating an Accounting Dept., a Stock Control Dept., a Shipping Dept., etc. with a traditional hierarchy of control, and thus miss the opportunity for Pre-Engineering a new organization.

The focal point of any Strategic Planning approach is the set of Organizational Objectives that defines where the organization is today, and where it expects to be in the future. Without this set of goals, the organization cannot define the processing and information it needs to support this movement.

The Key Organizational Questions

The key questions that an organization must answer in Strategic Planning are repeated and further clarified in Figure 11–1. The details of "how to" accomplish them are discussed in *Book Two: The Strategic Business Re-Engineering Methodology*.

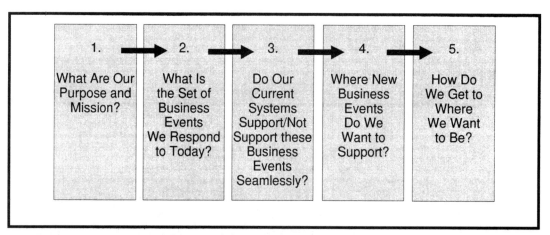

Fig. 11-1: Key Organizational Questions

1. What Are Our Purpose and Mission?

This is a description of the business our organization is in and what we want to be or do in current terms. This may be an overall purpose or it can be broken down into a set of Organizational Objectives. To be meaningful and useful, these objectives should be quantifiable and measurable. They contain the "vision" of the strategic planners. All projects use them to develop individual objectives. The objectives in the Mission Statement should be displayed throughout the organization. It is this that each and every employee and computer system are working to support.

2. What Is the Set of Business Events We Respond to Today?

We have already seen in previous chapters that the managers in each department of an organization will typically have their own view on what the actual business is. The heads of an organization and the Re-Engineers cannot take any particular department's view, so I recommend answering this question with:

- Definitions of existing business boundaries between the organization and the external world, and all Business Event Stimuli crossing the boundaries, and produce a *Business Event List* for the organization.

- Identification of organizational Business Events at the boundaries of the organization (i.e., a Business Event List).

- Identification of Critical Business Events. Define the set of Business Events that are our reason for being in business or our main revenue generators. (Identify Dependent and Regulatory Events, but don't include them in your critical Business Events List unless you are a government organization.)

- A high-level map of our existing implementation (e.g., departments, divisions, computer systems, and computer platforms).

- Using the Business Event List, an Organizational Business Event Objective or set of objectives can be developed for each Business Event. These Organizational Business Event Objectives are quantifiable, measurable statements of a Business Event Partition's required performance. The objectives must be stated such that it will be quite clear when they are, or are not, being met.

3. Do Our Current Systems Support/Not Support these Business Events Seamlessly?

We must evaluate how well our organization achieves its purpose and mission today. It does so by analyzing how the systems currently implemented respond and contribute to the organization's purpose and mission via the Business Events identified in question two, above.

One way of assessing how we are doing is to see how much any specific Business Event is fragmented across existing systems (manual and automated). Also, given each Organizational Business Objective, we should be able to assess how we are meeting these objectives by projecting the optimum response/performance statistics onto each Business Event and compare them with the current statistics. (*I tend to find that organizations have reasonable statistics or metrics of their operating costs for their manual systems, but not for their computer systems. So, this step may be difficult, but nonetheless essential, for the computer environment.*) Thus, the organization's purpose and mission objectives decompose into specific Business Event Partitioned objectives, which in turn decompose into specific Business Policy for each Business Event. I believe that the only way the organization can truly track its performance is by gathering honest statistics (metrics) for each Business Event Partition and how it is implemented in the current system(s) and in any future Re-Engineered system.

The Value of Current Systems

We can measure the value of each system based on the strategic value of how many of the critical Business Events (or how much of each Business Event) it supports.

As you now know, it may be difficult to measure the value of existing systems in terms of Business Events because most current systems will be partitioned almost opposite to Business Event Partitioning (i.e., many Business Events will travel through each and every system). So we may have to use a cruder and higher-level method to determine a system's strategic value such as shown in Figure 11–2.

In Figure 11–2 the high value/low cost systems can be found in the upper left quadrant. These are probably newer, engineered systems. In the upper right quadrant, we see the "nail biters" — high value/high cost systems that are probably older and non-engineered. The staff may hold their breath when they attempt to make changes to these systems. All this graph will really tell us is that we should probably pay more attention in our Strategic Plan to the high value/high cost systems.

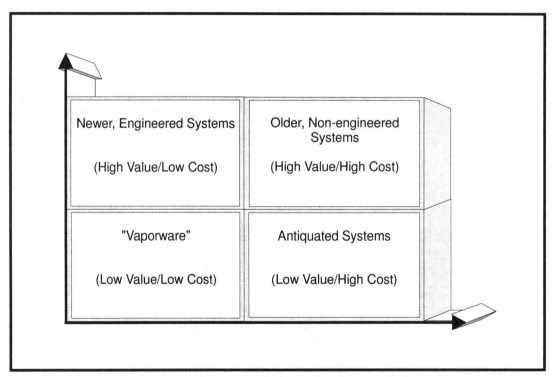

Newer, Engineered Systems	Older, Non-engineered Systems
(High Value/Low Cost)	(High Value/High Cost)
"Vaporware"	Antiquated Systems
(Low Value/Low Cost)	(Low Value/High Cost)

Fig. 11-2: Strategic Value vs. Operating Cost

Our second order of Strategic Planning importance would be systems falling into the lower right quadrant (low value/high cost). They may be antiquated administration systems or systems supporting unprofitable lines of business. These are systems that are not currently paying their way.

One of the main benefits of gathering the flow of critical Business Events through existing systems is that it provides us with some very important metrics for both devising a Re-Engineering Plan and monitoring its effectiveness over time. These metrics should reveal such things as:

- The long term savings in the cost of operations gained by Re-Engineering.

- How best to use limited staff resources, and hopefully avoid the all too common situation where a department is too busy keeping existing systems alive to give Re-Engineering its necessary commitment.

- Whether some or all of an existing system can be salvaged.

To answer this question of whether our systems currently support us seamlessly, we compare the capabilities of the organization's current automated and manual support systems with the Business Event List identified in the previous activities.

It is at this point that we analyze the internal configuration of the organization by:

- Modeling current system boundaries. This task examines *how* we do business today. It involves gathering information on existing manual and automated systems, and identifying boundaries and interfaces between systems. Knowing the current system boundaries allows us to identify the systems (manual and automated) making up the organization, and determine the cost of operating each system.

- Mapping Business Events to current business design. Given current design boundaries, we map Business Events to the current business systems, and see how the responses to these events flow through our systems. We are also interested in how the systems talk to each other when responding to the same Business Event. This yields a Business Event/System Matrix as in Figure 11–3.

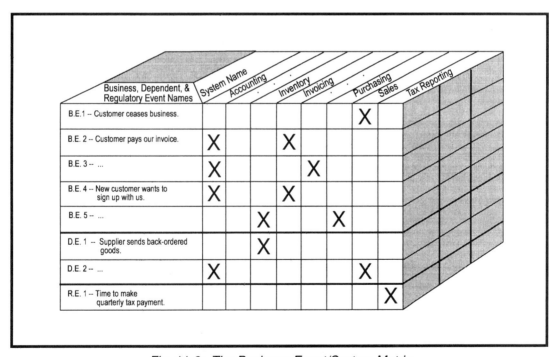

Fig. 11-3: The Business Event/System Matrix

- Identifying manual and automated system cost and deterioration. This task examines the history of each business system (manual and automated) to determine the rate of modification requests and the ease of satisfying them. Ideally, we would plan to first Re-Engineer the mission-critical Business Events. These are those that flow through the worst (in most need of replacement) systems. Or, we could choose to Re-Engineer those systems that comprise the bulk of our Business Event processing and memory.

4. What New Business Events Do We Want to Support?

In addition to evaluating the organization's current position, we must also identify what changes, additions, or deletions are required for future business opportunities. This can also be high level, but again, it must be measurable.

If we want to be more specific in our future goals, we can:

- Identify future Business Events — By reviewing any new business opportunities or the operations of competitive organizations, senior management can identify new Business Events to which the organization should respond in the future. Innovations in technology may also lead to new avenues of business and hence new Business Events.

- Assess feasibility and risk — We analyze the feasibility and risk of responding to (or not responding to) the new Business Events, examine the technological and resource implications, and look for any existing processes and data that can be re-used.

- Produce the future Organizational Business Event Model and future, high-level Enterprise Model (ERD). Having identified future critical Business Events, we show them on a new organizational high-level Business Event Model.

One of the major advantages of having a Business Event Partitioned Business Model is that it allows us to see the true details of the organization to realize where we can take advantage of strategic alliances. These will be easily identified where a Business Event Response causes a Dependent Event to come back into our organization. In this regard we should especially evaluate Dependent Events that are timing-oriented (i.e., those stimulated by a Control-triggered Stimulus from the clock or calendar). These types of Dependent Events are prime targets for one aspect of Strategic Planning. We can better serve our customers by being in control of every aspect of filling a Business Event including those that are currently beyond our organization and that show themselves as Dependent Events.

When forming strategic alliances we need to think "outside the box" (i.e., we need to ask what we could do for our customers before they even stimulate our organization). To do this, we should look at true External Interfaces. However, any Internal Interfaces that our organization has control over should be cleared up first.

Using the Business Model to Look to the Future

I want to talk about Business Events here, but through the use of implementation examples to show how to improve the organization. The first example involves the case of a Business Event that in turn triggers a Dependent Event. If we find that part of filling a Customer Order involves extracting materials from our inventory and we get these materials from a supplier, then we will see these materials return to our organization as a Dependent Event on the Business Model. This Dependent Event is where we respond to that supplier based on an outgoing requisition for more materials.

Using this example we can see an opportunity to improve the business by bringing the Dependent Event under the wing of the Business Event. We accomplish this by easily seeing on the Business Model that the materials are extracted based on a Customer Order. It's at the point of extraction that items in our inventory store can fall below a re-order level. It is at this time that we can immediately issue a requisition for more supplies. In other words, the Business Event Stimulus, Customer Order, triggers the requisition and not a disjointed Control-triggered Business Event Stimulus.

Having the Business Model available to us allows us to see that we can go one step further and form a strategic alliance with that Supplier where they keep track of our reorder levels and our current inventory levels. *(In this case we may not even have to keep track of our own inventory.)* Instead, we send them a record of every item purchased as part of a Customer Order Business Event. Therefore, they know before we do that it's time for them to fabricate and/or ship us the materials (still on a just-in-time basis if that's part of the alliance agreement). After all, the Supplier is the one who has the most incentive to keep our materials in stock to meet our customers' needs because we pay them for what they supply us.

In a service-oriented example the Dependent Events on our Business Model may point out aspects of our business that are currently outsourced. These may be services that we want to take back within our organization in order to have more direct control over satisfying our own customers' Business Events. I mentioned at the front of the book that I expect Re-Engineering to be just as likely to make an organization grow rather than be downsized. If strategic planners are really interested in satisfying customers' needs, then I would expect the organization to take on more things that it currently doesn't do as opposed to outsourcing or downsizing.

Vendors with whom an organization outsources some of its tasks must prove that they produce efficient and effective products and services just as the people inside an organization must prove to their management that they are the most efficient and effective providers of products and services. This is just another example of the healthy nature of competition except that it is between an organization's staff and that of a vendor (as opposed to their organization's competition).

The Dependent Events on a Business Model will also indicate areas that strategic planners may want to study that are beyond the organization. They may want to produce a new Business Model (or even buy one, if available) that extends their area of business into new Business Events.

An organization's strategic planners need to charter the Re-Engineers to create radical new designs. For example, when Re-Engineers invent new System Events to support an implementation of the Business Model, the new implementation will probably call for human beings. This will introduce System Events such as one for Pay Employees. As Re-Engineers thinking radically, we may suggest implementing a "real-time" payroll system. In this case payroll is no longer performed on a periodic batch basis. In the new implementation, payroll machines would be installed at the building exits. Employees could use a personal PIN and/or have a face scanning device to access their earned payroll on demand. The employees could get paid in any increment they wish (e.g., they could withdraw their last hour's earnings or get all their earnings since the last time they made a withdrawal — which may be hours, weeks, or months).

The payroll funds would be kept in the organization's internal bank and the company would earn interest on the balances. This may make the organization assume the task of managing the investments that earn the interest on the payroll dollars. The proceeds from the interest earned could be split between the organization and its employees. Part of this interest money could help fund things such as employee benefits programs providing more incentives for employees and employers. This way the money doesn't leave the organization to pay a bank that in turn pays the employees. In addition, the organization gets the benefits of having the funds available to it and the employees take on the responsibility of managing their own payroll disbursements.

As a third example at this point, let's use one based on the government because, as I say in my seminars, the older and larger an organization is, the harder it will be to Re-Engineer. In this light, the government has two strikes against it, because in the U.S., organizations don't get much older or much larger. However, please keep in mind that it is exactly this type of institution that stands to gain the most potential benefits from Re-Engineering provided that the Re-Engineers are not aligned with (or remove themselves from alignments with) any particular Department, Bureau, Senator, etc.

So that I don't get associated with any political alliance, let me use the Post Office as an example. This scenario assumes I have a Business Model as input for my new designs. When I look at the operations of the Post Office, I see very little logical difference between its business requirements and those of any other shipping, package delivery, or courier service. We could Re-Engineer such an environment by forming an alliance with a phone company or cable TV service company to provide a new type of service. This service would be where letters are formed on an interactive, voice recognition-based TV system. The system would of course have automated grammar and spelling checking to correct the idiosyncrasies of speech on the fly. In addition, the system would replace the current addressing scheme with an absolute longitude/latitude based addressing system with no need for Zip codes, mail stops, or other addressing schemes. Since the new addressing system would be entirely logical, the "mail" (if it was still called that) would be delivered to a person no matter where they were, instead of ending up in a mail box waiting for them to retrieve it. This new system would allow the Post Office to become the "on-ramps" and "off-ramps" to the Information Super Highway.

Radical solutions should win praise from the Re-Engineer's management, even though the budgeting of such an ambitious design has not been taken into account. After all, it's up to the Re-Engineer to come up with the new ideas and, it's management's job to come up with the money.[1] As strategic planners, we should create an award for the most radical ideas that our Re-Engineers propose, even if we don't implement them.

---

1   Of all of the people I've trained in Re-Engineering, what comes in second to their primary obstacle of being warped by existing designs, is their self-imposed restraint and second guessing based on their perception that management will reject their ideas based on budget restrictions.

5. How Do We Get to Where We Want to Be?

Unfortunately, we can't do a "big bang" repartitioning of an organization without completely shutting down the business, so we have to Re-Engineer organizational activities *in situ* by:

- Prioritizing the sequence of system replacement so that the critical Business Events are Re-Engineered first. (We can also identify the risks inherent in implementing these Business Events.) Ideally, we would want to replace all the systems that support a complete Business Event Partition at the same time, but in practice, due to budgets and schedules, we may have to replace them one by one. It's important, however, that we do this in full knowledge of how the responses to our current Business Events traverse our existing systems and with a clear understanding of which existing systems need to be replaced first. Depending on how detailed we want to get in Strategic Planning, we can document this plan with the help of a set of models as shown in Figure 11–4. This shows that based on our assessment of the Stock Control System as being high value/high cost, that we will start the Re-Engineering project with this area.

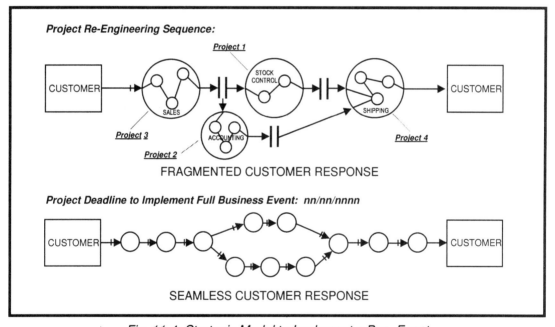

Fig. 11-4: Strategic Model to Implement a Bus. Event

- Creating a Re-Engineering Plan by knowing how the responses to critical Business Events traverse our existing systems. We can develop a Re-Engineering Plan for a more functional repartitioning of existing systems based on Business Events. The plan will be based on:
  - existing partitioning of the organization,
  - the Business Event/System Matrix,
  - the resources available, or
  - our Business Event Methodology.

This plan shows the Business Event implementation sequence and the phasing in of Business Event-partitioned systems, and the phasing out of classically partitioned systems.

- Assessing the budget for future projects to determine both the immediate budget and long-term future budgets. Hopefully, the new budgets will be based on the number of Business Events fulfilled and on the complexity and importance of those Business Events (and not on design boundaries).

We may be Re-Engineering over several years and *must* have the big picture within which to work. From the high-level Business Event Model and the Business Event/System Matrix, we can identify implementation subsets of full partitions, or identify subsets of the business community to receive all or part of a new partition and document this in the Re-Engineering Plan.

As stated previously, because we can isolate Business Events that are connected only by files, we can treat each Business Event (or collection of Business Events) as mini-projects. This becomes very helpful when developing a Strategic Plan for phasing out old systems and phasing in Business Event Partitioned systems. When we look at how we might phase out old systems and Re-Engineer the entire organization, the problem is choosing what strategies to use. We could use a number of strategies for this.

One would be to identify the set of Business Events to implement first by:

- Identifying the most critical Business Events in your organization (i.e., those that pay the bills).

- Identifying the Business Events that occur most frequently.

- Identifying the Business Events that are mandated by laws or regulations.

Another strategy would be to identify the collection of Business Events that create the most important set of Data Elements for running the organization within the Business Event/Data Element Matrix. Once these are identified, the strategy would be to combine the Business Events that create this data with their appropriate Retrieve, Update, and Delete events as the first phase of the Re-Engineering project. With this strategy of implementing whole Business Events at a time we would immediately arrive at Scenario C in Figure 11–5.

A third strategy would be to turn off (comment out of code and procedure manuals) all existing fragments of one Business Event at a time and trap their initial entries into the organization and route them to new, Business Event implemented systems.

A fourth strategy (as mentioned before) would be to use our system value quadrant to identify those systems that are currently causing the most problems and/or costing the most to maintain and to identify the Business Events that would replace these systems. While we are implementing the new Business Event systems and turning off their corresponding old implementations, we may need to provide temporary interface logic and procedures. With this strategy we would end up with Scenario B in the Scope Limited portion of Figure 11–5.

Let me give you an example. If I were new to an organization and were expected to prepare a Strategic Plan, I would probably want a model of all existing systems (i.e., a Design Model showing manual and automated systems). This model would also show the boundaries of these systems as well as their interfaces. Most importantly, I would need a complete Business Event List for the organization. With these tools (or if I were already familiar with the organization), I could use the Business Event List to set up a series of projects over the next "n" years based on the events in the list (if the project team is chartered with ignoring any existing human or computer system boundaries). Otherwise, I may want to rely on the existing system boundary model with the use of Internal Interfaces (see Scenario B of Figure 11–5) and then use this model to phase out the old system boundaries to streamline the organization by Business Event boundaries (and not by Internal Interfaces as shown in Scenario C of Figure 11–5).

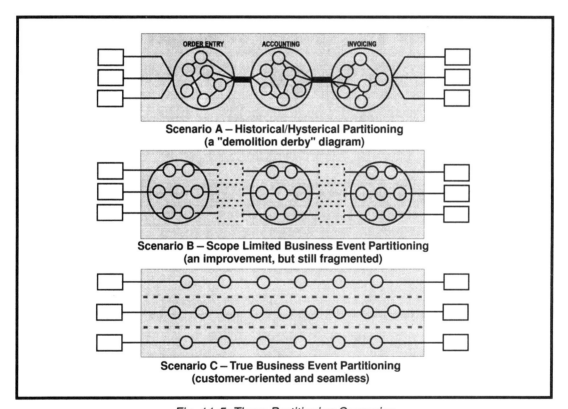

Fig. 11-5: Three Partitioning Scenarios

Note that for some of the above strategies, we will need to create some intermediate databases and files to support the migration of data during the conversion efforts.

Summary

Now that you understand the Business Event Methodology, I can give you my **real** succinct definition of Re-Engineering.

Re-Engineering is the re-alignment of an organization and its resources along Business Event lines.

I believe that the Business Event Methodology is a significant new direction for the entire business community. Applying this approach to an organization as a whole shows clearly what the business *is*, what it *should be*, and why there is a difference.

The greatest achievement was at first and for a time a dream. The oak sleeps in the acorn; the bird waits in the egg. Dreams are the seedlings of realities.

James Allen
As a Man Thinketh

A Logical Conclusion

In this book, we have examined how organizations took some archaeological wrong turns as they tried to implement new systems based on their old ones. I hope that I have shown you the benefits of using the Business Event-based Business Re-Engineering Methodology to eliminate these archaeological wrong turns.

I believe that we need to shift away from the outdated organizational structures of boss-subordinate relationships and departmentalization based on similarity of task. These old paradigms, based on the writings of Adam Smith and Frederick Winslow Taylor, have served us well to get to where we are today, but they have started to hinder us. The need to get beyond these old paradigms is the basis for the Re-Engineering movement. The key question is what new paradigm to use as a replacement.

I propose that the shift be to an organizational partitioning based not on human departmental or computer system boundaries, but to a paradigm that is more fundamental to the true business view — Business Event Partitioning. I believe that this Business Event-based Business Re-Engineering Methodology is a significant new direction for the entire business community and for the systems industry. Applying the approach to an organization as a whole yields significant clarity as to what the organization's business **is**, what it **should be**, and why there is a difference. The structure I'm proposing to replace the old paradigms is one that is organized around:

- Empowered, Business Event Partitioned employee roles.

- Business Event Partitioned computer programs.

- Business Event Partitioned departments.

- Business Event Partitioned systems.

The Re-Engineered organization's budget will be divided along these same lines rather than by traditional Smith/Taylor structures.

I am convinced that the Business Event Methodology, as described in this book, reveals a true business view, and as such, it is the only logical basis for Re-Engineering organizations. These Re-Engineered organizations should grow and last as long as the business need they satisfy is present.

If we apply engineering principles to the processes of creating manual and automated systems, we can gain the benefits of centuries of experience in building safe, high-quality, cost-effective systems. This book has shown three ways in which this could be done:

- Firstly, by using the quality methods and modeling tools available to us.

- Secondly, by re-using components (from single modules up to entire Business Event Partitions).

- Thirdly, by bringing together the preceding two approaches into a Partitioning by Business Event to create seamless, customer-oriented systems.

Re-Engineering's Goals and their Conclusions

It's important to not lose sight of the goals of Re-Engineering as stated in the first chapter. Now we can look back and reiterate these goals and see how to use the Business Event based Business Re-Engineering Methodology to attain them.

- To put the customer first — satisfy customers' needs and expectations by structuring our organization to seamlessly respond to these needs.

  The logical Business Event Partition is completely customer focused. It is not based on any existing implementations or old designs within an organization. Instead, it is driven entirely by the customer's need — the Business Event.

- To get back to business basics — focus on **what** we do rather than **how** we do it by knowing and following the organization's Mission Statement.

  Given the Mission Statement, applying the concepts of logical modeling allows us to focus in on the **what** (analysis) and to not be warped by the old **how** (design).

- To cut red tape — achieve dramatic and measurable improvements in the performance of the organization's implemented systems by creating the most effective processes for delivering products and services.

  The majority of all of the red tape will be at the existing seams (departments, bureaus, etc.) and will therefore represent System Events. The Business Events should be implemented without any old (or new) design seams or old System Events. Therefore, a Business Event based system removes a significant amount of data and processing required by the old design.

- To replace old systems that may be hurting the organization today with quality engineered systems. The new engineered systems (be they manual or automated) will be faster and easier to install and maintain.

  Engineered systems based on Business Events will never hurt the organization; they are the business. When the new implementation follows a Business Event Partitioning, systems will be easier to maintain and install because they are based on Business Issues (as opposed to technical or internal political issues).

- To create systems that promote data conservation and that take advantage of the opportunities for re-using data and processing whenever possible.

  The Business Event Conservator, using the collection of Business Event Matrices and the Business Event Library, ensures the reusability and data conservation of both data and processes.

- To attain the highest quality in the development and delivery of our products and services — use an engineering development discipline and empower employees and use the best available technology in implemented systems.

  We will only realize the benefits of using the best technology and of having empowered employees after we have a Business Model to understand how to take advantage of the technology and how to best use the empowered employees.

- To satisfy the organization's strategic goals — allow for constant improvement in the organization by producing a flexible environment for future change. This means that we create an environment in which we can make business changes that will not affect technology issues and where we can make technology changes without affecting Business Issues.

  The Business Event based Business Re-Engineering Methodology works in perfect unison with the principles of Total Quality Management. Constant system improvement becomes a far more powerful influence when applied at the analysis and design stages in addition to during the implementation phase. The Business Re-Engineering Methodology deliberately separates technology issues from Business Issues as shown in the Business Event Library entries. It is this separation of technology issues from Business Issues that makes it possible to change technology issues independently of Business Issues and vice versa.

Putting together the facets of engineering that we've seen in this book, and applying the principles of Strategic Business Re-Engineering, we're in a position to Re-Engineer the entire organization.

I believe that we now have proven methods and models to successfully Re-Engineer an organization. Before now, the main ingredient I've found missing is a business-oriented methodology that encompasses these proven methods and models. The Business Re-Engineering Methodology described in this book (and from a management perspective in Book II of the series) allows us to bring the entire business view together into one unified model.

I hope that it won't be too long before we find retail outlets for engineered Business Models that an organization can adapt to their particular business needs before using them as the basis for creating new manual and automated systems. In the near future it may be possible that any new systems needed to satisfy a customer's Business Event may be generated automatically (e.g., procedure manuals and computer code generators).

The Author as a Stimulus-Response System

Just as the Smith/Taylor paradigm was refined incrementally over the years to arrive at a system that got us to where we are today, I fully expect (and hope) that the Business Re-Engineering Methodology will be refined more than I have already done.

I believe that all work is, in a sense, iterative and that we should constantly be refining our ideas. This book has gone through many iterations and reflects my latest thinking on the *need for* and the *how to* of Re-Engineering.

Of course, this refinement can't occur in a vacuum. It depends on the critical thinking and input of my audience including Re-Engineers, Business Policy Creators, Business Event Conservators, and other champions of change for the better. I refine my thinking based on this input, so I welcome both your questions and comments about what you encounter in this book. If you do have any comments, please write to me at the address below.

Brian Dickinson
Logical Conclusions, Inc.
P.O. Box 699
Kings Beach, CA 96143

Quality, value, <u>creates</u> the subjects and objects in the world. The facts do not exist until value has created them. If your values are rigid, you can't really learn new facts. This often shows up in premature diagnosis, when you're sure you know what the trouble is, and then when it isn't, you're stuck. Then you've got to find some new clues, but before you can find them, you've got to clear your head of old opinions. If you're plagued with value rigidity, you can fail to see the real answer even when it's staring you right in the face because you can't see the new answer's importance.

Robert Pirsig
Zen and the Art of Motorcycle Maintenance
— An Inquiry into Values

Quality in Re-Engineering

F irst the good news — there is now an accepted movement towards quality conscious management where we recognize that we should approach zero defects with such things as continuous improvement and error-free software for computer systems. The Systems Development profession has finally evolved to a point where we can now build quality systems that have **zero** defects (i.e., no bugs) and that do not deteriorate during production and modification (they can last as long as the business they support). Thank goodness, because systems are becoming more complex. Lives are dependent on them in medical systems and air traffic control systems. Bad computer systems can shut down an organization and put many people out of work.

Now the bad news — there aren't many Systems Development "professionals" around and the vast majority of systems in production today don't even come close to zero defects. Even my mother knows what a programming "bug" is, and she can't read a line of computer code. Most computer systems software suffers from hidden bugs that cause them to fail frequently and are so difficult to modify that even the people who built them expect them to blow up and to have short production lives.

Its not uncommon to have Data Processing (D.P.) systems last as little as 2-3 years. Even though these and other aspects of businesses are subject to constant change (both technology- and business-related), many existing D.P. systems on which they depend were not built for flexibility and maintainability. In fact, Systems professionals at most companies are familiar with the large, old, monolithic, difficult-to-change D.P. system that "bites back" whenever they attempt a change. Systems developers who are accustomed to this kind of system and don't know a better way to develop systems, will generally tend to create new systems in the same style — thus perpetuating the same undesirable system characteristics. Systems developers should not make an organization be at the mercy of technology, allowing it to dictate the lifetime characteristics of business systems. I should also point out that manual systems that support a business have an equal number of reasons for obsolescence and also suffer from unnecessary defects.

There is very little point in practicing all of the techniques covered in this book without applying high quality standards.

A Working Definition of Quality

Having been involved in teaching engineering disciplines for systems development since the 1970s, I've often wondered what quality really is. It's always seemed to me to be an ethereal idea, a feeling if you like.

For many years I felt that quality was "attention to detail." But that didn't seem to ring true when I found myself in my home life building something in my garage like a dog kennel and literally putting it together in a matter of hours using 2 by 4s and plywood. I knew that even though I hadn't paid too much attention to detail, I was quite satisfied with the resultant kennel. It actually served my needs and I felt satisfied with the product.

One of the books I read that was fairly significant to me in this area of quality was *"Zen and the Art of Motorcycle Maintenance"* by Robert Pirsig. I found it interesting that in one of the chapters of this book, Pirsig thought that the divorce of art and engineering was an archaeological wrong turn and quite unnatural. That seemed to satisfy my inner feelings that there was some sort of pride that went into work which had more affinity with art than it did with engineering discipline. However, this feeling wasn't an easy thing to teach in my seminars. It's quite difficult to instill a feeling of quality in one's students.

Then I read a book called *"Quality Is Free"* by Philip Crosby that summed up something that I could put my finger on, nail down, and teach. That something was that quality is simply "conformance to requirements."

What I consider to be quality is the consistent satisfaction of ethical requirements. The requirements and their satisfaction must both be measurable. Based on what I've just said, here's my definition of Quality — building on Crosby's definition.

Quality is recognized in a product or service when it satisfies both the ethical and measurable requirements of the requester. It is accomplished with pride of ownership on the part of everybody involved in satisfying those requirements.

This definition satisfied the reason that I felt comfortable after having built a dog kennel that I knew hadn't had too much attention to detail paid to it. The kennel satisfied what I was trying to produce and that was something that would satisfy my requirements for a temporary home for my dog. (Notice that I was the requester, not my dog — identifying the real customer is important.)

Although I do still believe that there's something to do with art and engineering brought together in pride in your work, that might have something to do with my value systems. But certainly we can all agree that quality is "conformance to requirements", especially when you look on requirements as having many different faces. What I mean by this is that we can have requirements for the system to build systems (what we call the Meta Model — see Figure A–1) as well as requirements for the system that results from it. In other words, you can have quality built into a methodology (into the practices and the step-by-step procedures) for building a house as well as for the resulting house that would come from using that methodology.

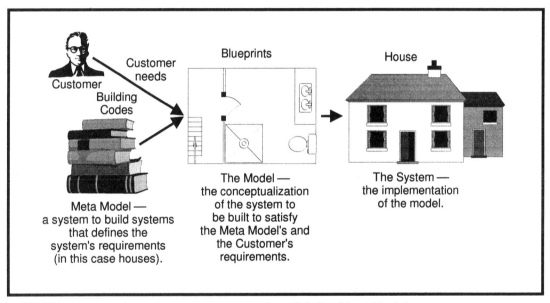

Fig. A-1: Example of an Existing Meta Model

So we can have requirements for the methodology, we can have requirements for the analysis, we can have requirements for the design, and we can have requirements for implementation (see Figure A–15). By building in the quality at each one of these stages, we can produce a resulting system that has quality (or at least something that everyone would agree has quality) because it conforms to the customer requirements in analysis, to what the designer wanted as requirements in the solution, and to what the implementor wanted in requirements for the implemented product.

Some History of the Quality Movement

What follows is a brief outline listing the milestones of the evolution of attaining quality in processes and systems.

In 1930 a Professor Shewart working at Bell Laboratories identified that most of the problems resulting from a system were in the system itself and not in its implementation. He recognized that we could measure a process that produced some product or service by focusing on the process' inputs and outputs. The areas of his study were the tasks and functions that took place in the office environment. One of his ideas was to use those measurements of the input into and the output from a process to eliminate the variations in the quality of a final product that came out of that process. This approach was called Process Control and its goal was to ensure an acceptable range of quality in some finished product.

Then, an individual by the name of Dr. W. Edwards Demming advocated the principles of quality management in production to put over the idea that we should eliminate after-the-fact inspections and improve the quality of the process itself. Demming introduced the concept of being aware of the customer as the person who ultimately had to be satisfied with the results of a process. He also recognized the quality added value to a product or service. His approach therefore extended the ideas of Process Control to include the customer who up to that point was an entity totally external to the organization that produced the product or service.

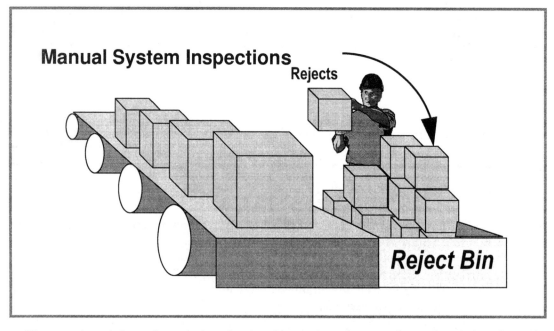

He questioned the value of after-the-fact inspections because he realized that the only thing you can do if an inspector finds a bad product is to throw the product away. Demming was a revolutionary when he said that we shouldn't produce the bad product in the first place. Unfortunately, the managers in the United States did not listen to Demming, but the Japanese in the late 1940s and 1950s did. Anybody reading this book who is old enough to remember the products that came out of Japan in the 1940s and 1950s probably relates to the term "Japanese Junk." The kind of products that I remember the Japanese companies exporting in those days were small gadgets and toys that were flimsy and cheap.

The next phase of the evolution occurred when Dr. Demming and another person by the name of Dr. Joseph M. Juran convinced the Japanese to look at the principals of statistical control and process control and built-in quality. They introduced some of the basic graphical models that we now almost take for granted as a means of representing processes.

In the short space of a few decades, we no longer think of Japanese products as junk or cheap. The quality of the products of that nation has been completely turned around. This does not mean that a car coming out of Japan never breaks down. What it does mean is that we think of that car as being of higher than average quality. I believe that Demming and Juran were the only Americans who were given medals by the Emperor of Japan. An award was created, called the Demming Award, that is still sought today by companies looking to be associated with quality products and services.

In the 80s we saw a lot of these ideas come back to the United States from Japan. One such idea was that of "Quality Circles" as put forward by Professor Ishikawa. This idea centered around a process where teams would manage themselves and introduce quality on their own (and not be managed by a hierarchical system). The idea here was that the best people to come up with quality suggestions were the people who were doing the work, not the people who were <u>managing</u> the work.

One of my own modest contributions to the evolution of ensuring quality in the processes that create systems or products was that of introducing the importance of understanding the Stimulus/Response and Process/Memory nature of systems. Another of my contributions to the field was the idea of using a collection of modeling tools based around Business Events to aid in obtaining quality. I have also advocated for many years the creation of "seamless" systems to respond to customer needs along Business Event lines (ignoring traditional departmental or other organizational boundaries).

Today we see many organizations adopting the ideas of quality management. Some people know this as *Total Quality Management (TQM)*. Once you've got a process in place in a human system, it can be continuously improved on the fly. This is one of the basic ideas of Professor Ishikawa (building on the work of Juran and Demming) — that we should apply continuous improvements by the people who do the work themselves.

Unfortunately, it's rather difficult for a computer program to improve itself once it's been written and installed on a system. A production computer system typically keeps the same level of quality for its life cycle as it had on day 1 of its installation (or its quality could even deteriorate due to poor maintenance).

An implemented computer program doesn't care about satisfying customer needs, but a human being should. The basic idea here is that as a human being in a job, you should no longer look upon the procedure that is put in place today as cast in concrete. In fact, the focus should be on the question: "Is this satisfying the customer's needs?" And, when it isn't, we need to constantly change that process. Of course this involves everyone. It involves the people who conduct the customer interaction, the people inside the system who may never see a customer (but who nevertheless are satisfying the customer's goals), and the people who are the leaders and facilitators helping/facilitating those workers do the process itself.

I see a number of companies now seeking awards such as the Demming Award. (In the United States we also have the Malcomb Baldridge Award and in England, the ISO 9000 Award.) All of these awards are aimed at recognizing the introduction of quality in organizations.

We can sum up the idea of Total Quality Management as making sure that we don't satisfy customer needs after the fact, but rather that we try to do it the first time, every time. It also means that we constantly improve the process to be able to improve how we deliver the product.

The ironic thing about this discussion is captured in Philip Crosby's book, *"Quality Is Free."* The irony is that actually producing a quality product ends up being cheaper overall by the time you include customer satisfaction (and not losing customers) — never mind the cost of throwing away products during the process and all of the costs of installing inspections and testing mechanisms in system (and, of course, the costs of fixing problems and "putting out fires" while producing a product). So, as I said earlier, I would even go further than Philip Crosby's statement that "QUALITY IS FREE" and claim that QUALITY SAVES YOU MONEY IN DEVELOPMENT AND MAKES YOU MONEY IN PRODUCTION.

Quality in Human-based Systems

When I teach the concept of Business Engineering in management seminars, most people can relate to the following comparison with the construction industry.

When a buyer contracts to have a house built, they expect the correct house will get built. But it may not measure up to the level of quality that the buyer wants if the buyer doesn't get involved during the development stage. If, however, the buyer relates their requirements to the architect up front in the development stages and agrees with the blueprint model produced, no after-the-fact "Acceptance Testing" is needed on their part. Building inspectors ensure conformance to established design and technological standards, but they cannot ensure conformance to a purchaser's requirements.

I'm not saying here that we can eliminate all errors and defects in systems. I am saying that we should reduce them to the same level as other engineering disciplines by holding proper reviews and inspections. The errors that get through will be natural human errors, not errors caused by the engineering methodology. We have many quality assurance techniques available to us: Total Quality Management, walkthroughs, reviews, iterative user/analyst dialogue, and presentations. But I want to emphasize that these will be effective only if we have clear, representative requirements and design models that customers and Business Policy Creators can understand.

You could take a big picture and say that everybody who has brought new ideas into the business world (such as producing a good mission statement and a good set of objectives in a project initiation document or Project Charter) has had the intention to document the quality required at each level (strategic, tactical, etc.).

The JFK goal of putting a man on the moon was an example of a good, measurable objective. It was a requirement that we could measure against and use to produce all lower level requirements to accomplish that goal. That excellent one-liner was a measurable requirement that could be developed at the lower levels into individual objectives, goals, and requirements that would aim at satisfying that one global and measurable requirement.

Of course we have both managerial and technical requirements. So, we could look at this idea of quality being conformance to requirements from more than a single- or two-dimensional view. We can only resolve conflicts between product, project, and business requirements if we specify these aspects, quantify them, and model the potential alternative solutions. A vital component of Business Re-Engineering is a project life-cycle that advocates engineering disciplines.

The space shuttle, which was an implementation of JFK's one-line requirement, can have technical quality. However, these quality requirements can then be overridden by some managerial requirements. We saw the result of this when the Challenger blew up. We could conclude from this that not all requirements then have a positive outcome. In which case, we could say that not all requirements have positive quality. So we must introduce the word "ethical" into our definition of quality.

People Issues and Quality

Let me address the subject of quality in another context. In striving for systems quality, we have to be aware of the many different issues in systems development. Figure A-2 shows one view of these issues — Project, Product, and People.

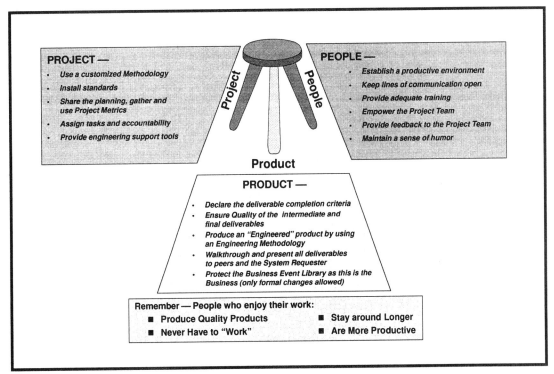

Fig. A-2: People Issues and Quality

This book concentrates on **product** issues (deliverables — both intermediate and final system) and Book II focuses on **project** issues (how deliverables are actually developed via plans and schedules). But there's a third issue, one that I've come to see as being of paramount importance—the **people** issue.

None of the latest techniques and methodologies can compensate for poor people management. Two of my colleagues, Tom DeMarco and Tim Lister, have done some good work in the area of people management, and I strongly recommend their book, *Peopleware*, for the people aspects of the Systems profession.

Quality in Automated Systems

Note, if we look at the software side of the computer industry, we don't find anywhere near the same advances as we do in hardware (see Figure A–3). In general, we don't even see a 50% increase in system maintainability, reliability, or programmer productivity over the old days of programming (never mind orders of magnitude in improvements). [1]

Over the 30 years plus of my observing the development of computer hardware and software, I have noticed that hardware became much more reliable with the most dramatic improvements starting in the 1970s. This improvement has continued steadily, although more slowly. We now more or less take the hardware's reliability for granted. Software on the other hand got slightly better in the early years of systems development, but starting in the mid 1980s, overall software quality began to decline. The early gains were due to the fact that many software systems were designed to accomplish fairly simple tasks and that Software and Information Engineering techniques were introduced to clean up the development process and eliminate bugs. In the mid 1980s with the proliferation of the PC and its software, many programs' tasks got increasingly complex while their developers did not follow any kind of engineering disciplines when creating PC software. A crash that brought down a mainframe was (and is) treated very seriously while a bug that brought down a PC was (and unfortunately still is) somehow accepted by the product's customers.

---

1   I believe one reason for this is that while people regard hardware as a tangible asset, they do not treat software the same way; after all you can't touch software, see it, or feel it. Nonetheless, software is a major asset, especially when we consider the amount of processing that can be done by a well-programmed machine. Think of the army of clerical staff you would need to do the equivalent volume of work, and then figure in the costs of staff accommodation and benefits. The vast majority of companies today simply couldn't function without computer support.

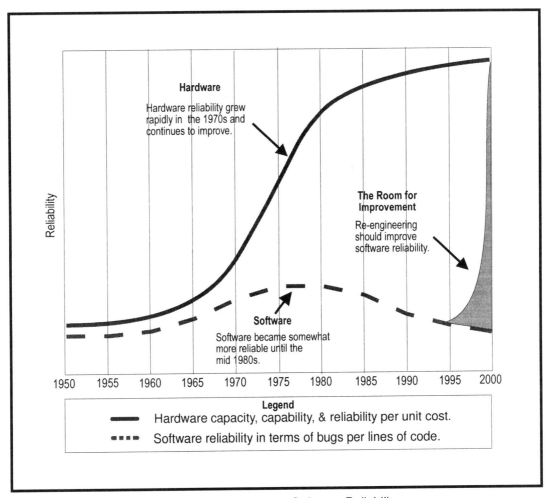

Fig. A-3: Hardware vs. Software Reliability

As an example from my own background, people in the Data Processing (D.P.) Industry often say that you can't guarantee zero defects in software. This strikes me as odd. Why can we build reliable computer hardware, subject though it is to variations in temperature and humidity, and to damage by dropping and misuse, but we can't build robust software which isn't vulnerable to any of these? In fact, quality software's only natural predators are untrained maintenance programmers. So I find it very strange that people bounce a laptop computer around on an aircraft, expecting it to withstand such abuse, but don't expect their software to have zero defects. This simply indicates the immaturity of the software industry. The only excuse for these defects are development management's and the purchasing public's willingness to accept them.

I believe the software industry is headed for engineering status. The question is, "how quickly, and how smoothly?" My intent, and that of many others, is to promote a speedy and easy transition of software development practices to those of an engineering discipline. For the business people reading this book, what follows is the ammunition to take back to the data processing folks who say zero defects can't be achieved. We've already talked about what's meant by the term "engineering" in the preface.

I was lucky enough to come to the United States in the mid-1970s when the equivalent of the human-based system quality revolution (via Demming, etc.) was taking place on the Data Processing side. Let me identify the history that I saw (and luckily was a part of) of introducing quality to the Data Processing world.

In the early days of D.P., the requirements for a system were gathered together haphazardly by someone called a "programmer", using no particular formal method, and possibly in collaboration with the requester of the system, typically known as the "user."

Sometimes a unit called Quality Assurance attempted to ensure that the system was "correct", (i.e., that it conformed to user requirements). However, the only modeling and documentation tools available for verifying systems and programs were logic flow charts and often just the completed program listings themselves. In fact, quality was usually evaluated "after the fact" by testing the programs exhaustively via unit testing, system testing, integration testing, acceptance testing, and observing the system in production. As errors were discovered during these tests, programmers made "patches" to the actual code and did not usually reflect these patches in the flowcharts. And the patches often resulted in additional errors being generated inadvertently — the so-called error "ripple effect."

Typically, the programmer delivered systems to the final production environment knowing that a number of errors still remained undetected. These defects were usually regarded as inevitable and were affectionately known as "bugs." *(I call this the "What's a few bugs between friends?" syndrome in System development efforts.)*

Because of the unreliability and expense of modifying these bug-ridden systems, very few of them seemed to last beyond seven to ten years in production, even though business requirements hadn't changed. And if they did last longer, there was usually some poor maintenance programmer begging to have the system rewritten.

If, as Philip Crosby has observed, "Quality is conformance to requirements" — analysis requirements, design requirements, and implementation requirements, and so on — then the problem of proving that a system had quality was further compounded by the fact that business and system requirements were seldom formally defined. Thus a good yardstick may not even have existed for measuring or proving quality. Finding errors, omissions, and "undocumented features" (i.e., bugs) during the user acceptance testing of the final code became an industry substitute for good analysis. In other words, analysts simply relied on acceptance testing to specify final requirements.

The Introduction of Quality into Data Processing

I started in D.P. in 1964 and Figure A –4 summarizes what I've seen of the evolution of the D.P. Industry. Referring to Figure A–4, the 1980s seemed to be an incubation period for Software and Information Engineering. People either attempted to use the new methods but only with paper and pencil, or held back to see if this stuff was just another fad.

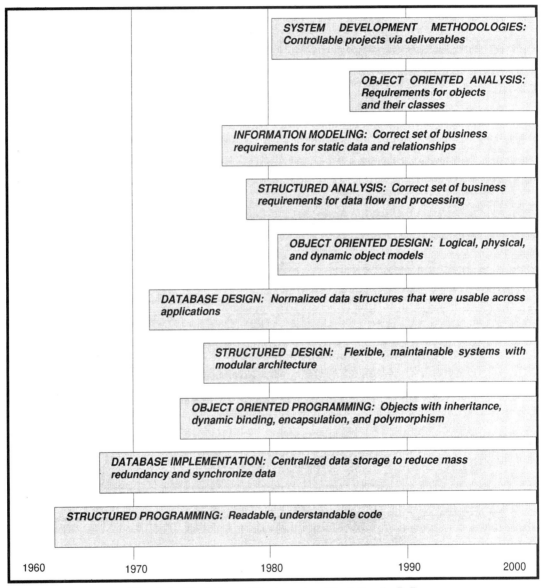

Fig. A-4: Evolution of Engineering Discipline in D.P.

Of course, we did see Object Oriented Analysis and Design introduced during this same period. As engineers, we owe it to ourselves to be absorbing Object Oriented techniques into our tool-kit. A true engineer will select the appropriate techniques to use on each project depending on the type of system being studied and what best depicts their business view.

Figure A–5 shows the major engineering trends over the four decades of data processing history. In the following pages I will use my background to look at the Systems and Information Engineering aspects in a little more detail so that we can see why each was necessary, how it came about, and how it formed a foundation for later enhancements that enabled the D.P. Industry to deliver higher quality products and systems to its customers.

Quality during Implementation — Processing

The serious lack of quality in computer systems was obviously a cause for concern in the newly emerging D.P. profession. In the latter part of the 1960s, a global conference was held in the United States on the so-called "software crisis." Edsgar Dijkstra, a concerned D.P. pioneer, offered certain recommendations for cleaning up poorly constructed, unreadable computer code, and for providing a way to prove the correctness of code logic. These recommendations became the foundation for Structured Programming, and include the following:

- The use of only the fundamental logic constructs of sequence, selection, and iteration

- Improved code readability through the use of indentation to show logic subordination and block structure

Figure A–5 shows a sample of structured logic. Here we see selection, iteration, and sequence structures and how the use of indentation clearly exposes the structure of the logic.

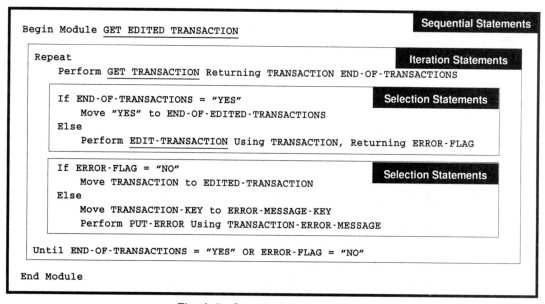

Fig. A-5: Sample Structured Logic

It took a long and slow period of infiltration to get Structured Programming into the D.P. Industry. It assists the software-building process by bringing the necessary degree of quality into the coding effort and by defining how to produce readable, non-idiosyncratic computer code.

Quality during Implementation — Data

During the same era of the 1960s, data structures (e.g., files) were just as idiosyncratic as programs. We found mass redundancy across sequential files that required sorting, merging, and extraction in order for a particular program to use their data. This also led to non-synchronized data, for example, changes were made to the data in one file but not to their sorted or extracted derivatives. These files were obviously difficult to change because of their rigid, sequential structure.

Indexed and direct-access file structures were introduced, but these were still organized around complex, monolithic files. Databases were introduced to overcome this type of problem where we could hold partitioned segments of data in a centralized repository of data, accessible by multiple programs, thereby improving the quality (in this case, integrity) of the data.

Unfortunately, some of the first databases of this era tended to be based on access and storage characteristics, and on physical descriptions of things in the company at that time, such as customer orders, transactions, and accounts (see Figure A–6). Such databases also had great difficulty absorbing changes. Despite these shortcomings, however, databases greatly helped to clear up many data problems. Today, databases are widely accepted as a major aid in reducing redundancy and obtaining synchronized data.

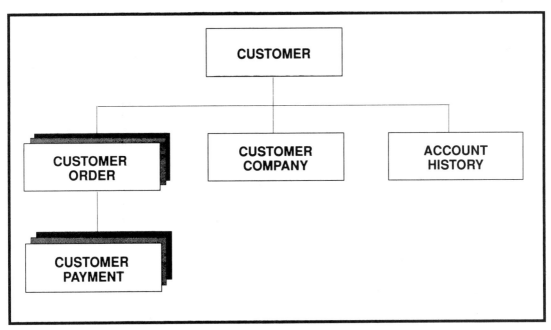

Fig. A-6: Sample Hierarchical Database Structure

Quality during Design — Processing

As with many clean-up operations, Structured Programming exposed the pollution upstream, that is, in the computer system design activity. In fact, historically, many representations of the total system development life-cycle did not even portray a separate "design" activity — design just happened somewhere during the analysis and programming phases.

The design activity lays out the architecture, or overall structure, of the system before the actual code is written. In the early 1970s, other D.P. pioneers, such as Ed Yourdon and Larry Constantine, introduced the ideas of Structured Design, bringing quality to the internal system architecture. Systems were becoming more complex and computers were being used for more than just simple reporting and data summarization. Structured Design injected quality into systems architecture by *partitioning* large, complex systems into small, manageable pieces, or *modules*, organized hierarchically under the management of control modules. The intermediate control modules made it possible to push responsibility down to lower-level modules and hide data and data structures that were not important to the main activities of the program.

We found that small, partitioned modules were easier to test, to prove correct, and to maintain. Also, they could be re-used in other parts of the system and in other systems, thus avoiding the need to rewrite everything from scratch — the "reinventing the wheel" problem found in many D.P. environments.

A modeling tool called a *Structure Chart* (see Figure A–7) was introduced to show the system architecture graphically. This model provided D.P. professionals with a tool to show the:

• Partitioning rules,

• Hierarchical levels of control, and

• Levels of understanding necessary for complex computer solutions.

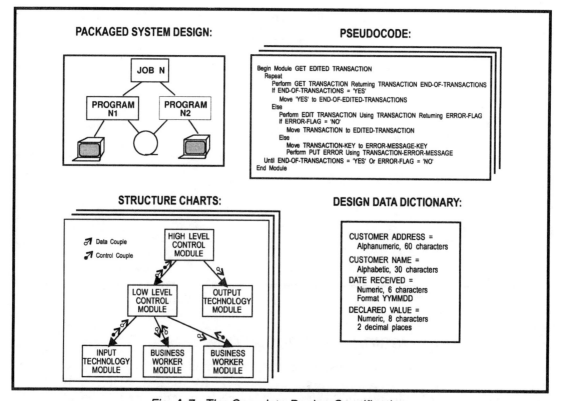

Fig. A-7: The Complete Design Specification

With the introduction of Structured Design, the quality of system architecture could now be established prior to writing the code. The quality could be evaluated by observing:

- How well the system was partitioned into manageable "single-minded" modules — the measure of "cohesion."

- How minimally a module was connected to, or dependent on, other modules — the measure of "coupling."

- How easily the resultant system could absorb future changes.

Structured Design assisted the design effort by advocating the use of:

- Structure Charts — hierarchically-partitioned, modularized models.

- Design Data Dictionary — common, detailed definitions of all input and output data with their formats.

- Module Specifications — detailed, verifiable logic or pseudocode.

- System and program design quality rules — measurable levels of coupling and cohesion.

Figure A–7 shows how these parts form the complete Design Specification. Today, Structured Design is accepted, in one form or another, by the majority of D.P. professionals.

Quality during Design — Data

With physical databases in place, the need for database design emerged. We needed a view of the data structure that did not get involved in a particular database implementation, but concerned itself with the structure of cohesive data groupings and their associations. Pioneers such as Edgar Codd and Chris Date introduced the ideas of normalization and partitioning of data in the early 1970s. These techniques produced cohesive, logical data structures that did not depend on their physical implementation. These normalized groupings partitioned the data to a degree of independence where the data could be used across many systems (see Figure A–8).

SEMINAR INDENT	SEMINAR CLIENT	SEMINAR LOCATION	SEMINAR START DATE	SEMINAR INSTRUCTOR
ASA03	SMITH IND.	DENVER	01/07/94	DICKINSON
ASA05	SMITH IND.	SAN FRAN	01/07/94	BROWN
ASD02	D&O INC.	SAN DIEGO	01/14/94	RYMER
ASD03	WILSON'S	SAN FRAN	01/28/94	STUBBS
ASD04	SMITH IND.	SAN FRAN	02/04/94	EDGEHILL
MSE02	D&O INC.	SAN DIEGO	02/14/94	BARSTAD

STUDENT NAME	STUDENT DEPT	STUDENT TITLE
R. LEE	H18	SNRANLYST
K. STEPHENS	Z45	PGMR/ANYLST
J. JOHNSON	A14	MNGR
A. SMITH	B34	SNRANYLST
D. LUI	Z45	PGMR
F. WATSON	G23	MNGR
K. JWOSKY	X19	PGMR/ANYLST
J. MARTIN	TOB	ANYLST/DSNR
R. COSTA	VEN	DSNR
P. GRAHAM	198	ANYLST
D. KRUGER	078	DSNR
R. MECHLER	023	SNR DSNR
V. BRANNING	C29	ANYLST/PGMR
P. HWANG	GRT	MNGR
F. KRUIL	URD	ANYLST

SEMINAR IDENT	STUDENT NAME
ASA03	R. LEE
ASA03	K. STEPHENS
ASA03	J. JOHNSON
ASA05	A. SMITH
ASA05	D. LUI
ASA05	F. WATSON
ASD02	K. JWOSKY
ASD02	J. MARTIN
ASD03	R. COSTA
ASD03	R. LEE
ASD03	P. GRAHAM
ASD03	D. KRUGER
ASD04	R. MECHLER
ASD04	J. JOHNSON
ASD04	V. BRANNING
MSE02	F. WATSON
MSE02	P. HWANG
MSE02	F. KRUIL
MSE02	D. LUI

SEMINAR CLIENT	OPEN CLIENT
SMITH IND.	Y
D&O INC.	Y
WILSON'S	N

Fig. A-8: Normalized Data Tables

The data groupings and their elements were defined in textual or simple graphical specifications. At this point in database design, many practitioners were mainly concerned with access to data, and many models depicted access paths rather than relationships. Access Path Diagrams are now used for this purpose (see Figure A–9). Also, in order to obtain efficient physical database structures, many of the database designs were implemented without being fully normalized. Today, database design concepts are widely-accepted in the D.P. Industry.

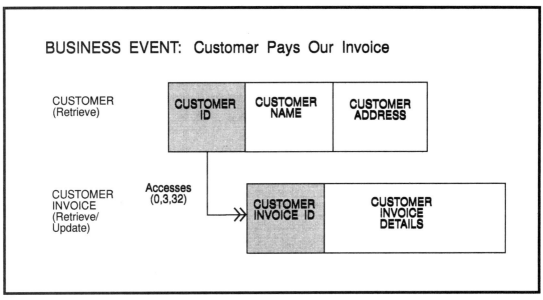

Fig. A-9: Logical Access Path Diagram (LAPD)

Quality during Analysis — Processing

The introduction of Structured Design exposed the lack of clarity and rigor in the existing methods of requirements analysis — the activity before design. The problem of poor requirements specifications prompted other D.P. pioneers such as Tom DeMarco, Chris Gane, and Trish Sarson to introduce the ideas of Structured Analysis in the late 1970s, bringing quality to the process of defining the business requirements for a system. Using a set of graphical and semantic models, based on the users' non-D.P. views of the flow and transformation of data, Structured Analysis helped D.P. professionals to deliver systems that conformed to business needs. Structured Analysis allowed them first to model the business needs in a way that users could easily confirm as correct.

Structured Analysis took the viewpoint of *data* first providing a smooth development transition to Structured Design. By using partitioning concepts similar to those of Structured Design and by advocating a graphical model called a *Data Flow Diagram*, the analyst could now pre-establish the quality of the users' requirements without ambiguity. In this way, the analyst could ensure that the statement of user requirements conformed to the actual business requirements and that those requirements could be easily verified prior to considering any design technology.

To assist the analysis activity, Structured Analysis advocated using:

- Data Flow Diagrams — network *flow-of-data* models.

- Analysis Data Dictionary — detailed data composition definitions.

- Process Specifications — partitioned descriptions of data transformations (i.e., processing).

Figure A–10 shows how these components together make up the Structured Analysis Specification.

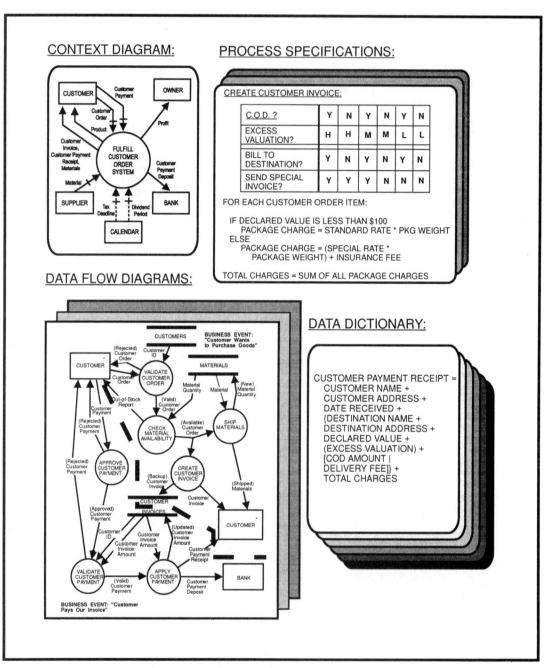

Fig. A-10: A Complete Process Specification

Quality during Analysis — Data

The introduction of database design, in turn, exposed the lack of clarity about business needs in the analysis of data. The *static* view of information systems has evolved into the discipline of Information Modeling, bringing quality to the specification of business-related information needs. Pioneers such as Peter Chen and Matt Flavin focused on the analysis of data. Information Modeling introduced another level of quality by identifying conformance to requirements based on the users' non-D.P. view of business entities and the relationships between them.

Again, the concepts of partitioning (this time of *business data* using a graphical model — the Entity Relationship Diagram or ERD) were used to verify the quality of the static business view of data. Figure A–11 shows two styles of Information Model.

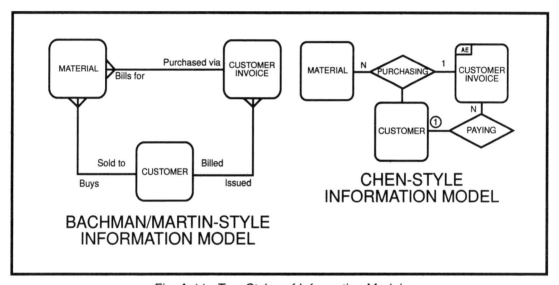

Fig. A-11: Two Styles of Information Models

Information Modeling assisted analyzing static data needs by advocating the use of:

- Entity Relationship Diagram — an implementation-independent model of stored data partitioned into entities and their relationships

- Entity Specifications — definitions of business data groupings

- Relationship Specifications — optional definitions of associations between entities

- Data Element Specifications — definitions of detailed data facts and data integrity rules

Quality for Real-time Systems

The analysis models we've looked at so far satisfy requirements for:

- Data flowing through a system

- Data grouping and the structure of an organization

However, when we have a requirement to specify a system characteristic that is not based on data flow or data structure, but rather on situations and conditions (i.e., control) that occur as part of the business, we need additional analysis symbols. Simple control issues such as the one shown in Figure A–12 can be indicated on a Data Flow Diagram, but not complex control issues.

Scientific and real-time environments create the need to specify control requirements. It's worth noting that many books that address control models tend to focus in on design problems, for example, the control of an automated teller machine (ATM), computer terminal, and printing devices. We need to separate design control issues from analysis control issues. That is, during analysis we are interested in those issues that depict business controls.

In a non-real-time (commercial) environment, the external interfaces and what happens in them provide the *context* for our system and are beyond our control. That's why we make them "external" interfaces. In a real-time environment the external interfaces, or system context, may be devices like sensors, gauges, and switches. We should not class these as design issues, just as we would not class a customer as a design issue in a commercial environment.

When we think of requirements for applications like controlling an elevator bank in a large building, controlling the traffic lights at a complex road junction, or monitoring a process control device (see Figure A–13), we find it very difficult to specify all the requirements using Data Flow Diagrams or an Entity-Relationship Diagram.

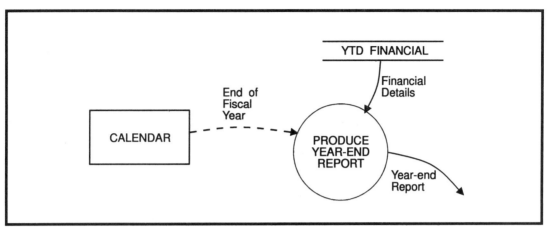

Fig. A-12: A Simple Control Issue

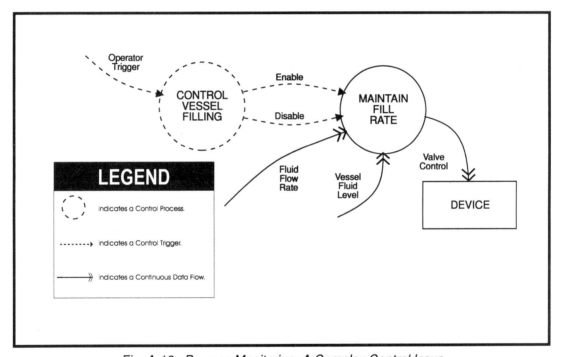

Fig. A-13: Process Monitoring: A Complex Control Issue

During real-time systems analysis, we encounter:

- Flows that do not have data content such as the fact that someone in an elevator wants to stop it

- Situations that require our system to respond to the same stimulus in different ways depending on the current conditions such as someone wanting to go up when all the elevators are on the way down

These situations force us to find a new way of modeling them. Notice that these conditions will not be affected by the design (automated or manual), so we still need some additional way of specifying the control requirements.

We can use a State Transition Diagram (STD) for specifying complex control. For example, Figure A–14 shows a State Transition Diagram for a coin-operated vending machine and Table A–1 shows the corresponding State Transition Table.

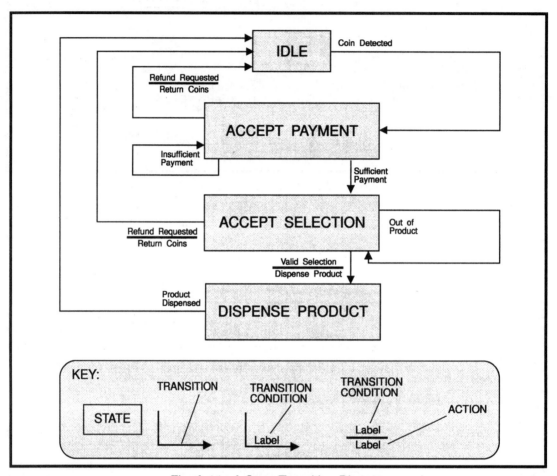

Fig. A-14: A State Transition Diagram

STATE	EVENT	ACTION	TRANSITION TO
Idle	Coin Detected		Accept Payment
Accept Payment	Sufficient Payment		Accept Selection
	Insufficient Payment		Accept Payment
	Refund Requested	Return Coins	Idle
Accept Selection	Valid Selection	Dispense Product	Dispense Product
	Out of Product		Accept Selection
	Refund Requested	Return Coins	Idle
Dispense	Product Dispensed		Idle

Table A–1: State Transition Table

As seen in *Chapter 4*, it's very important for the synergy of modeling methods (and for the Unified System Model) that the different models do not usurp each other.

I've also found that a State Transition Diagram helps the business world when a particular on-line device is identified during the design activity. If the device has states of operation that are not stimulated by data but by compound conditions, the State Transition Diagrams help show protocol issues.

The Management of Quality

Once the D.P. Industry had identified at least one new set of methods that would bring technical quality to analysis, design, and implementation, the next important question was how to integrate all these new methods and their models into a cohesive discipline. Many individuals (including yours truly) and organizations have proposed methodologies, or guidelines, on how to combine the new technical set of methods into a System Development Life-Cycle (SDLC). Such methodologies also include the control management aspects of software development such as planning, scheduling, budgeting, and quality assurance.

To aid leadership in ensuring quality and controlling the development of a system, methodologies also recommended management models that enhanced planning, provided direction, identified a particular project's intermediate deliverables, and monitored project progress. Many models, such as Program Evaluation and Review Technique (PERT), Critical Path Method (CPM), and Gantt Charts have been recommended.

Methodologies based on the emerging engineering approach aided leadership in bringing quality to the task of managing a project's activities and building quality into each intermediate deliverable, and therefore, to the final deliverable (the installed system). We'll explore this issue in Book II of this Re-Engineering Series which specifies the *Strategic Business Engineering Methodology* and how to manage it.

The Use of Models for Obtaining Quality

What pervades all the new methods that have been introduced into systems development? They all use graphical models as their documentation and communication medium. These models form the system's documentation as a by-product of the development work itself rather than documentation being created in a boring, resource-consuming, and error-prone after-the-fact task.

The reason I got into teaching in the first place was to improve poor quality systems that I saw in my profession. Each time I taught the ideas of Systems Analysis or Information Engineering, it always seemed to me that you could look at the resultant models and specifications that I was advocating and ask: "Are those quality too?"

Professionals can obtain quality by ensuring, as a pre-planned and pre-determined project characteristic, that each intermediate deliverable in the system development life-cycle has the necessary level of quality.

Computer Support for Re-Engineering

By the time you've read to this point you must have realized the amount of effort needed to capture and manage the information required to fully Re-Engineer an organization. I strongly recommend that you have computer assistance for keeping track of this information.

The Data Processing world introduced CASE (Computer-Aided System Engineering) tools to meet this challenge. In the D.P. Industry CASE emerged in the 1980s, spurred on by the personal computer and such technologies as local-area networking. Many systems shops have been quick to embrace the new CASE tools and have already built systems more easily because CASE helps handle the sheer volume of development information about the system.

Before we discuss CASE further, however, I feel that it's necessary to state that unfortunately some CASE vendors are compounding D.P.'s problems by promising that their CASE tool will help solve analysis problems. Unless the tools contain powerful artificial intelligence programs (and I haven't yet seen one that does), this is not true. Certainly, they "aid" System Engineering with computers (maybe that's why they are called Computer-*Aided* System Engineering tools), but many buyers fail to notice the "aided" part of the acronym. We can do a lot of damage a lot faster and more efficiently with CASE, just as it's dangerous for someone who doesn't know how to fly to pilot a jet plane.

Please don't regard these comments as criticism of the usefulness of CASE tools. When I have conducted Systems Engineering projects without them, it's been a real pain to keep documentation in good order and up-to-date, while maintaining integrity between the various models. I do want to emphasize the letters in the acronym — we must know *SE* (System Engineering) before we can use *CA* (Computer-Aided) tools.

Any automated tools used in a Re-Engineering effort should provide on-line facilities to support:

- Graphical assistance in modeling either computer or manual-based systems.

- Integrity and syntax verification within and across engineering models.

- A Central Repository for information (often termed an *Encyclopedia*).

- Prototyping to generate a working model of an automated system's interfaces — menus, screens, reports — without necessarily incurring the overheads of coding the internals. Some form of prototyping should also be available to allow testing of the physical environment present in a human-based system.

- Support should also be present for project and methodology management in efforts to develop either human- or computer-based systems. Because a project is a "system to develop systems," an entire methodology can be held as a Meta Model from which project managers can produce customized project models for their particular project.

- For automated systems, some form of code generation should be included to create computer source code directly from the comprehensive information captured in the Central Repository.

At the time that this book was in production Logical Conclusions, Inc. was building a computer aided Re-Engineering tool for both manual and automated systems. This tool is the Logical Conclusion's Business Re-Engineering Automated Toolkit (BRAT). It is designed to help keep track of the information used in the course of Re-Engineering an organization.

The Benefits of Computer Supported Re-Engineering

The following are some of the benefits of using computer aided tools when developing human- or computer-based systems.

- *Lower Resistance to Change*

  These tools automate many of the tedious, time-consuming tasks of computer system or human procedural documentation. This automation makes it easier to produce high quality specifications of requirements, functions, and information. With the model right on the screen, the analyst interacts directly with the emerging design, being able to manipulate it and review the results immediately. Because change is easier, there is less psychological resistance to it.

- *Faster Response to Change*

  Staff productivity savings alone may not justify a computer assisted system. The major benefit comes from using an automated tool as the documentation tool as well as the data integrity tool. High-quality documentation automatically improves the quality of analysis and design work and enhances the usability of the resulting system.

- *Uniform Standards*

  While automated tools offer enormous power to the analyst, they also offer a standard set of symbols and conventions that avoid idiosyncratic representations. Because of the standards incorporated in the tool, all members of a project team must work within an agreed syntax. Initially this may seem like a constraint, but it actually proves to be a very useful framework if the standards are well thought out ahead of time.

- *Project Consistency*

  Several analysts can work with the same design simultaneously via a local-area network (LAN). In this shared environment each developer can look at the same version and is able to see how all the pieces tie together. Holding the methodology as a design within an automated development tool provides a project management tool which encourages a standard representation of project phases, tasks, deliverables, durations, and so on, so that senior management is presented with consistent project plans. Ease of use also actively encourages the project manager to plan, control, and to keep the plans updated.

- *Improved Documentation*

  Smaller, clearer, graphical specifications encourage the project team to update documentation, especially since changes made in one place are automatically reflected in every associated model.

By far the most important benefit, however, is the improved quality of the end product. An automated development tool allows the analyst to focus on the real nature of their job — that of building the right system to meet the business need.

Prototyping

One of the most powerful features of a sophisticated automated development tool is support for prototyping so that various aspects of a system can be represented as working models. These aspects may just drive the system's requirements or they may go on to be installed. Prototyping is a large subject in its own right. I include only a brief outline of it here to illustrate one of the applications of an automated tool set.

There are many kinds of prototyping:

- *High-level requirements prototyping* — to speed up requirements definition by including users on the team for greater quality, and avoiding communication problems in determining data and processing requirements.

- *Analysis prototyping* — to determine data models and to assess the correctness/completeness/consistency of process logic.

- *Design prototyping* — to represent scenarios (i.e., screens, reports, and logic execution sequence in a computer-based system or process flow in a human-based system).

Once built and tested, the prototype is ready for user sessions in which analysts and users conduct walkthroughs simulating real work. They use the prototyped procedures or the computer system's simulated screens, menu paths, databases, reports, and so on, and modify the prototype right then and there. Obviously, very careful version control is needed to avoid creating several different working copies of the system. As requirements firm up, the prototype designers can flesh out the prototype software and files until they arrive at a final version. For medium-to-large systems and for smaller integrated systems, I would recommend that the prototype then be used to develop good requirements models to ensure integrity of data and processing.

Quality Assurance

Over the years, I've come to see that quality in system development falls into four areas, and I encourage project managers to partition their quality assurance efforts accordingly. These four areas of quality are:

- *Correctness of requirements for data and processing by conducting user/analyst interviews and/or code analysis*

  User interviews are iterative dialogues that elicit the correct detailed business requirements. Code analysis is an inspection of existing computer code in order to extract the correct detailed business requirements.

- *Clarity and conformance to standards by conducting walkthroughs*

  Walkthroughs should be scheduled in advance (but can be informal) and are technical in nature. They verify that intermediate and final deliverables conform to company standards, are clear and readable, and that they follow the technical rules of the modeling tools utilized (see a following section for guidelines in conducting walkthroughs).

- *Project consistency by reviewing deliverables*

  Reviews ensure consistency across deliverables and with the project methodology. The review should be formal and technical in nature and attended by the project team and representatives from other affected areas of the organization.

- *Fiscal and organizational acceptance by making formal presentations to user and D.P. leadership*

  In these presentations we inform and obtain concurrence on major deliverables and obtain resource approval. (The deliverables are rarely pre-circulated for these non-technical presentations.)

Quality Assurance is an on-going activity throughout the system development life cycle. In fact, it can be looked on as a progressive activity starting with the Business Plan dictating the Project Charter. The Project Charter, in turn, dictates the analysis requirements which dictate the design architecture. The design will govern the manual procedures and code, which in turn dictate the production system. Pollution of a project and its system can occur anywhere in this progression. Therefore, each stage of the life cycle must be staffed with skilled, professional developers and supported with good technical tools. Probably the most useful tools I have encountered for ensuring quality are *walkthroughs* and *product reviews*.

PLAYER	DELIVERABLE	GOAL ORIENTATION	METHODS/MODELS
Strategic Planners/ Upper Management	Mission Statement	Strategic/Organizational	Long Range Forecasting/ High-level Business Models
Project Manager	Project Charter/ Customized Methodology/ Project Plan	Project	Metrics/Communication/ Organizational Methodology
Project Team	Manual & Automated System(s) (via Analysis, Design, & Implementation)	Technical	Development Models/ Implement Technology
Business Policy User/ Operations	Completed Work	Production	Manual & Automated Systems/ Schedules

The <u>Mission Statement</u> dictates

The <u>Project Charter</u> dictates

The <u>Analysis Requirements</u> dictates

The <u>Design Solution</u> dictates

The <u>Procedures Manuals/ Computer Code</u> dictates

The <u>Implemented System</u>

Insuring Quality at each and every stage of these dependent deliverables avoids pollution in the final product.

Fig. A-15: Building in Quality at Each Step

Walkthroughs

The methodology in this book places reviews after the completion of a significant deliverable. However, walkthroughs can and should be performed on complete intermediate deliverables for either a human- or a computer-based system. These intermediate deliverables should include things such as Data Flow Diagrams, Entity Relationship Diagrams, Logic Specifications, or a Data Dictionary.

A walkthrough is a quality assurance/control procedure to find errors, ambiguities, or omissions in a deliverable, to ensure that company standards are observed in a deliverable, and to ensure that a deliverable is readable and understandable by all who need to reference it.

Let me give some guidelines for conducting walkthroughs.

• The make-up of the walkthrough participants will depend on the material being reviewed but should mainly consist of the deliverable developer's peers, such as other analysts or designers. The developer(s) of the deliverable can also attend, provided they do not verbally add any assumptions that should have been in the deliverable.

Reviews and walkthroughs are for finding problems, not solving them.

- A feature I see being adopted frequently in walkthroughs is the presence of "someone borrowed", that is, someone engaged in the activities on either side of the activity producing the deliverable. For example, when you're reviewing an analysis specification, borrow a user and a designer, and in a design review borrow an analyst and a coder. The walkthrough participants may also include representatives from database administration, standards, auditing, maintenance, and so on.

- The project manager may attend if he or she is involved in the technical side of the product, but no upper-level management should attend. Unfortunately, when upper-level management is present, the developer of the deliverable being reviewed can become defensive and reviewers may try to look good by concentrating on how *they* would have developed the document, or by inventing instant solutions to problems. The product, not the developer, is under review. For the same reason, a walkthrough report should never be used for personnel evaluation or salary review.

A walkthrough must be cost-effective. Therefore, the time, number of reviewers, and degree of formality will depend on the amount and importance of the deliverable being reviewed. For example, a preliminary level walkthrough will demand fewer resources than a detailed level walkthrough.

The producer can incorporate solutions to minor problems into the material, with verification outside the walkthrough process by the person who discovered the problem. Major problems may require cycling back to previously affected processes in the methodology to rework them and of course, for another walkthrough.

Reviews

In Book II, *A Strategic Business Engineering Methodology*, I place *reviews* after major complete deliverables, such as a completed analysis specification. Reviews are used to assure technical project consistency and are attended by the whole project team, whereas walkthroughs are peer group sessions. Reviews serve as a way of sharing and communicating project knowledge, rather than a means for uncovering errors. Like walkthroughs, reviews should not normally be attended by upper D.P. or user management.

I advocate both internal project reviews (in which the developers of the product participate) and independent reviews (in which more objective, outside reviewers participate).

As a by-product, reviews and walkthroughs provide a training ground and communication tool for different development styles and insurance that someone other than the developer is familiar with, and can use, a product if the developer leaves the team.

I recommend Ed Yourdon's book, *Structured Walkthroughs* for more information on this subject.[2]

---

2   *Structured Walkthroughs* by Ed Yourdon — see Bibliography

I do hope the ideas in this book will introduce even more quality when you realize that a business is not its implementation and that you must first understand what the business is and model it before getting involved in any implementation.

By applying an engineering discipline, we can provide *quality* in terms of:

- Conformance to the business requirements of the larger enterprise through the use of customer/analyst dialogues, effective models, and "power tools",

- Conformance to established industry practices through the use of walkthroughs, reviews, and presentations, and

- Conformance to naming standards and data conservation.

Summary

We have seen in this appendix how we can obtain quality in systems by applying engineering tools and techniques within the context of a modern methodology. System engineers can then perform their partitioned activities to produce quality deliverables using the appropriate methods and models correctly.

Objective Quality Assurance with TQM applied to the project's intermediate deliverables will certify the final quality of the completed system.

Quality should be dictated from outside. Also, we as customers should start expecting quality systems from professional engineers. Engineering in systems must become the rule rather than the exception. Only then can we enter a quality Information Age.

B

Glossary

Analysis	The methodical study of a system or systems to understand, define, and document their business requirements independent of any existing design or implementation considerations.
Attribute	An indivisible item of data that takes on a value (also called a Data Element).
Automated	A qualifier for a portion of a system that is implemented with a computer.
Batch Processing	A processing approach in which transactions are accumulated over time for processing in a single execution of a system.
Bundled Store	A type of data store that contains multiple unrelated items of data.
Business	The essence of **what** an organization does. Those operations that pertain directly to the act of satisfying the organization's customers' needs.
Business Customer	Individuals, clients, agencies, systems, and other forms of impetus that are external to an organization and over which it has no control. Business Customers do not regulate an organization in any way nor do they modify its Business Policy.
Business Event	An incident that places a demand on the organization to which it responds in order to accomplish its strategic mission. Business Events are the most important type of event for the Business Re-Engineer.
Business Event Conservator	The person or persons in an organization who are chartered to maintain the integrity of the organization's Business Event Library and its associated matrices.
Business Event Library	The documentation (the set of models and supporting specifications) for all Business Events in the organization. When complete, each Business Event's entry in the library will show the essential business view of the event with its design and implementation.
Business Event List	A list of all the Business Events (as well as Dependent and Regulatory Events) to which an organization responds.

Business Event Memory

The collection of all the stored (i.e., non-transient) Data Elements necessary to accomplish the processing contained in one Business Event Partition.

Business Event Methodology

The collection of techniques used for analysis, design, and implementation when Re-Engineering an organization's systems along business lines to achieve ultimate customer satisfaction.

Business Event Name

A unique and descriptive name for a Business Event, preferably consisting of a whole sentence.

Business Event Partition

A Business Event Stimulus plus all associated processing, stored memory, and outgoing responses that constitute the organization's complete reaction to a Business Event.

Business Event Partitioning

The process of identifying and documenting the processing and data used by an organization to satisfy a single Business Event.

Business Event Partition Elements

The constituent parts of a Business Event Partition including the Business Event Source (the need), the Business Event Stimulus, the Business Event Processing, the Business Event Memory, the Business Event Response, and the Business Event Recipient.

Business Event Processing

All business logic (processing) and its transient data required to produce a Business Event Response.

Business Event Recipient

Who (or what) receives an organization's response to a Business Event.

Business Event Response

All outgoing data, control, products, or services resulting from a Business Event.

Business Event Source

This is a customer. It may be individuals, clients, agencies, systems, and other forms of impetus that are external to an organization and over which it has no control and that create a stimulus to the organization.

Business Event Specification

The complete set of models and supporting specifications and textual documentation needed to describe a Business Event Partition.

Business Event Stimulus

A demand (input data, condition, or material), that activates part of the business, resulting from a Business Event .

Business Issues

Those things pertaining to **what** an organization does regardless of **how** it's implemented.

Business Logic

The rules governing the processing of data and/or control within an organization.

Business Model	A non-redundant set of facts that describe the Re-Engineered business of an organization. This is a business tool for declaring an implementation-independent view of what has to happen to satisfy an organization's customers' needs.
Business Objective	A description of a business need that should be satisfied.
Business Policy	The essential data and processing, as defined by the Business Policy Creator, that must be put in place to satisfy the organization's mission.
Business Policy Creator	The organization's decision makers who are authorized to dictate which data, processing, and control are used by the organization to respond to its customers' needs.
Business Re-Engineer	The person chartered to Re-Engineer an organization along Business Event lines using an engineering discipline and a Re-Engineering Methodology.
Business Re-Engineering	The re-alignment of an organization and its resources along Business Event lines.
Cardinality	The numerical relationship between any two or more Entities on a data-oriented model (i.e., one-to-one, one-to-many, and many-to-one).
Cohesion	The measure of how closely related, that is, how strong is the association of instructions/functions that are packaged together. There are various levels of strength of cohesion.
Cohesive Entity	A grouping of all strongly related Data Elements. This collection of Data Elements is typically associated with one identifying key.
Control Flow Diagram	A control oriented model that can also show data movement or be tied to an associated Data Flow Diagram. This model is helpful for modeling the complex control issues of a system.
Control Oriented Model	A type of model suited for modeling the flow of control between different states in a system.
Control-triggered Stimulus	A type of Business Event Stimulus that contains no data. One typical source of this stimulus is the calendar or a clock reaching a predetermined point in time.
Convenience Store	A data store that is created to satisfy design or implementation reasons. A convenience store is not an essential business store.
Customer	The external individuals, clients, agencies, systems, and other forms of impetus that are external to an organization and over which it has no control and that have the need that is the organization's Business Policy to satisfy.

Critical Business Event	A Business Event that is essential for carrying out an organization's mission. In an organization that exists to make profits, this event is their main revenue generator.
Data	The factual information used by an organization as the basis for calculations or processing.
Data Cohesion	The property that binds a set of related, but individual Data Elements.
Data Conservation	**(1) For Processing:** The practice of ensuring that data entering and leaving a process, procedure, or system is conserved (i.e., all data are used to derive the outputs and all outputs could be derived from their inputs). **(2) For Memory:** The practice of ensuring that any data that is Created (captured) by a process, procedure, or system must be Retrieved (and optionally Deleted) by at least one other process, procedure, or system. Conversely, any data that is Retrieved, Updated, or Deleted must have been Created by at least one other process, procedure, or system.
Data Coupling	Data that is communicated between two or more processes — usually related to a design.
Data Definition	A description of a Data Element or a Data Aggregate.
Data Dictionary	A repository or encyclopedia that contains supporting specifications for a Business Model and its implementation.
Data Element	An indivisible item of data that takes on a value (also known as an Attribute).
Data Flow	A conduit for moving information between processes, data stores, or external interfaces.
Data Flow Diagram (DFD)	A model that is both process and data-oriented. This particular model allows the analyst to look at the data and the processing acting on that data as it travels through a system, business, or organization.
Data Integrity	A feature of a Data Element indicating that it is either dependent or independent of another Data Element.
Data Oriented Model	A graphical representation of the static data of a system or an organization.
Data Primitive	A data item that does not require any further breakdown in order to be defined.
Data Transformation	A process that changes the status or content of an item of data.
Data-triggered Stimulus	A Business Event Stimulus consisting of a cohesive set of data necessary for processing the event.

Deliverable	A defined result — usually the output of a process or procedure.
Dependent Event	An event that is in response to an outgoing request that an organization has made in order to satisfy one or more Business Events. Dependent Events typically originate with the vendors used by an organization.
Design	**(1) as a verb** — The process of inventing a solution to a problem.
	(2) as a noun — The solution to a problem or requirement.
	(3) as an adjective for data and processes — It indicates that implementation features are specified such as the media and format or the people or program I.D.s.
Dynamically Defined Business Event	An event that is put together to completely satisfy the specific need of a customer at the time they interface with an organization.
Engineering	The application of science and mathematics by which the properties of matter and the sources of energy in nature are made useful to man in structures, machines, products, systems, and processes.
Engineering Discipline	Applying the concepts of Engineering in the production of a product or service.
Entity	A cohesive set of related Data Elements captured by an organization.
Entity Relationship Diagram (ERD)	A model declaring Entities (cohesive sets of data) and the associations between those Entities that are needed to support an organization's Business Policy. An ERD can show "n-ary" (multiple) relationships.
Essential Boundary	Those boundaries over which an organization has no control — they must exist for the business to run.
Essential Business	Those things to which the organization must respond now and in the future.
Entity Specifications	The definitions of cohesive sets of data.
External Interface	A point beyond the organization where a need occurs to which the organization responds.
Flow Chart	A model that depicts processing in a linear (flow-of-control) manner.
Fragmented Store	A data store that does not contain a complete, cohesive set of data.
Fragmented Event	A portion of a Business Event that has been broken apart or batched to accommodate an existing design.

Functional Decomposition Diagram

A process oriented model that provides a process-only view. These models are a good way to decompose a process or a problem and to break down that process or system from a high-level to a low-level view.

Functional Primitive

A detailed-level, specific process that does not require further decomposition to be understood.

Hierarchical Relationship Diagram

A data-oriented model that shows the design structure of a manual or automated file system.

Implementation

The process of building and testing a design prior to in-stallation.

Information/C.R.U.D. Event

A Business Event that requires a simple Create, Retrieve, Update, or Delete.

Interface

A point at which an event is initiated or terminated (e.g., a Customer or the Outside World).

Internal Interface

A point where a Business Event stopped in relation to our area of study (i.e., it's a point where a Business Event got fragmented).

Leveling

The process of decomposing a single-function process into discrete sub-processes.

Logical

An implementation-independent view. A qualifier for data or processing indicating that all design charac-teristics of the item have been removed.

Logical Access Path Diagram

An implementation-free diagram that models the access paths among Entities and that shows how processing navigates from one logical data group to another.

Maintenance

The clean-up process performed on a production system to remove features that were inserted by error during its development.

Manual

A qualifier for a portion of a system that is implemented with human beings.

Material-triggered Stimulus

The actual products or items that arrive at and stimulate an organization.

Memory

A record of relevant stored data that an organization needs to respond to a stimulus.

Message

The communications between Objects on an Object Ori-ented Model.

Method

A reusable process acting on shared variables — Data or States— within an Object.

Metrics

Detailed historical records of deliverable related usage of project resources (also known as statistics).

Mission Statement

A brief, clearly stated expression of an organization's reason for being in existence.

Model	A representation to be used as a pattern or guide for conceptualizing, specifying, planning, or executing a system or deliverable.
Modification	The necessary change to a product or system initiated by the Business Policy Creator when business needs change.
Network Structure Diagram	A data-oriented model used to show the access of one Entity (cohesive set of data) from any other.
Non-essential Boundary	Those boundaries based on some implementation or historical reasons.
Normalization	The process of systematically eliminating redundancy and dependence within the items of an Entity.
Object	An encapsulation of data and processes.
Object Oriented Model (OO)	A model that declares Objects and the interactions between those Objects via Messages.
Physical	A qualifier for data or processes, indicating that implementation features are specified. For data, the definition or composition may include the media and format used for transmission and/or storage. For processes, the specifications may include the people or program I.D.s performing the tasks and how the processes are procedurally accomplished.
Pre-Engineering	The application of the discipline and the methodology of Re-Engineering to a new organization.
Process	The set of forces, actions, laws, rules, and operations that act on a stimulus, generate the response, and usually alter the state, memory, or material within the system.
Process Hierarchy Diagram	A model used to depict top-down control issues such as showing who is in charge of whom in an organization. Process Hierarchy Diagrams are also used in the Data Processing Industry when modeling the structure of computer systems to show "boss" modules and "subordinate" modules that are invoked by these "boss" modules.
Process Integrity	A feature of a single-function process indicating that all data input into it is utilized and that all data output from it is derived only from its input and that therefore, the process can be used across Business Events and applications.
Process Oriented Model	A type of model that focuses exclusively on processing and process flow.
Process Specification	The specification of a functional primitive process that describes the policy or procedure necessary to transform incoming data into outgoing data.

Project Charter	A public document that declares the scope and objectives of a specific project.
Project Model	A methodology or life cycle for building systems. This is a management tool for declaring an organization's systems development standards.
Project Objective	The directions as to the manner in which a project should be conducted.
Quality	Quality is recognized in a product or service when it satisfies both the ethical and measurable requirements of the requester. It is accomplished with pride of ownership on the part of everybody involved in satisfying those requirements. Succinctly, quality is conformance to requirements.
Re-Engineering	The re-alignment of an organization and its resources along Business Event lines.
Re-Engineering Plan	A well defined series of steps to Re-Engineer an organization's activities *in situ* without impacting the organization's day-to-day operations.
Regulatory Customer	This is typically an external organization that regulates an organization and with which it has to interface because of the business it is in and its location.
Regulatory Event	An incident that places a demand on an organization to which it responds in order to comply with legal requirements.
Relationship	An association between two or more Entities that is important to an organization.
Relationship Specification	The optional definitions of the rules of association between Entities.
Reusability	A characteristic of data or a process that determines its suitability for use across Business Events or applications.
Reusable Library	A well documented and cataloged collection of quality-engineered processes and Entities that are available for re-use.
Reusable Process	An engineered, single-function process available for use across Business Events or applications.
Seamless Business System	A system in which a Business Event Partition is implemented as a unit with no artificial boundaries or stores.
State Transition Diagram (STD)	A control-oriented model used to model the flow of control between the different states of a system.
Strategic Event/ Meta Event	An event that makes the Business Policy Creator change the way their organization does business and hence changes their Business Model in some way.

Strategic Objective	A quantifiable and measurable statement of a specific line of business' required performance. A goal contains the "vision" of the strategic planners.
Strategic Planning	A planning approach aimed at organizational issues that address where the organization is today, and where it expects to be in the next decade and beyond.
Structure Chart	A graphical tool used to hierarchically model the design solution (architecture) of a computer system.
System	A connected or related set of activities that works toward a result.
Systems Analyst	A person who studies, models, and documents an organization's Business Policy.
System Builder	The persons (Technical Writers and Programmers) who implement an organization's Business Policy.
System Customer	These are internal persons, departments, or systems that exist because of the existing structure of an organization.
System Designer	The person who designs the implementation of the Business Policy.
System Development	A sequence of steps that involves a progression of specifications from gathering objectives in a Project Charter, to identifying requirements in an Analysis Specification, to creating solutions in a Design Specification, and on into building the systems in an Implementation Specification.
System Event/ Internal Event	An event created during the design of an organization's structure and systems in order to implement its business.
System Issue	A thing that pertains to **how** an organization is designed to run its day-to-day operations. A System Issue involves technology aspects (e.g., human beings, computers, robots, etc.).
System Model	An implementation view of the Business Model. This is a design tool for declaring how the business runs in the real world.
System Store	A memory store that is not shared across Business Events. These are invented to satisfy a design.
Transient Data Flow	The intermediate data between two processes within a Business Event. The data in these Transient Data Flows is not stored and "burns up" after the processing has terminated.
Walkthrough	An informal quality control/assurance inspection of a deliverable in which the reviewers are the peers of the author of the deliverable.

Bibliography

Chen, Peter. 1976. The Entity Relationship Diagram — Towards a Unified View of Data. The Transactions of the IEEE.

Constantine, Larry, and Yourdon, Ed. 1979. Structured Design. New Jersey. Prentice-Hall.

Crosby, Philip. 1979. Quality Is Free. New York, New York. Mentor.

Ram Dass. 1975. Be Here Now. New York, New York. Crown Publishing.

DeMarco, Thomas. 1978. Structured Analysis and System Specification. New York, New York. Yourdon, Inc.

DeMarco, Tom, and Lister, Tim. 1987. PeopleWare: Productive Projects and Teams. New York, New York. Dorset House.

Demming, W. Edwards. Industry Week.

Dickinson, Brian. 1981. Developing Structured Systems. New York, New York. Yourdon Press.

Dickinson, Brian. 1989. Developing Quality Systems: A Methodology Using Structured Techniques. New York, New York. McGraw-Hill.

Dickinson, Brian. 1991. Strategic Business Engineering: A Synergy of Software Engineering and Information Engineering. Brisbane, California. LCI Press.

Editors, Webster's Encyclopedic Unabridged Dictionary of the English Language. Springfield, MA. G. & G. Merriam Company.

Einstein, Albert. Out of My Later Years.

Flavin, M. 1980. Fundamental Concepts or Information Modeling. New York, New York. Yourdon Press.

Editors, 1975. A Course on Miracles. Glen Ellen, California. Foundation for Inner Peace.

Gane, C., and Sarson, T. 1977. Structured Systems Analysis: Tools and Techniques. New York. Improved System Technologies.

Hatley, D., and Pirbhai, I. 1987. Strategies for Real-time System Specification. New York, New York. Dorset House.

Humphrey, Watts. 1989. Managing the Software Process. Reading, MA. Addison–Wesley.

Martin, James. 1989. Information Engineering — a Trilogy by James Martin. Englewood Cliffs, New Jersey. Prentice-Hall.

McMenamin, Steve, and Palmer, John. 1984. Essential Systems Analysis. New York, New York. Yourdon Press.

Mellor, S. J., and Ward, P. T. 1985. Structured Development for Real-time Systems. New York, New York. Yourdon Press.

Page-Jones, Meilir. 1995. What Every Programmer Should Know About Object-Oriented Design. New York, New York. Dorset House Publishing.

Page-Jones, Meilir. 1988 (Second Edition). The Practical Guide to Structured Systems Design. New York, New York. Yourdon Press.

Pirsig, Robert. 1991. Lila — an Inquiry into Morals. New York, New York. Bantam Books.

Pirsig, Robert. 1974. Zen and the Art of Motorcycle Maintenance — an Inquiry into Values. New York, New York. Bantam Books.

Santayana, George. 1905. The Life of Reason — Volume 1 – Reason in Common Sense. New York, New York. Charles Scribner & Sons.

Smith, Adam. 1776. The Wealth of Nations.

Taylor, Frederick Winslow. 1911. Scientific Management.

Yourdon, Ed. 1989. Modern Structured Analysis. New Jersey. Prentice-Hall.

Yourdon, Ed. 1989. Structured Walk-Throughs. 4th edition. New Jersey. Prentice-Hall.